The Child and the Caribbean Imagination

The Child and the Caribbean Imagination

Edited by

GISELLE RAMPAUL

and

GERALDINE ELIZABETH SKEETE

University of the West Indies Press
Jamaica • Barbados • Trinidad and Tobago

University of the West Indies Press
7A Gibraltar Hall Road   Mona
Kingston 7   Jamaica
www.uwipress.com

© 2012 by Giselle Rampaul and Geraldine Elizabeth Skeete

All rights reserved. Published 2012

A catalogue record of this book is available from the
National Library of Jamaica.

ISBN: 978-976-640-267-9

Cover illustration: J. MacDonald Henry, *Shine Eye*.
© The Estate of J. MacDonald Henry. Courtesy of John Simpson.

Cover and book design by Robert Harris
Set in Constantia 9.5/14.5 x 27

Printed in the United States of America

In memory of Dr Patricia Ismond

Contents

Acknowledgements / **ix**

Introduction
Imagining Caribbean Childhoods / **1**
Giselle Rampaul and Geraldine Elizabeth Skeete

PART 1. DISCOURSE AND REPRESENTATION

1   Towards a Poetics of Childhood / **13**
Sandra Pouchet Paquet

2   The Child as Symbol of "Challenge" in Michael Anthony's
The Year in San Fernando / **32**
Jennifer Rahim

3   "The Thing Without a Name": The Child as Narrative Strategy
in *Miguel Street* / **48**
Ryan Durgasingh

PART 2. UNSTABLE IDENTITIES

4   Child's "I" and Other in Olive Senior's Narratives of
Self-Invention / **67**
Barbara Lalla

5   "How the Mirror Broke": Deconstructing Colonial Fairy Tales in
"I Remember Pampalam" / **81**
Giselle Rampaul

6   "What Child Is This?": Same-Sex Desire among Children in the Anglophone Caribbean Short Story / **99**
Geraldine Elizabeth Skeete

PART 3. LANGUAGE DEVELOPMENT

7   The Child and the Structure of Creoles, Pidgins and Signed Languages / **117**
Ben Braithwaite

8   "How Yuh Make a Story?": Narrative Development in Young Trinidadian Children / **136**
Kathy-Ann Drayton

PART 4. PEDAGOGY

9   Black Heart/White Heart: *The Chronicles of Narnia* as Literary Text in a Creole Space / **157**
Nicha Selvon-Ramkissoon

10   Using *For the Life of Laetitia* to Teach Character Development to Form 3 Special Students / **174**
Karen Sanderson Cole

11   "We Supposed to Have Fun": Voice and Resistance in the Primary School Classroom / **187**
Rowena Kalloo

12   Do Teachers Make Science Learning Fun and Relevant? / **212**
Rawatee Maharaj-Sharma

Contributors / **225**

Acknowledgements

THIS BOOK WOULD NOT HAVE been completed but for the significant contribution of many of our colleagues and friends.

We are grateful indeed to Jennifer Rahim, the driving force behind the Conference on Caribbean Childhood, which yielded the chapters in this book. Without her hard work, determination and belief in the project, this book would have remained simply a good idea. We are also grateful for her contribution to the writing of the introduction.

Paula Morgan and Barbara Lalla, who were part of the initial editing team, were also always generous with their advice and time despite their own demanding schedules.

We would also like to thank Valerie Youssef and Jo-Anne Ferreira for reviewing the chapters that deal with language issues.

Andra K. Ramdeen deserves special mention for her careful formatting of the manuscript and her willingness to work on this project despite the demands of her postgraduate degree and her undergraduate tutoring.

A grant awarded by the University of the West Indies Research and Publications Fund also provided much-needed finances to complete this book.

Adel Bain, Jacintha "Jessy" Mitchell and so many others have also contributed in one way or another and for this we are truly grateful.

Most of all, we would like to thank the contributors of the chapters who saw this as a worthy project. Thank you for your infinite patience and for helping us to see this book to completion.

Introduction

Imagining Caribbean Childhoods

» GISELLE RAMPAUL AND GERALDINE ELIZABETH SKEETE

THE ADAGE "CHILDREN MUST BE SEEN and not heard"[1] points to an inherent ambivalence in the Caribbean's collective psyche about the place and role of children in its social order, since it simultaneously recognizes and silences their presence. The child and adolescent have occupied a seminal place in the region's culture and creativity. Children, for instance, have key roles in folk tales, songs and games. Novels of childhood and adolescence, such as Merle Hodge's *Crick Crack, Monkey*, and Jamaica Kincaid's *Annie John*, have been central to Caribbean literary culture, often analogizing the developing nation and its cultural consciousness, as well as its citizenry's migratory practices.[2] However, despite the long-standing interest in representing the child in different kinds of media, the issues surrounding Caribbean childhood have not been given sufficient academic attention.

The current social climate of the region demands that the conditions under which children live, the issues that directly have an impact on their holistic development and the valuable contribution they make to society be brought into focus. A number of issues affecting and surrounding the Caribbean child and the experience of childhood are in dire need of critical enquiry and analysis. It is hoped that this multidisciplinary book will have direct bearing, not only on guiding the understanding of childhood's cultural significance in the region, but also on social policy development and the influencing of necessary attitudinal changes – for example, in childhood rights and education.

Internationally, the study of childhood and adolescence has developed fairly rapidly, particularly in the United States and in the United Kingdom, where increasingly popular and highly theoretical postgraduate programmes exist. For example, the University of Reading and the University of Newcastle, UK, both have well-established and well-subscribed postgraduate programmes in children's literature. The University of Pittsburgh, Pennsylvania State University and San Diego State University in the United States also offer postgraduate degrees in children's literature. Further, there are many publications devoted to the scholarly analysis of representations of the child in literature and arts, which have both sprung out of the study of children's literature.

Yet this is an area of scholarship that has been largely overlooked in the Caribbean. There are only a few publications devoted to Caribbean childhood, including Christine Barrow's *Caribbean Childhoods: "Outside", "Adopted" or "Left Behind"*; Debra Curtis's *Pleasures and Perils: Girls' Sexuality in a Caribbean Consumer Culture*; Zanifa McDowell's *Elements of Child Law in the Commonwealth Caribbean*; and a few handbooks like Emiliana Vegas's *The Promise of Early Childhood Development in Latin America and the Caribbean*; Rosamunde Renard's *Handbook for Caribbean Early Childhood Education Caregivers*; and the Children's Issues Coalition's annual serial, *Caribbean Childhoods: From Research to Action*. However, these publications largely deal with sociological or pedagogical issues.[3] A collection of essays on trauma, social policy and popular culture as they relate to Caribbean childhood is being compiled for the inaugural issue of *Tout Moun: Caribbean Journal of Cultural Studies*. These forays into representations of the child and Caribbean childhood are but starting points for what is an increasingly important area of critical enquiry.

The chapters in this collection were initially presented at the very successful International Cultural Studies Conference, "First They Must Be Children": The Child and the Caribbean Imagi/nation, hosted by the Department of Liberal Arts at the University of the West Indies, St Augustine campus, in May 2009. The presentations have since been extensively revised and upgraded to form the present book, which engages in multidisciplinary discussions on the representational patterns related to the Caribbean child and childhood. The chapters, taken together, provide analysis of the ideological perspectives and discursive practices employed in constructions of children as social and imaginative subjects; the roles, language and identities they have been assigned; their acts of resistance and transgression as cultural agents; and the multiple meanings of their presence in traditional and contemporary Caribbean mythologies of being and becoming. It is hoped that this book will provide distinctly Caribbean perspectives on the role of childhood in the making of societies and cultures.

The chapters in part 1, Discourse and Representation, examine Caribbean novels of childhood and move, as Sandra Pouchet Paquet's chapter title indicates, towards a poetics of childhood. These chapters explore issues relating to representing the child in literary discourse, focusing on problems of child characters being represented through adult consciousnesses, autobiography and memory, for example. Ryan Durgasingh also examines the marginalization and subordination of children to the fringes of their own narrative. The chapters in this section also analyse the problems of identity formation in societies dominated by specific sociopolitical agendas, the tendency to construct narratives about children as allegories of national development, and, as Jennifer Rahim points out, the preference for child characters as symbols of social change and renewal.

In "Towards a Poetics of Childhood", Sandra Pouchet Paquet examines narratives of childhood by men and women of different ethnicities from various parts of the Caribbean. Through these autobiographical narratives, she explores the constituent elements of childhoods remembered and expressed in self-narration, the functional relationship of adult consciousness to the childhood self and the idea of childhood that mediates the temporal world of childhood, as well as the adult's perspective and memories of childhood. Pouchet Paquet assumes that the intimate connection between childhood and adulthood that drives this study can contribute to our understanding of the nature of human consciousness in our world, and she invites us to reflect on the recurring themes of childhood experience and the burden of consciousness that the literature of childhood represents.

This idea is picked up by Jennifer Rahim in "The Child as Symbol of 'Challenge' in Michael Anthony's *The Year in San Fernando*", in which she points out the tendency for Caribbean authors to use the child figure to represent, if not vicariously theorize, the region's myriad sociocultural issues, political evolutions and articulations of identity. Rahim argues that, more often than not, these narratives function as avenues for social protest and allegories of national development. Michael Anthony's novel, *The Year in San Fernando*, is revisited in light of the dialogical strain Martin Carter illuminates between dream and disappointment and vision and reality in which the child is cast in his poem "The Child Ran into the Sea". Rahim discerns, in the novel's early but covert engagement with the social politics of multi-ethnic, pre-independence Trinidad and Tobago, the author's effort to theorize a pathway for national development in which the twelve-year-old protagonist, Francis, plays a major role as symbol and agent of "challenge" and, therefore, of transformation.

In "'The Thing Without a Name': The Child as Narrative Strategy in *Miguel Street*", Ryan Durgasingh also draws attention to narrative issues involved in representing childhood by focusing on the unnamed child narrator of V.S. Naipaul's novel. The child narrator relates the picaresque exploits of his neighbours to the reader while his past-self, the child who has ostensibly experienced these events, remains peripheral throughout most of the narrative. The child's own development follows an anachronous path and complicates notions of the Bildungsroman as his life is often overshadowed by the colourful characters with whom he associates. In this chapter, Durgasingh analyses "the child" as narrative strategy and as a character who is not allowed to be central to what first appears to be his novel of development.

In part 2, Unstable Identities, the focus on literary texts continues but the focus is on the subjectivities that are available to child characters in the narratives. These chapters, taken together, reveal the "constructedness" of identity as the child characters, through various means and for different reasons, "try on" different personas that are significant to the formation of their personhoods. These chapters concern ideological, conceptual and psychological perspectives on identity formation and tackle political issues related to patriarchy, colonization and sexuality. In Barbara Lalla's essay, the child character's story becomes a means of creating reality in the face of psychological trauma. Giselle Rampaul examines the borrowed images of colonial culture that are fed to the child, who is ultimately torn between competing realities. The section ends with Geraldine Skeete's discussion of the issues surrounding same-sex desire in children as depicted by contemporary, Caribbean diasporic short fiction writers.

Barbara Lalla, in her chapter, "Child's 'I' and Other in Olive Senior's Narratives of Self-Invention", analyses how Senior conveys the displaced child's attempts at self-construction through a range of narrative strategies. By focusing on the unmothered child character, Lalla reveals the psychological crisis that results from worlds where game and reality horrifyingly intersect. In such circumstances of dissociation, Senior characteristically identifies potential for adult intervention, but the alignment of vision may never be achieved in the narrative, even as narration becomes the crucial mechanism for imposing coherence on a shattering consciousness. In this chapter, Lalla examines how the child's "I" experiments with alternative identities may become a desperate effort to impose order on her life as she searches for a sustainable story for going forward.

Drawing upon a quotation from Olive Senior's poem "Colonial Girls' School", which alludes to the irrelevance of colonial education and its dissemination of European cultural myths in the Caribbean, Giselle Rampaul examines the effects of the colonial fairy tales passed down to the child character in Joyce Gittens's 1947 short story "I Remember Pampalam". These fairy tales, especially *Snow White*, include assumptions about race, colour and class and serve to indoctrinate the child into social norms involving gender performance and sexuality, patriarchy and family structures. These norms become an imitation of and are measured by inevitably European standards, which have very little to do with the character's reality of living in a barrack yard in Trinidad. The difficulties involved in shattering the colonial mirror and attempting to construct a Caribbean identity and world view become clear in this chapter.

In "'What Child Is This?' Same-Sex Desire among Children in the Anglophone Caribbean Short Story", Geraldine Skeete analyses the short story as a literary form considered in dialectical and binary opposition to the novel, as children are to adults, and as heterosexuals are to homosexuals. In this chapter, Skeete includes award-winning writer Lawrence Scott, who has actively focused on the gay, intersex or transvestite youngster in his long and short narratives. She also includes the writers Dionne Brand and Shani Mootoo, among others. Skeete examines how some literary critics' description of short stories as, in part, being peopled with characters that are "non-hegemonic", "peripheral" and "at odds with the dominant culture" can also fit the subject position of the non-heterosexual. Of interest are the links between form and content; gender and genre; and the writers' use of the short narrative with its paradoxical features of brevity and tightness, flexibility and openness to explore the sometimes fraught, sometimes satisfying experiences of Caribbean gay and lesbian children in the literary discourse.

In part 3, Language Development, Ben Braithwaite and Kathy-Ann Drayton consider the ways in which Caribbean children, through their own creativity, contribute to the development of languages and discourses. These chapters take a linguistic perspective and present children not simply as cultural products of society but as individuals who are producers of language and who have a hand in shaping the cultural terrain of their societies. Whereas Drayton explores the ways in which children use their imagination to construct linguistically coherent stories, Braithwaite argues that children have played a key role in the development of the very languages used to tell these stories. The chapters in this section, therefore, emphasize the role of children as active social participants and cultural agents.

Ben Braithwaite, in his chapter, "The Child and the Structure of Creoles, Pidgins and Signed Languages", focuses on some linguistic similarities between creole languages and signed language and discusses the special role of children in the development of language. Braithwaite reviews some recent typological findings relating to creoles, sign languages and pidgins, paying particular attention to Caribbean languages, and considers what these findings tell us about the role of children in the formation of these languages. He argues that the productivity of reduplication found in signed and creole languages (but not in pidgins) may be attributed to the regularizing role of child learners. He also suggests that further comparisons between these three types of language may contribute to a better understanding of the ways in which children aid the development of languages.

In "'How Yuh Make a Story?': Narrative Development in Young Trinidadian Children", Kathy-Ann Drayton examines narrative development as part of children's linguistic, cognitive and social development. Narrative development helps them to organize their experiences, construct multiple and changing identities, analyse events as logical episodes and develop metalinguistic and metacognitive skills to reflect on their own thinking and communicative processes. Drayton charts children's growing ability to produce narratives from their employment of basic chaining of events and little use of complex phrase structure or evaluative devices to being able to narrate complex and coherent stories with well-organized story grammar and increased linguistic sophistication.

In part 4, Pedagogy, the authors raise issues regarding the advantages of cross-disciplinary instruction and considerations of how children's everyday lives are beneficial to decisions relating to pedagogy, how they should be given more agency in the teacher-pupil relationship, and how children can be taught subliminal messages from instructional material that may seem inimical to ideals of ethnic and racial harmony necessary for productive relationships in a Caribbean space. Descriptors usually define this space with the *multi*-affix, yet teachers can use such material as countermeasures to teach valuable lessons about discrimination and prejudice, tolerance and acceptance. These chapters therefore explore the real-life situation of the Caribbean classroom – three of them present actual case studies with a Trinidad and Tobago context – and the philosophies and practices that engender a learner-centred and learner-autonomous environment. They interrogate the pedagogical implications of using traditional versus modern teaching and learning methods and of allowing the voice of Caribbean children to be heard as a factor both in the teacher-pupil relationship and in the development of educational policy at the primary and secondary levels in Trinidad and Tobago.

In her chapter, "Black Heart/White Heart: *The Chronicles of Narnia* as Literary Text in a Creole Space", Nicha Selvon-Ramkissoon discusses how literature can teach vital life lessons to twelve- to fourteen-year-olds in Trinidad and Tobago's secondary school classrooms. Using a literary linguistic approach and a close reading of the novels, she investigates and uncovers the perceived subtext or underlying messages of C.S. Lewis's *The Chronicles of Narnia*, which is recommended reading material in the language arts curriculum for the aforementioned age group. Selvon-Ramkissoon examines the novels' perpetuation of racism, misogyny and fundamentalist religion. She explores how the ideological orientation of characters, narrator and implied author is betrayed through the use of language, of which teachers should be mindful and which they should be able to identify. While acknowledging the challenges of reading and studying a book like this in a Caribbean classroom that typically includes children of diverse groups based on race, class, gender, colour and religion, Selvon-Ramkissoon nonetheless offers perspectives on why such a text can still be retained on the reading list and also be used for counterdiscursive purposes.

In "Using *For the Life of Laetitia* to Teach Character Development to Form 3 Special Students", Karen Sanderson Cole recounts and analyses her teaching experience with low-achieving students in a secondary school in Trinidad. This chapter provides a provoking and sobering insight into the struggles of underachieving students in the Trinidad and Tobago secondary school system and the extent to which teachers need to painstakingly apply creative ideas to enhance students' critical thinking, reading and literature skills. The chapter is a revealing pedagogical discourse on how to improve the academic and life skills of "special" children. Thus, it reads as an inter- and cross-disciplinary paper, encompassing the fields of literature, family life education, reading and writing. With this remedial class, whose members are, on average, fourteen years old, Sanderson Cole uses both qualitative and quantitative assessment and employs the principles and methods of critical literacy to teach a lesson on character development so that students can make meaningful correspondences between their real-life context and that of the fictional character in the Caribbean novel, *For the Life of Laetitia*, by Merle Hodge. The statistics, analysis, recommendations and appendices are very informative to the reader who may not belong to the field of education.

Rowena Kalloo's chapter, "'We Supposed to Have Fun': Voice and Resistance in the Primary School Classroom", centres on the pressures affecting students preparing for the Secondary Entrance Assessment examination and, as a consequence, the learning and behavioural outcomes evident both in and out of the classroom. As participant-observer, Kalloo traces how this preparation impacts students' cognitive and affective development, their attitudes to study and play, and their perceptions of and relationship with their teacher, and vice versa. She uses as her representative study a co-educational elementary institution and one of its classes, investigating concepts of power and how student voice is a means of resistance in such a setting. She presents the direct speech and first-person narratorial voices of the students, as well as the teacher and captures the nuances of the speakers' maturational age, sex and ideological orientation towards the questions posed. Kalloo highlights the human aspect of the process, rather than emphasizing the rigorous requirements of a syllabus for an examination that is a rite of passage from childhood to adolescence and from primary to secondary school.

In the final chapter, "Do Teachers Make Science Learning Fun and Relevant?", Rawatee Maharaj-Sharma focuses on the implementation of the primary school science syllabus in ways that are both fun and relevant. She argues that although teachers purport to use a variety of strategies during science lessons, they ultimately rely on traditional resources and methods because of time constraints, limited resources, restrictive physical accommodation, lack of creativity and insufficient support from administration. Like Kalloo, Maharaj-Sharma also interrogates the cognitive and affective domains of teaching and learning in the real classroom setting, but she examines the psychomotor domain, as well. Whereas Kalloo focuses more on the learner, Maharaj-Sharma turns her attention more specifically to the teacher. Like Kalloo, she bases her findings on classroom observations and personal interviews with teachers, offering their direct statements and reflections on their delivery of the science curriculum. Because Maharaj-Sharma is involved in teacher education, she critiques this delivery, providing statistical data to track the use of traditional versus modern and dull versus interesting teaching and learning strategies used in a sampling of classrooms in

Trinidad to determine if an optimum balance is being struck between the child as learner while enjoying the world of science and that same child acquiring the requisite knowledge and skills.

Childhood is largely an overlooked topic in the Caribbean, as is evident in the surprising dearth of publications devoted to it. And yet understanding childhood is crucial to the perpetuation and preservation of culture and necessary to the formation of stable and productive societies. By foregrounding the experience of the child as far as possible and by examining childhood from a variety of disciplinary lenses, these chapters offer a variety of new perspectives on the importance of childhood as an area of critical enquiry and provide a foundation for further study and for effecting practical improvements in the lives of children.

Notes

1. Although this saying is not of Caribbean origin, it is often quoted to describe attitudes towards children in the Caribbean. See, for example, Jaipaul L. Roopnarine and Janet Brown, eds., *Caribbean Families: Diversity among Ethnic Groups* (Greenwich, CT: Ablex, 1997), 5; Simon Taylor, *A Land of Dreams: A Study of Jewish and Caribbean Migrant Communities in England* (London: Routledge, 1993), 150; and Zanifa McDowell, *Elements of Child Law in the Commonwealth Caribbean* (Kingston: University of the West Indies Press, 2000), 91.
2. Merle Hodge, *Crick Crack, Monkey* (London: André Deutsch, 1970); Jamaica Kincaid, *Annie John* (New York: Farrar, Straus and Giroux, 1997).
3. Christine Barrow, *Caribbean Childhoods: "Outside", "Adopted" or "Left Behind"* (Kingston: Ian Randle, 2010); Debra Curtis, *Pleasures and Perils: Girls' Sexuality in a Caribbean Consumer Culture* (New Brunswick, NJ: Rutgers University Press, 2009); Zanifa McDowell, *Elements of Child Law in the Commonwealth Caribbean* (Kingston: University of the West Indies Press, 2000); Emiliana Vegas, *The Promise of Early Childhood Development in Latin America and the Caribbean* (Washington, DC: World Bank Publications, 2009); Rosamunde Renard, *Handbook for Caribbean Early Childhood Education Caregivers* (Stoke-on-Trent: Trentham Books, 1998); Children's Issues Coalition, *Caribbean Childhoods: From Research to Action* (Kingston: Ian Randle, 2003).

Part 1.

DISCOURSE AND REPRESENTATION

1.

Towards a Poetics of Childhood

» SANDRA POUCHET PAQUET

IN APPROACHING THE SUBJECT of the child and the Caribbean literary imagination, I am keenly aware that writers like Olive Senior carve out the space of childhood that others like me struggle to occupy with some understanding of Caribbean childhood in the time and place they designate. It is in this spirit that I attempt to lay out some of the parameters of childhood experience remembered and expressed in self-narration and to explore the functional relationship of adult consciousness to the childhood self in enduring works of art created by men and women of different races and ethnicities from different parts of the Caribbean, wherever they may now reside.

The literature of childhood mediates the temporal world of childhood as well as the adult's perspective and memories of childhood. The field is large, and in the interest of time and manageability, I have chosen to focus on the aesthetic contours of select texts as a way into a discussion of the poetics of childhood in Caribbean literature. My emphasis will be shaped by specific works that have guided my understanding, chief among them George Lamming's *In the Castle of My Skin,* Maryse Condé's *Tales from the Heart: True Stories from My Childhood,* Judith Ortiz Cofer's *Silent Dancing: A Partial Remembrance of a Puerto Rican Childhood* and Patrick Chamoiseau's *School Days.* All are autobiographical in varying degrees but this is important to my quest for an understanding of the relationship between adult consciousness and the childhood self in Caribbean writing.

Uppermost in my mind as I started organizing my thoughts were two perspectives on childhood experience that seemed to disturb each other in ways that invited further investigation. One is from George Lamming's *The Pleasures of Exile*: "Equally noble in their origins, Father and Child are different only in the degrees of their knowledge. What comes between them is the distance which separates Age that apprehends, from Innocence which can only see."[1] The other is a statement by Maryse Condé about the composition of *Tales from the Heart: True Stories from My Childhood*.[2] At the New York University Institute of African-American Affairs in late May 2002, where she had given a reading with her husband and translator Richard Philcox, an audience member asked whether *Tales from the Heart* was autobiographical. Condé responded:

> Because I was sixty when I was writing about myself being ten. Everything that I could say about me was a kind of fiction. Of course it is true, all the facts are true, all the elements are autobiographical. For example, the stories that Richard read earlier this evening – I remember vividly even the day when they happened, but I am not sure that I felt the way I say in the book. It is no more autobiography. There is a distance that you create between your text and the reality you are talking about. So when I say *contes vrais* – "true tales" – means that it is true, but with the distance of age, the gap of time, and so on, it has become a kind of fiction.

If we trust their statements, Lamming's observation that "the distance which separates Age that apprehends, from Innocence which can only see" (*Pleasures*, 103), is also Condé's "distance that you create between your text and the reality you are talking about".[3] I want to focus first on the theme of age and innocence, not the novel by that name also written by Lamming, but the concept in relation to childhood as a distinct and separate state of being that is nonetheless intimately related to the adult's way of seeing and knowing. In autobiographical narratives, age and innocence assume self-reflection and evaluation in the light of then and now. The temporal hierarchy imposed by the process of remembering assumes a vantage point of wisdom in tension with the innocence of childhood. The quest for a poetics of childhood is a quest for recurring themes and the strategies employed in the recovery and representation of childhood.

My points of reference will be *In the Castle of My Skin* and *The Pleasures of Exile*. Then I will briefly explore *School Days*, the second of Patrick Chamoiseau's three autobiographical narratives of childhood, which underscores Lamming's *In the Castle of My Skin*'s thematics and strategies of narrating childhood, despite the authors' generational and national differences. Chamoiseau is from Martinique rather than Barbados and was born in 1953, the year in which Lamming's *In the Castle of My Skin* was first published.

Next, I will focus on two women writers, in particular, the thematic of memory and the mother/daughter dyad in Condé's *Tales from the Heart*. I consider Judith Ortiz Cofer's *Silent Dancing* a complementary quest for self-knowledge although Cofer, born in 1952, like Chamoiseau, belongs to a different generation and has a different ethnic and national history. All these writers invest an acute island consciousness in their narratives of childhood, and I hope to suggest some areas of marked gender difference.

Age and Innocence

When Lamming writes that, "Father and Child are different only in the degrees of their knowledge" (*Pleasures*, 114), he is equating innocence with ignorance and credulity. Ignorance, he adds, "is also the source of some vision. It is, as it were, a kind of creative blindness" (*Pleasures*, 115). Lamming posits the possibility of significant, even radical generational change, in that the experience of childhood and the growth to maturity can fashion a different quality of person, not only in relation to the child that was, but also in relation to the adults who share responsibility for nurturing the child. In *Of Age and Innocence, The Pleasures of Exile* and *In the Castle of My Skin,* Lamming tests the possibility of generational transformation based on this principle in a series of dramatically rendered relationships among children and between old or older caretakers and the young.[4] The immediate context for Lamming is decolonization, and the developmental promise of social and political change is cast as the backdrop to individual growth and development. *In the Castle of My Skin* is allegorical in this sense: the innocent and credulous child of native community is the emblematic child of national belonging.[5]

Despite ongoing debates about the Jamesian framework of national allegory, *In the Castle of My Skin* sets the mould as a paradigmatic narrative of boyhood.[6] It is national allegory that assumes the epic contours of a literary assertion of a previously denied subjectivity. On one level, it is the subjectivity of one boy among others in the temporal space of a colonial childhood in a community that, like many others, is a mixed bag of those who are nurturing and well intentioned, and those who are unconsciously or intentionally criminal and abusive. On another level, it is the linked subjectivity of the child who resides in the double consciousness of the adult who is both witness and creator of a narrative that traces the development of a sympathetic imagination that is engendered in a literary reassertion of the boy's experience of native community.

The structural arrangement of the narrative is both linear and circular. As the child matures into a young man and leaves home, that experience is first isolated as the innocence and credulity of childhood in a particular place and time, and then through a discernible process of rupture and displacement, the adolescent begins to open up to the possibility of knowledge and experience gleaned from other worlds. Adult recollection and reflection in an indeterminate space and time are constituted in interludes of omniscient narrative, as an enduring part of the adult's sensibility.

Still another element of narrative structure is the village voice, rendered plurally in the direct speech of the boys talking to each other at school or at the beach, and others like the Old Man and the Old Woman. In the process, specific images of childhood and adolescence, some joyous and others terrifying and unbearably sad, are all linked in the writer's creative vision, which, located in the occluded space and time of writing, collapses the boundaries of time and place in the autobiographical inscription of self in the designated landscape of his self-formation.7

Among the most powerfully rendered of these points of connection is not the mother/child dyad, as one might expect, although mothers struggle to manage the socialization of the boys, but experiences of male bonding. Such bonding is evident among the boys of the village who attend elementary school together, play together and together create myths and rationalize the vagaries of an adult world not of their making. There is the Shoemaker's shop where the men of the village gather to talk and learn more about who they are as individuals and subjects of the British Empire. There are also instances of cross-generational male bonding in which the relative social isolation of the boys from nurturing adult male company is interrupted quite dramatically, to register the power of individual choice and the necessity of individual responsibility to the community. On one occasion, a fisherman at the beach risks his life to save Boy Blue, one of the gang of boys who play together, from certain death by drowning and delivers an important lesson in what it means to be a Man (*Castle*, 153):

> We were afraid of the fisherman. The way he looked at us! He was like someone who had been sorry for what he did, and yet not sorry since he knew it had to be done. He looked so terribly repentant and at the same time there was an expression which we could not define. Under the marble eyes and the impenetrable

stare there must have been something that cried out for life. He knew the catch was not a fish, but he hauled the net with the earnestness that could only have meant a desire beyond his control for the other's survival. (*Castle*, 152)

Another example occurs at the end of *In the Castle of My Skin*, as the villagers are dismantling their homes to accommodate a housing development into which they cannot afford to buy. The protagonist G, still stumbling about in the darkness of his innocence and credulity on the eve of his departure to take up a job in Trinidad, has a farewell encounter with the Old Man Pa, a guardian and community elder. It is a fond farewell in which Pa puts a hand on his shoulder, kisses him on the forehead and wishes him well. It is unmistakably an encounter between "Age that apprehends" and "Innocence which can only see" (*Pleasures*, 103), as Lamming described it in *The Pleasures of Exile*. G is both confused and overwhelmed by the finality of the encounter. He senses the significance of the moment through a flood of recollections that crowds his thoughts in the darkness: "The earth where I walked was a marvel of blackness and I knew in a sense more deep than simple departure I had said farewell, farewell to the land" (*Castle*, 303).

The reader is left to intuit a necessary connection between this fond farewell and the narrative imperative that links the adult's consciousness to the signal events, companions and guardians of his childhood in a village that, in a sense, ceases to exist except in the creative imagination that structures *In the Castle of My Skin* as autobiographical fiction. Yet, Lamming must have been dissatisfied with this ending because he returns to this farewell scene at the end of *The Pleasures of Exile* and embellishes it considerably with autobiographical detail about the spiritual nature of his relationship with "old Papa Grandison, my godfather" (*Pleasures*, 226), on whom he modelled Pa of *In the Castle of My Skin*. Shortly after he begins high school on a scholarship, he recalls the shattering experience of seeing Papa Grandison forced to move his small house from the site it had occupied for generations (*Pleasures*, 226):

> The carpenters knew me as a gentleman by daylight; and I don't think I would have liked anyone from the school to see me that night; for I walked all the way – *not me so much as the force within which binds me eternally to the root that was Papa* – miles and each mile an eternity I walked, crying like an infant, every step of the way beside that push cart with Papa's watch dog on my left. And the meaning of Papa's departure is the story of *In the Castle of My Skin*. (*Pleasures*, 228; emphasis added)

Lamming takes time at the end of *The Pleasures of Exile* to elaborate on the moral imperative implicit in the natural bonds, both humorous and moving, that he shared with his godfather. Papa Grandison kept pigeons and chickens under his house and called the pigeons home to feed them corn out of his hand at five o'clock each evening. Papa kept goats and before Lamming started high school he would take the goats out to graze, enjoying the pretend "role" of foreman to a group of boys who played along. He had his first meal every Sunday with Papa when the latter returned from church. He recalls the occasion when he witnessed, "Papa helping a goat to deliver its young":

> It was my first conscious experience of what happened at birth, and what birth did actually look like. Had spies informed, my mother would have murdered the devil in me with her Victorian rod. But it was valuable; because there was something between Papa's hands and the goat's travail: the way he helped the young kid out of its tangle of night and blood into life; there was something between that life and Papa's hands which made you feel that the animal was human; for Papa certainly wasn't any goat. (*Pleasures*, 227)

These experiences of Papa at one with the natural world are recalled and narrated as a wellspring of the author's creativity and moral compass, his sympathetic bonds with the individuals and community that shaped his life and gave it meaning. Childhood is recollected and imagined as the alignment of the past and the present on a scale of values that endures in the writer's commitment to an idealized native space.

Childhood, Language and the Creative Imagination

The complexity of language forms and uses is an important subtext in *In the Castle of My Skin*. Language is a source of puzzlement to the gang of boys who speculate in Creole on its relative values in the shifting contexts of school and home, the preacher and the politician.

I want to broaden my frame of reference by turning to Patrick Chamoiseau's *Chemin-d'école*, translated into English as *School Days*, where Chamoiseau constructs a narrative of childhood that in some ways parallels the preoccupations and aesthetic design of Lamming's *In the Castle of My Skin*, suggesting key strategies of imaginative return, recovery and narration.[8] In *In the Castle of My Skin* the fashioning of autobiographical consciousness rests on the juxtaposition of distinct narrative elements in the voices of the third-person adult narrator, the first-person narrative of the child and assorted dramatic interludes. In Chamoiseau, it is the voice and perspective of the author and writer as *raconteur* who narrates his childhood in the third person, in dialogue with the *Répondeurs*, who provide a running commentary on the unfolding narrative. The ensuing drama not only inscribes salient features of oral storytelling, to which Chamoiseau is committed, but also the process of transforming memory into narrative. As one of the authors of the cultural manifesto *Éloge de la créolité*, translated into English as *In Praise of Creoleness*, it is as though Chamoiseau puts aspects of the manifesto to the test in the recollected experience of childhood, which is recuperated and refashioned to harmonize with the adult's consciousness in *School Days*.[9] "In short, *we shall create a literature*, which will obey all the demands of modern writing while taking roots in the traditional configurations of our orality," wrote Bernabé, Chamoiseau and Confiänt in *Éloge de la créolité* (98). Childhood is in fact summoned and recreated as source and evidence, as filter and purifier of the writer's at-oneness with his native landscape.

Language and childhood are also a primary focus of Chamoiseau's *Au temps de l'antan: contes du pays Martinique*, translated by Linda Coverdale as *Creole Folktales*.[10] In the latter, Chamoiseau's narrative persona plays the role of a Creole storyteller, or the Master of Words. In a short introduction entitled Tales of Survival, he explains the socio-historical context that shaped the tales and gave them a utopian and emancipatory twist; they are utopian because they celebrate inventiveness and creativity as a cultural inheritance, and they are emancipatory because they celebrate survival and anticipate freedom from oppression as a community in the process of naming itself and its moral compass. There are twelve tales, and in each the Creole storyteller or *conteur* recreates with all the sophistication of an accomplished writer, "many features of oral storytelling, such as call and response ('cric . . . crac'), formulaic introductions and conclusions, parenthetical self-reference, enumerations and onomatopoe[i]a (among others)".[11] There is a lot more to be said about the aesthetics of adapting the oral to the written, but my point is that in *Creole Folktales,* Chamoiseau creates a poetics of childhood as he seeks to recover the interconnections between the oral folk tale and the world of the child's imagination in "the hypnotic power of the voice, the mystery of the spoken word" (*Creole Folktales*, xiii). Childhood may be a distinct and separate state of being but its boundaries are permeable. Assuming the masque of the Creole storyteller at the end of his introduction, Chamoiseau adroitly merges the worlds of the writer and the *conteur*:

Allow the strange words to work their secret magic, and above all, read these stories only at night. Remember, I wrote them with the moon as my sole companion, for fear of being changed into a basket without handles – a fate described by the old Storytellers, who must have been amused even then to know that I would never, oh never, tempt such a fate as that, just to see. (*Creole Folktales*, xiv)

In *School Days*, the child persona is rendered as the "*negrillon*", translated by Coverdale as "the little black boy", and at times as "the little boy". The Word Master or Creole storyteller narrates a childhood that must contend with the colonial school and the dedicated colonial conflict between Creole and French, oral and written. It is a narrative of childhood that explores the enigma of language and consciousness that culls inspiration from both worlds. The first part of the narrative, called "Longing", is just that: the child's irrepressible desire to go to school. The second part is called "Survival", and again, is just that: how the child survives the repressive, Creole-hating environment of the French colonial school. The binary "Longing" and "Survival" parody the innocence and experience of the adult's narrative of childhood; this is immediately evident in the author's self-placement as *raconteur* in the novel's dedication:

> Youngsters,
> of the West Indies, of French Guyana, of New Caledonia, of Reunion, of Mauritius, of Rodriguez and other Mascarenes, of Corsica, of Brittany, of Normandy, of Alsace, of the Basque country, of Provence, of Africa, of the Four Corners of the Orient, of all national territories, of all far-flung dominions, of all outlying posts of empires or federations, you who have had to face a colonial school, yes, you who in other ways are still confronting one today, and who will face this challenge tomorrow in some other guise: This voice of bitter laughter at the One and Only – a firmly centered voice challenging all centers, a voice beyond all home countries and peacefully divers[al] in opposition to the universal – is raised in your name.
> In Creole friendship,
> P.C.

The narrator, in the persona of the Creole storyteller, signs himself noncommittally as P.C., introduces the little black boy with all the self-deprecating mockery he can compress into what is tonally Creole: "My brothers and sisters O! I have something to tell you: the little black boy made the mistake of begging for school. I must add in his defence, that his sucking days were long gone and that by exploring the endless possibilities of his home, he had wrung them dry. This humble conquistador now developed a taste for window sills" (*School Days*, 11).

A chorus of *Répondeurs*, whom the storyteller introduces and calls upon whenever it suits him and who, at times, intervenes at will, embellishes the playful and performative aspects of the narrative. It is in this context that Chamoiseau playfully charts the boy's quest for language in a series of chalk adventures; the little boy alternately nibbles at the chalk and covers every space in the outer hall of the apartment where he lives with chalk scrawls. The breakthrough comes when his older brother, Jojo the Math Whiz, writes the little boy's name in chalk on the walls and confronts the little boy with the symbolic power of the written word:

> "That there is your first name . . . and you're inside it!" he revealed, with a wizard's mocking grin.
>
> *Wo yoyoy!* . . . Jojo the Math Whiz had just plunged the little boy into a fine predicament: he saw himself there, captured whole within a chalk mark. *Which means he could be erased from the world!* Pretending he wasn't scared shitless (which would have tickled Jojo), he began to copy out his first name a thousand times, in order to proliferate and avoid genocide. (*School Days*, 21)

The saga continues with the *Répondeurs*' endless interruptions and the storyteller's flourishes. "So he took to trapping scraps of reality inside his chalk marks" (*School Days*, 21), and from there he begins clamouring to go to school: "This ability to capture pieces of the world seemed to come from school. No one had confirmed this, but the chalk, the satchel, the morning departure toward this unknown place seemed to link a ritual of power into which he longed to be initiated" (*School Days*, 22). Once in the colonial school, he must weigh the situations where Creole rules against those where French is exclusive and absolute and where they intrude on each other's territory. Yet his passion for language and for the imaginative stimulation of books and writing continues to grow and assume a life of its own.

In *School Days,* a poetics of childhood is constructed around alignment of the child's irrepressible quest for language with the adult storyteller's refinement of a Creole literary aesthetic. Childhood's innocence is measured by language, first as a site of longing and increasingly as a means of survival. Wisdom is the Master of Words' prerogative in a call-and-response performance with the *Répondeurs*, which also mimics the storyteller's participatory audience and the writer's creative process. The child's delight in the sounds and shapes that he tries to capture with chalk on his apartment's outer walls finds a correlative in the narrative's sounds and shape – the orality – which lends coherence to the twin dimensions of experience that the child and the adult share.

In *The Poetics of Childhood*, Roni Natov sums up age and innocence's trajectory in the literature of childhood in this way:

> Through exploring this literature and the states of mind inherited from childhood, we might identify the images through which we saw the world: we might approximate the lenses through which we view the world even now. . . . The poetics of childhood draws attention to the ways in which we might see the flux of our imaginations more clearly. We might be able to distinguish between projection of the values and attitudes we associate with images from our early experiences and an illumination of the object or moment itself, as it stands more revealed.[12]

That said, I am struck by the relegation of the maternal to the background in both Lamming and Chamoiseau. In Lamming, male community is privileged at every stage of development in childhood's recovery and renewal, which begins when G is about nine years old. In *School Days*, I am again struck with the humorous assertion that, once the little boy's sucking days are over, he develops "a taste for window sills" (*School Days*, 11) and exploring the street outside. One key may lie in the windowsill that the little boy shares with G in *In the Castle of My Skin* (8) and C.L.R. James in *Beyond a Boundary* (46).[13] The focus of all three at the onset of childhood recollected is on the world outside and away from mothers and aunts, who hover in the background as caretakers and discipliners. This seems in keeping with Christopher Bollas's view that the individual's personal aesthetic is shaped first by interaction with the mother, which eventually "yields to the aesthetic of language . . . With the word, the infant has found a new transformational object, which facilitates the transition from deep enigmatic privacy toward the culture of the village."[14] Following this line of thought in Maryse Condé's *Tales from the Heart: True Stories from Childhood* takes us to another place of childhood altogether.

The Thematics of Mother Discourse

Dedicated to her deceased mother, *Tales from the Heart: True Stories from Childhood* brings us to a liminal place in adulthood. Childhood is elusive at age sixty, when memory is filtered through revolutionary issues of race, colonialism and women's freedom. A tentativeness, perhaps a hesitation, exists in the design of the text, which consists of fourteen stand-alone narratives held together by the narrator. She revisits her childhood in Guadeloupe seemingly in an attempt to recover the "truth" of her relationship with that place – with her parents and in particular with her mother – and the ways in which her parents attempted to mediate her perspective and experience. In design, this autobiography recalls the fragmentation of Jean Rhys's unfinished autobiography, *Smile Please*, where the lack of coherent memory over time and space remains unresolved.[15] The fragmentary poetics of Condé's childhood focuses on a much-loved youngest child who is precocious and rebellious, on her formation and development amid a growing alienation from her parents, and on a need to escape the constrictions of black middle-class life on a French colonial island.

In discussing the text, Condé stresses the challenge presented by "the distance of age, the gap of time, and so on": "in the French it is *contes vrais de mon enfance*. Why *contes vrais*? Because I was sixty when I was writing about myself being ten. Everything that I could say about me was a kind of fiction. Of course it is true, all the facts are true, all the elements are autobiographical."[16]

A serious tone exists in recovering her childhood's remote past and unravelling its significance, which recalls a literary Ceremony of Souls.[17] The narrator airs her grievances against her parents, and her mother in particular, whose fierce preoccupation with colour, class and respectability prompts Condé to reject her. She was a vain and beautiful woman who embarrassed her children by wearing stockings much lighter than her skin yet paradoxically disavowed any intimation that whiteness might be intrinsically superior. The narrative sequence's fault-finding bias is clear in the first of the stories, "Family Portrait". Smarting under the perceived condescension of a waiter in post-war Paris, her mother protests: "We're more educated. We have better manners. We read more. Some of them have never left Paris, whereas we have visited Mont Saint-Michel, the Riviera, and the Basque coast" (*Tales*, 5). Condé's comment is explicitly condemnatory: "There was something pathetic in this conversation which, though I was very young, upset me" (*Tales*, 5). When she asks her older brother, Sandrino, to help her understand her mother's seeming overreaction, he sums it up as alienation: "Papa and Maman are a pair of alienated individuals" (*Tales*, 6). That night she vows never to become alienated like her parents, and she initiates her fraught relationship with them as a way of defining herself. Condé is orphaned when she is twenty. "Family Portrait" poses the question: "Were my parents alienated?" (*Tales*, 8).

Through the filter of memory and the desire to recover the "truth" of her relationship with her mother/other, *Tales from the Heart* attempts to answer this question and explore its significance by isolating events and experiences that help Condé to understand two great losses: (1) her initial rejection of her mother as an alienated individual and her resolution at that time to be anything but the aesthetic personality (character) that her mother has constructed for herself and (2) her mother's death. Throughout, the narrator subjects her now-distant childhood self to rigorous self-questioning and harsh self-judgement in the shifting double consciousness of then and now, even describing herself while a student at the *lycée*, as "the incarnation of intelligence combined with spitefulness" (*Tales*, 125).

After a nomadic life as a young adult in West Africa, France and the United States, her eventual return to Guadeloupe appears to necessitate this line of self-enquiry. While Condé doesn't ever retreat from her assertion of difference and entitlement to an identity of her own making, she narrates the splintered mutually destructive relationship with her mother in a mixture of admiration and scorn, yet appears to achieve some enduring resolution in a deeply moving night of love, sympathy and perhaps atonement before she leaves Martinique to continue her education in Paris. In the fifteenth story, when as a teenager who has stayed out too late exploring the city and its environs on her *Motobécane*, a present from her parents on her sixteenth birthday, her mother berates her in ignominious racial terms: "What was I doing racing around like a crazy under the sun? Wasn't I ugly enough and black enough as I was? I looked like a Kongo girl. If it was a man I was looking for, I was wasting my time" (*Tales*, 127). What follows is a stunning reversal of their mutual hostilities. From the self-imposed isolation of her room, she hears her mother struggle up the stairs:

> I could hear her bump into the furniture and climb into her bed, which creaked like a boat being put to sea. Under the deceptive colors of pity, all the love I had for her surged into my heart and almost suffocated me. I went into her room without knocking, which was forbidden. Lying in the middle of her bed she was propped up against a pile of pillows, for she complained of breathlessness during the night. Her prayer book lay open in front of her. She had removed her *postiche*

and there were bare patches on her scalp. She was old and alone . . . Old and alone. I climbed on to the bed like I used to do when I was small, when nothing was refused me, when nothing was out of bounds. I hugged and hugged her and showered her with kisses. Suddenly, as if a signal had been given, we both began to cry.

I slipped my hand between her now withered and useless breasts which had breast-fed eight children, and we spent the whole night together, her clinging to me and I curled up against her side amidst the smell of old age and arnica, lost in her warmth.

That is how I want to remember her. (*Tales*, 128)

Her mother's body is restored to its original contours of intimacy with the child as a palpable experience of mutual recognition, affirmation and need. The poetics of childhood here is rendered as the thematics of home and mother love.

Moments of Being

The quest for the aesthetic moment, the transformational experience somewhere in childhood, is constituted differently in Judith Ortiz Cofer's *Silent Dancing: A Partial Remembrance of a Puerto Rican Childhood*.[18] Cofer is a Puerto Rican–American poet who writes in English like other women writers from the Caribbean, among them, Edwidge Danticat, Julia Alvarez and Esmeralda Santiago. Cofer's remembrance of childhood takes an unusual turn. As in Condé's *Tales from the Heart*, the title announces its fragmentariness and its incompleteness. It begins with a self-reflective critique of her undertaking in her preface, which is subtitled "Journey to a Summer's Afternoon" (as in Virginia Woolf's *Moments of Being*: "I dream, I make up pictures of a summer's afternoon").[19] This is followed by thirteen short stand-alone *ensayos* (Spanish for "essays"), which include oral tales, fables, songs, games and rhymes; each is followed by one or two poems related thematically to aspects of the narratives that precede them (*Silent Dancing*, 12). As she observes in a subsequent interview with Dolores Carmen Hernandez, poetry and prose "are different ways of seeing . . . one is like a microscope and the other like a telescope".[20] Moments of being are explored relationally in a variety of forms, crystallizing insecurities of perspective that mirror the construction of the subject self.

Cofer is bilingual and intersperses Spanish words, phrases and proverbs with English. She was born in Puerto Rico of Puerto Rican parents, and her childhood is spent moving back and forth between the rural village (*pueblo*) from which her mother comes, and Patterson, New Jersey, where there is a large Puerto Rican population from which her father would like the family to keep their distance. To support his family, Cofer's father joins the US navy; when he is away on a tour of duty, his wife and children return to their Puerto Rican *pueblo*, and when he returns to base in the United States, they join him in Patterson. He was gone for over two years during the Cuban Missile Crisis. His goal is children educated in the United States who will enjoy the privileges his navy life has procured for them. When her father dies prematurely, her mother returns to Puerto Rico; it is arguable that her mother ever really left Puerto Rico. However, Cofer chooses to remain in the United States. The divergent paths of mother and daughter have a specific social and cultural history; the narrative quest is for an enduring connection to her mother and her mother's "matriarchal tribe" (*Silent Dancing*, 139) across language, culture, time and space so that she can better understand the source of her creativity.

The text's self-consciousness always calls attention to its discursive limits. Cofer chooses a spiritual guide and mentor in Virginia Woolf. Her epigraph is from *A Room of One's Own*: "A woman writing thinks back through her mothers."[21] Yet, she dedicates *Silent Dancing* to her mother and her daughter. She uses Woolf's aesthetic design to tease out specific concerns and preoccupations when faced with the task of recovering from her childhood what has been intuited, and consciously or unconsciously repressed before it was understood. Like Condé, Cofer is sensitive to gaps in memory and the role of the creative imagination/art in fleshing out the truth: "memory for me is the 'jumping off' point; I am not in my poetry and in my fiction writing, a slave to memory. I like to believe that the poem or story contains the 'truth' of art rather than the factual, historical truth. . . . Art gives me that freedom" (*Silent Dancing*, 12).

Although Cofer's mother is alive, and she visits her in Puerto Rico with her daughter, her literary mentor and model text is that of a woman who is trying to recover and situate moments of experience shared with her deceased mother, whom she lost while still a child. In "A Sketch of the Past" Woolf says, "But if I turn to my mother, how difficult it is to single her out as she really was; to imagine what she was thinking, to put a single sentence in her mouth."[22] This model suggests a disconcerting quality of absent interiority, considering that Cofer acknowledges that she has all the documentation one could need for a biography. Or is it something else?

In *Sexing the Self*, Elspeth Probyn observes "the very mediated nature of speaking the self; it is not a transparent self who speaks from the heart".[23] Strategies of reference problematize any single narrative of the self in Cofer's case, inscribed in the dizzying operational space of childhood and adolescence spent moving back and forth between two cultures, two languages and two homes. While conflict with her mother persists, for example, in their different definitions of "words such as 'woman' and 'mother'" (*Silent Dancing*, 152), it assumes the contours of an open-ended dialogic quality.

In her preface, Cofer charts her illumination by quoting directly from Woolf's "A Sketch of the Past": "many bright colors; many distinct sounds; some human beings, caricatures; several violent moments of being, always including a circle of the scene they cut out: and all surrounded by a vast space – that is a rough visual description of childhood. This is how I shape it; and how I see myself as a child" (*Silent Dancing*, 11–12). She concludes: "This passage illustrates the approach that I was seeking in writing about my family. I wanted the essays to be, not just family history, but also creative explorations of known territory. I wanted to trace back through scenes based on my 'moments of being' the origins of my creative imagination" (*Silent Dancing*, 12).

The poetics of childhood constructed here identifies specific sites and conjunctural moments in the formation of consciousness where there is no clear line of origin and return between the lived experience of local community in the *pueblo* and Woolf's discursive struggle to find the appropriate images of self-articulation. Chief among these is Cofer's *pueblo* home of childhood, her maternal grandmother's house: "Then Mamá's house belonged only to us women. The aroma of coffee perking in the kitchen, the mesmerizing creaks and groans of the rockers, and the women telling their lives in *cuentos* are forever woven into the fabric of my imagination, braided like my hair that day I felt my grandmother's hands teaching me about strength, her voice convincing me of the power of storytelling" (*Silent Dancing*, 19). Storytelling emerges as an enduring link between generations of "my mother's matriarchal tribe" (*Silent Dancing*, 139), as a female space of resistance and self-empowerment as well as the transmission of oral history and instruction. The narrator recalls that as a child she begins to make up her own stories in imitation of her grandmother's authoritative style: "as I embroidered my own fable, listening all the while to that inner voice which, when I was very young sounded like Mamá's . . . And later, as I gained more confidence in my own ability, the voice telling the story became my own" (*Silent Dancing*, 85).

Unspeakable Things Unspoken: The Nightmare of Childhood

The trajectories of a poetics of childhood introduced here in specific reference to selected narratives of childhood cannot offer more than a partial recognition of the genre under study. But there are other childhoods in our literature that are not constituted with a goal of spiritual recovery and coherence of consciousness as these autobiographical narratives are; rather, they are crafted to register the unrelieved nightmares of childhoods lost, absent mothers and orphanages; narratives of abandonment and rejection, psychic disfigurement and abuse irrespective of gender.

Foremost in my mind is Fred D'Aguiar's *Dear Future*, where the poetics of childhood is constituted as a state of mind and a point of view that thrills to discoveries of language and experience, that hardly distinguishes reality from fantasy, daydream from nightmare, that longs for the safety and reassurance of an absent mother, only to be killed by the vengeful actions of a mob attack. The emotional foregrounding of childhood is explicitly a way to foreground ethical failures of the community and the state.

In a similar vein, Shani Mootoo's *Cereus Blooms at Night* is the harrowing account of children abandoned by their mother to incest and systematic abuse. The community recognizes these events and, instead of rescuing the children, condemns them to marginalization, universal contempt and flight in one case and madness in another. The images that cluster around such childhoods are distorted and deformed as in a garden gone wild and are a testament to maternal betrayal and social failure.

In D'Aguiar's novel, lost childhood assumes the contours of a stasis that resembles some kind of Catholic limbo where innocence is eternally innocence or life cut short; in Mootoo's novel, the childhood penchant for creating myths, rationalizations and magical rituals of control and release, freeze time and all possibility of becoming.

This is not the case in childhoods without mothering: Dionne Brand's *At the Full and Change of the Moon* and Jamaica Kincaid's *Autobiography of My Mother*. The poetics of childhood here are difficult to unravel because the aesthetics of being in each is so deeply implicated in the local historical and the epic, thus allegorical contours of experience.

Jamaica Kincaid's *Autobiography of My Mother*, however it is read, revolves around irrecoverable damage to the infant's nascent ego in the absence of a nurturing mother. The transformational moment of being is recoverable seemingly only in a re-enactment of abandonment and loss; the present is dedicated to the past.

Dionne Brand's *At the Full and Change of the Moon* comes at the same problem of being, however, webbed across generations in time and space. Faced with death or survival, Marie Ursule, Bola's mother, chooses death for herself and survival for her daughter, for whom she anticipates making a new life in an ever-widening diaspora of her generations. The novel suggests that making life is not the problem; it is the absence of nurturing and the emptiness, agony and rage, endlessly reproduced without a facilitative maternal environment. If, as Christopher Bollas argues, the grammar of our being is shaped by maternal interaction, if "we learn the grammar of our being before we grasp the rules of our language" (44), then the first human aesthetic is "the mother's tongue (the word)" (43), and the second human aesthetic is "the finding of the word to speak the self" (43).[24] Marie Ursule's vision of death delivering life is, in fact, so spiritually deficient that her generations never quite recover from this fundamental lack. That said, I'd like to add that Dionne Brand's *At the Full and Change of the Moon* is one of the grimmest and most beautiful Caribbean novels I have ever read.

I began this study with the dialectic of age and innocence constituted as a quest for moral compass and ethical being through the entanglements of memory and the creative imagination. As Elspeth Probyn observes in respect to autobiographical discourse, "The self here is both an object of inquiry and the means of analyzing where and how the self is lodged within the social formation."[25] A poetics of childhood anticipates a harmonious alignment of consciousness, past and present. The nightmare of childhood provides no such option except as a work of mourning in which the reader is invited to participate.

Notes

1. George Lamming, *The Pleasures of Exile* (Ann Arbor: University of Michigan Press, 1992), 103. Subsequent references to the book appear parenthetically in the text.
2. Maryse Condé, *Tales from the Heart: True Stories from My Childhood*, trans. Richard Philcox (New York: Soho Press, 2001). Subsequent references to the book appear parenthetically in the text.

3. Barbara Lewis, "Tales from the Heart: A Conversation with Maryse Condé", *Black Renaissance /Renaissance Noire* 5, no. 2 (Summer 2003): 94–106.
4. George Lamming, *In the Castle of My Skin* (Ann Arbor: University of Michigan Press, 1991). Subsequent references to the book appear parenthetically in the text.
5. I use the phrase "national belonging" in the context of migration studies and intercultural relations. It is meant to emphasize the writers' identification with national origins as a mark of belonging.
6. Initially, Aijaz Ahmad, "Jameson's Rhetoric of Otherness and the 'National Allegory'", *Social Text* 17 (Fall 1987): 3–25, written in response to Frederic Jameson, "Third-World Literature in the Era of Multinational Capitalism", *Social Text* 15 (Fall 1986): 65–88. For a Caribbean perspective on this debate, see Roberto Strongman, "A Caribbean Response to the Question of Third World National Allegories: Jameson, Ahmad and the Return of the Repressed", *Anthurium: A Caribbean Studies Journal* 6, no. 2 (Fall 2008), http://anthurium.miami.edu/volume_6/issue_2/strongman-acarribeanresponse.html.
7. I have written extensively about this novel before, for example, in *Caribbean Autobiography: Cultural Identity and Self-Representation* (Madison: University of Wisconsin Press, 2002), and my foreword to *In the Castle of My Skin* (Ann Arbor: University of Michigan Press, 1991).
8. Patrick Chamoiseau, *School Days*, trans. Linda Coverdale (Lincoln: University of Nebraska Press, 1997).
9. Jean Bernabé, Patrick Chamoiseau and Raphaël Confiänt, *In Praise of Creoleness*, trans. M.B. Taleb-Khyar (Baltimore: Johns Hopkins University Press, 1990).
10. Patrick Chamoiseau, *Creole Folktales* (1988), trans. Linda Coverdale (New York: New Press, 1994).
11. Lewis Carl Seifert, "Orality, History, and 'Creoleness' in Patrick Chamoiseau's *Creole Folktales*", *Marvels and Tales* 16:2 (2002): 214–15.
12. Roni Natov, *The Poetics of Childhood* (New York: Routledge, 2006), 5–6.
13. C.L.R. James, *Beyond a Boundary* (Durham, NC: Duke University Press, 1993).
14. Christopher Bollas, "The Aesthetic Moment and the Search for Transformation", in *Transitional Objects and Potential Spaces: Literary Uses of D.W. Winnicott*, ed. Peter L. Rudnytsky (New York: Columbia University Press, 1993), 43.
15. Jean Rhys, *Smile Please: An Unfinished Autobiography* (Berkeley: Creative Arts, 1979).
16. Lewis, "Tales from the Heart", 94–106.

17. I have in mind the Ceremony of Souls as George Lamming described it in *Pleasures of Exile* (9–10).
18. Judith Ortiz Cofer, *Silent Dancing: A Partial Remembrance of a Puerto Rican Childhood* (Houston: Arte Publico Press, 1990). Subsequent references to the book appear parenthetically in the text.
19. Virginia Woolf, *Moments of Being* (San Diego and London: Harcourt, 1989), 87.
20. Dolores Carmen Hernandez, "Judith Ortiz Cofer", *Puerto Rican Voices in English: Interviews with Writers* (Westport, CT: Praeger Publishers, 1997), 102.
21. Virginia Woolf, *A Room of One's Own* (New York: Harcourt Brace, 1989), 69.
22. Cofer, *Silent Dancing*, 11.
23. Elspeth Probyn, *Sexing the Self: Gendered Positions in Cultural Studies* (London and New York: Routledge, 1993), 74.
24. Bollas, "Aesthetic Moment", 43–44.
25. Probyn, *Sexing the Self*, 91.

2.

The Child as Symbol of "Challenge" in Michael Anthony's *The Year in San Fernando*

» JENNIFER RAHIM

Introduction

THE POPULARITY OF THE child in the work of imaginative writers from ex-colonial nations invites consideration as to whether, as Meenakshi Bharat believes, these writers feel that "postcoloniality confers a special role to the child and to childhood".[1] The Caribbean's literary tradition has no shortage of short stories, novels and poems in which the child or adolescent is central to plots, the focus of themes and present in some symbolic capacity. Authors have used the figure to represent, if not vicariously theorize, the region's myriad sociocultural issues, political evolutions and identity locations. Usually, they construct narratives that function as avenues for social protest and allegories of national development.

One of the first critics to draw attention to this category is Kenneth Ramchand. His signature study, *The West Indian Novel and Its Background* (1970), references four representative works in a chapter entitled "Novels of Childhood".[2] These include Austin Clarke's *Amongst Thistles and Thorns* (1965), George Lamming's *In the Castle of My Skin* (1953), Geoffrey Drayton's *Christopher* (1959) and Michael Anthony's *The Year in San Fernando* (1965).[3] With Anthony's first-person approach to narrating as his focus, Ramchand supplies a foundational critical taxonomy for reading that category of fiction.

A great deal has happened since that early phase to expand the social realist (male) gendered and (pre-independence) nation-based architecture evident in Ramchand's selection of novels. The post-1970s appearance of Caribbean women writers, for instance, introduced accounts of girlhood in novels like Merle Hodge's *Crick Crack, Monkey* (1970), Zee Edgell's *Beka Lamb* (1982) and Jamaica Kincaid's *Annie John* (1985).4 Additionally, novels written by previously unrepresented ethnic groups, such as Lakshmi Persaud's *Butterfly in the Wind* (1990), and more recently Joanne Haynes's *Walking* (2007), give access to new terrains of experience in their respective accounts of the East Indian and Afro-Chinese girlhood.5 A cursory sample of contemporary novels like Merle Hodge's *For the Life of Laetitia* (1993), Nalo Hopkinson's *Midnight Robber* (2000), and Oonya Kempadoo's *Buxton Spice* (1998) and *Tide Running* (2001) demonstrates the varied ways in which experiences of growing up have been configured.6 Further, if one references texts like Shani Mootoo's *Cereus Blooms at Night* (1996 and *Valmiki's Daughter* (2008), Lawrence Scott's *Aelred's Sin* (1999) and *Night Calypso* (2004), David Dabydeen's *Molly and the Muslim Stick* (2008) and even Jamaica Kincaid's *Mr. Potter* (2002), the difficulty of approaching the category in generically pure terms or with rigidly defined expectations about plot designs and form becomes even more acute, as none of these texts are exclusively novels of growing up in the traditional sense.7 They nevertheless treat with or allude to significant aspects of childhood and adolescence that impact the maturation process and so warrant consideration if not classification as such.

Admittedly, Caribbean novels of development have always presented young characters in a complex matrix of interrelated histories and contingencies that defy the traditional Bildungsroman formula. The current writing culture, however, features bold experiments with fictional (auto)biography, historical re-narrativization, and realist and futuristic forms. This culture also depicts worlds and subjectivities marked by disjunctures related to time and spatial boundaries, memory and invention, and point of view and subjectivity that interrupt expectations about the linearity of narratives of development, the presumed "innocence" of childhood and the unity of narrative subjects. Previously underexplored issues such as sexuality, sexual orientation, abuse, incest, street violence, fatherhood, and the impact of tourism and media cultures complicate and expand the terrain of growing up beyond the usual (post) imperial thematic hubs with sometimes unbridled candour. Indeed, the era of Ramchand's rather straightforward classification has certainly passed.

Yet whatever the transformations in representational practices and thematic foci, childhood's transitory nature remains an attractive metaphor for figuring social/national development, even when its use, as is often the case of (ex) subject societies, means challenging some of the easy "universal" assumptions accrued to the state. Openness to discovery and pliability to change, which typify childhood and undergird the child's facility to be simultaneously iconic and iconoclastic, no doubt align well with the expectant but turbulent path of the Caribbean's diverse societies from colony to independence and beyond. Indeed, if as Edward Baugh notes, the long-standing attraction to the use of metaphor in Caribbean theorizing is its capacity to sustain "nuance, suggestiveness and latency", then the child seems a "natural" sign of that productive liminality.[8] Baugh, incidentally, does not include the child/adolescent in his wide-ranging classification of metaphors that have served to represent "paradigms to describe Caribbeanness". This is perhaps because the figure bifurcates into considerations of the allegorical and so goes beyond the scope of his taxonomy. One wonders, however, how the Caribbean's literary child, over time, might fit a theoretical praxis that, as Baugh argues, forges a marriage between "poetics" and the "poetic". In an archipelago marked by so many diverse race-based and ethnic allegiances, this union locates the child as ideally equipped to enable a "process of argument that avoids rigidity and fixity, static positions".[9]

In this regard, one finds in Martin Carter's short but philosophically pregnant poem "The Child Ran into the Sea" a useful organizing paradigm.[10] The poet profiles the child as a symbol of ontological restlessness, that is, possessive of an active "desire" for an arrival at some site or state of otherness that it simultaneously embodies and seeks. Carter interplays the symbolic and allegorical levels of interpretation, as the child is both an archetypal sign of promise and a historical agent of quest. Symbol is thereby grounded in the temporal and spatial so as vision-bearer/actualizer, the child is also subject to the contingencies that retard promise and force retreat:

> the child ran into the sea
> but ran back from the waves, because
> the child does not know the sea on the horizon, is not the same sea
> ravishing the shore.
> ("Child", 108)

This tension between forward and reverse motions is prompted no doubt by a learned differentiation between the sea that erodes and the aspired-after sea at the horizon. It therefore points to a chasm between vision and realization that leads the poet to a kind of Lacanian threshold of deferred "desire" as he writes:

"what every child wants is always in the distance, like the sea on the horizon". Yet, retreat or defeat is not foreclosed, signalled by the reference towards the end of poem to some other child, "who wants to run / into the sea, into the horizon". The perennial propensity of the human to hope, of which the child is archetype, is the quality that underpins even the vulnerability of the dream to suppression by "inarticulate mouths" ("Child", 108). Not disregarding the particular sociopolitical context to which Carter's poem speaks or the phase of political disillusion in which it appears in his oeuvre, the poem's meditation on change makes it readily applicable to the ongoing regional quest for more hospitable nation spaces, as well as to the literal journeys to other landscapes or horizons of possibility that are also part of the Caribbean's story.

This chapter revisits Michael Anthony's novel *The Year in San Fernando* in light of the dialogic strain Carter illuminates between dream and disappointment, vision and reality in which the child is cast. It discerns, in the novel's early but covert engagement with the social politics of multi-ethnic, pre-independence Trinidad and Tobago, the author's effort to theorize a pathway for national development in which the twelve-year-old protagonist, Francis, plays a major role as a symbol and agent of "challenge" and therefore of transformation. The word "challenge" evokes Sylvia Wynter's "challenging criticism", a practice that, as Norval Edwards explains, participates in the necessary "disenchantment" of subject societies from their "bewitchment" by the cognitive norms and systems of knowledge bequeathed them by their colonial histories, or what Baugh less accusatively calls their "imputed Eurocentric biases".[11] But more significantly, she points to the militancy of the text itself as the primary ground for a criticism of challenge since "to write at all for the West Indian was and is a revolutionary act".[12]

To draw Wynter into this revisitation of Anthony's novel, however, is to unsettle the dust of the heated debate that erupted between her and Ramchand, in which his *West Indian Novel and Its Background* is the text she severely criticizes in her essay, "Creole Criticism: A Critique". As Edwards reminds us, it features her "blistering" rebuttal to Ramchand's categorization of her (and others) as practitioners of a "brand of pseudo-criticism, 'neo-African theory' that reduces criticism to socio-political commentary".[13] In turn, she brands Ramchand's Leavisite formalism mere "colonial mimicry", an acquiescent, ambivalent "creolist" criticism that suffers the deficiency of reproducing Western modes of knowledge. As such, it is a denial of the African presence in the Caribbean and is indicative of the Indo-Caribbean's angst of unacknowledged subjectivity.[14]

My intention is not to rescue Ramchand from the intellectual tour de force Wynter unleashes in her defence. Perhaps both sides make useful foundational observations about the problems and pitfalls of theoretical and critical practice in a civilization like the Caribbean's. However, I draw into the conversation Ramchand's reading of Anthony's novel to consider how his concept of the child as an "open state of consciousness", not by the way to be mistaken for a tabula rasa, may function in the spirit of Wynter's "challenging criticism". How does the child unveil the "enchantments" and injustices of exclusive structural and perceptual orthodoxies? How does the child participate in laying the groundwork for stimulating new cognitive modes on which social change may be engineered? Can the literary child serve to revitalize the debate on the legitimate concerns expressed by Ramchand and Wynter with the limitations of either ethnocentric or sociohistorically delinked theoretical and critical practices?

"Shake Fresh": Open Consciousness towards a "New Century of Mind"

At the close of a rather hellish year in the Chandles household, Edwin extends an invitation to Francis to "shake fresh. You is a gentleman" (*Year*, 179). Edwin is Mrs Chandles's somewhat renegade son, who lives on his own for reasons upon which the text does not elaborate, but leaves the reader to deduce in light of the open antagonism between Linden, his brother and their mother. At one level, the handshake marks Francis's departure. At another, it is Edwin's way of acknowledging that there has been some violation of relations between the boy and the Chandles and so signals a genuine desire to lay the foundation for a fresh beginning. Francis left his rural Mayaro home for San Fernando to function as helper and companion to the ageing Mrs Chandles. In turn, the arrangement would offer some relief to his recently widowed and financially struggling mother. In the process, however, he becomes something of an exploited "house-boy" in the Chandles house, relegated to sleeping on a pile of old newspapers on the floor, fed on meagre meals and subject to the dictates of its ill-tempered and severely class-conscious owners. Further, he is witness to a vicious battle over the inheritance rights to the house and is a kind of voyeur to a triadic love affair that involves Linden; his Mayaro-based, socially approved fiancée, Marva; and his less well-positioned but alluring city girlfriend, Julia.

The book's pre-independence time frame makes it possible to locate its ideological treatment of the protagonist's journey to deepening awareness, if not full maturity, in the context of the society's imminent but uncertain movement towards independence, with the full weight of a colonialism in its trail. Set in the 1940s, that entrenched status quo is powerfully manifested by two key buildings: the embattled house of the Chandles in San Fernando and the newly fenced Forestry Office in Mayaro, complete with the figure of Mr Chandles leaning over its banister and looking disapprovingly at the unkempt yard of Francis's working-class household. Taken together, these structures echo the past only to signal that this is primarily a novel about the slow and painful process of social and ideological transition, in which the nation stands at the crossroads of a collapsing colonial hegemony and the as-yet-uncertain shape of its new day. The inevitable dismantling of the old order is powerfully foreshadowed by the image of Francis's mother slipping through an opening in the newly constructed tiger-wire fence that separates the Forestry Office from her yard. The space is her self-created shortcut to the building, but she is unconscious of the rebellious potential in her physical breach of barriers.

Her son, Francis, however, is the ground in which the latent seed of that revolution will spring, signalled by his decision to return to his native Mayaro after his year in the Chandles conflicted household. Given the mounting instabilities in the society's rigidly configured class structure, therefore, Edwin's invitation to Francis "to shake fresh, you is a gentleman" evokes the possibility of a reconstituted order of relations. The Creole register in which the term "gentleman" is deployed is in direct contrast to all that his brother, Linden, represents. Linden's is a mere superficial claim to civility and respectability, since these go no deeper than his debonair dress and refined manner. He is in every sense a "mimic man" whose real tragedy is his investment in a hollow materialistic ethic at the expense of his personal integrity and happiness. This greatly overlooked handshake, I argue, carries much of the ideological weight of the narrative's admittedly subtle allegorical possibilities.

Much has been said to challenge Fredric Jameson's claim that, for writers relegated to that troublesome category he calls "third-world literature", "the story of the private individual destiny is always an allegory of the embattled situation of the public third-world culture and society".[15] Jameson makes an awkward effort to salvage this literature from the "readerly disappointments" of those, perhaps Western consumers, who miss the allegorical connections. However, Doris Sommer concedes, to his credit, that to "simply dismiss the relationship between nation and allegory", as she claims Ahamad had done in his response to Jameson, is untenable.[16] Sommer's affirmation of Jameson's argument provides a useful bridge to the case she makes for the role of allegories in the literatures of (ex-)colonized societies. She develops an unexplored strand of Jameson's discussion, which hints at the possibility of approaching the allegory from a dialectical, or what she calls a "weave"-like interdependent model, as opposed to one that reflects a "metaphoric parallelism", in which the private, surface narrative is simply analogous to the state of the nation.[17] This is the vantage point from which she argues that, in the Latin American nineteenth-century national allegory, "romance" or "erotics is coterminous with politics in an interlocking, rather than parallel relationship".[18]

As different as the novels that figure in Sommer's Latin American study may be from the West Indian context to which Anthony's novel belongs, they intersect in at least two significant aspects. Both traditions are preoccupied with the politics of national development, and both have allegorical designs. Sommer's argument may therefore have some relevance to the West Indian literary treatment of growing up, in which case, like the challenges of romance, those of child/adolescent are not merely analogous to the sociopolitical, but are in a metonymic, "coextensive" relationship with it. In other words, the growth of the nation is codependent on the maturation of the child in a radically symbiotic way. This notion of codependency at the private and public levels of the allegory provides an avenue for rethinking Ramchand's foregrounding of Anthony's fidelity to Francis as an "open", "experiencing" "consciousness", as well as his apparent suppression of the text's allegorical double vision and, therefore, its politics. In fact, with the exception of Anthony's novel, and, to some extent, Drayton's *Christopher*, Ramchand is critical of Clarke's and Lamming's overt use of the child as an authorial mouthpiece to advance social and political agendas at the expense of creative credibility.

It is therefore against a spate of negative criticism that deemed Anthony's novel simplistic and divorced from the pertinent social issues of the time that Ramchand generously celebrates the author's successful management of a certain type of narrative fantasy, that is, the "illusion of living through the boy's consciousness".[19] That the narrative perspective is recognized to be "an illusion" indirectly points to its doubleness. Ramchand's analysis, however, acknowledges its allegorical ramifications only at the end, where he establishes a crucial analogy between Francis's particular circumstances and the West Indian condition at the time, which in turn images displacement as a universal human experience. He writes, "The image of Francis, deprived, and tethered to the Chandles house (even to having a lair below the house), in a circumscribed world of which he is trying to make sense, is an image of the condition of the modern West Indian. But out of this distress, Anthony has created an archetypal situation."[20]

Caribbean literature is replete with stifling households from which escape is essential for not just survival, but also the reconstitution, even reinvention of self. Leave-taking, however, is often cast in ambivalence as demonstrated by the curiously botched parting conversation between Edwin and Francis, to which I will return. The act, nonetheless, is linked to a necessary untethering from the debilitating formative codes that govern those spaces. Unlike Lamming's G, Hodge's Tee, and Kincaid's Annie and Lucy, Francis makes a different kind of journey.[21] He comes full circle with his decision to return to Mayaro. He does so, however, as a changed individual having arrived at a new stage of awareness at the end of his brutal baptism into life's crude realities and their enablement by the status quo. That individual journey, however, mirrors the society's slow and painful decolonization process through what Ramchand praises as an "art of fiction of a very subtle kind".[22]

Sommer's observations about the intense weaving of the "two levels of desire", that is, between romance and nation, in her Latin American study, apparently meets its opposite in Anthony's and Ramchand's privileging of a more "discreet" or unobtrusive allegorical practice.[23] In *The Year in San Fernando*, the association between the growth of the child and the emergence of the new nation is merely suggested by the author's masterful mask of authorial distancing. But the reverse is actually truer, in that the subtlety of Anthony's allegorical thread makes the two levels appear almost inseparable, indeed an almost seamless intensity.

My interest, therefore, is not with the very worthy arguments about the (im)possibility of authorial objectivity, because Ramchand already addresses that in his recognition that Anthony's objectivity is an exquisitely managed "fiction". My interest is rather with the writer's and his critic's investment in elucidating a certain type of response to experience, typified by the child, and on which the future of both the child and the nation depends. This dialectic has a special benefit for the diverse, multicultural and evolving nature of the Caribbean post-independence societies. More than the achievement of verisimilitude in abstaining from authorial intrusion, therefore, the real political force of Anthony's narration of childhood/adolescence in *The Year in San Fernando* is, in Ramchand's formulation, its mobilization of "a vision for the reader in which each 'known' factor of experience is restored to a more primordial condition of latency".[24] The statement's overtures to the Romantic's ideal of the unfettered imagination and its ability to liberate one from the staidness of "known" are unmistakeable.[25]

I choose, however, to arrive at its interpretative possibilities by another route. I turn to Wilson Harris and Ramchand's reading of his work to facilitate the unravelling of this rather cryptically expressed restorative process. Such an approach is favoured, in part, because Ramchand had been already shot down by Wynter for his mimicry of Western critical practice. In his cogent 1968 preface to Harris's first novel, *Palace of the Peacock*, Ramchand not only succeeds in unlocking the workings of Harris's complex imagination, but displays an unbridled admiration for the author's treatment of character and its relevance to the region's historical realities.

He, therefore, consolidates the author's objectives as follows: Instead of creating characters whose positioning on one side or the other of the region's conflicts consolidates those conflicts and does violence to the make-up of the person, the West Indian novelist should set out to "visualise a fulfilment, a reconciliation in the person and throughout the society, of the parts of a heritage of broken cultures".[26] Harris's ultimate subject is is always the human "person in context" and the essential unity of that condition across races, histories and cultures. Ramchand gleans in the author's radical approaches to character and narration a creative response to the particular recuperative needs of the fractured, but diverse and emergent, West Indian sensibility. These are ostensibly strategies for articulating or visualizing a reconstituted sense of the human on which the possibility of a renewed social order may be generated. He therefore concludes part 1 of his preface to *Palace of the Peacock* as follows: "So the ground of loss or deprivation with which most West Indian writers and historians engage is not for Harris simply a ground for protest, recrimination and satire, it is visualized through the agents in his works as an ambivalent condition of helplessness and self-discovery, the starting point for new social structures."[27]

In a more recent essay, "Creoleness? Crossroads of a Civilization?" which extends the thinking he rehearsed in his first novel, Harris revisits the need for a radical break with "conquistadorial habits" of seeing and behaving. Such a rupture, he stresses, requires a decisive turning away from "a perverse commitment to privileged frame or family, a hidden authoritarianism".[28] This "will to rule" manifests itself in different ways as a malady of relations that plagues contemporary civilizations, eclipses the inherent unity of the human and the bridges of connections that often lie "latent" in consciousness and, therefore, in culture. For

Harris, the seminal paradox of the New World's history of conquest is its role in instituting modernity's culture of violence which is, paradoxically, at the same time, the "womb" of new possibilities. In this, the region exists as a kind of representational theatre for the outworking of a global crisis of relations that all must confront as an essential starting point for exorcizing prejudicial histories, their modes of perception, exclusory value systems and preferential structures. This perpetually staged and restaged human drama of reconciliation, therefore, informs Harris's emphatic pronouncement in his novel *Carnival* that "violence is *not* the corner-stone of a civilization".[29]

The link to Frantz Fanon's formulation of this very task of atonement and healing seems unavoidable. He writes in *Black Skin, White Masks* that "freedom requires an effort at disalienation", that is, the formation of new modes of engagement with the Other by turning our backs "on the inhuman voices which were those of [our] respective ancestors in order that authentic communication be possible".[30] The human horror that results from the enactments of learned prejudice leads to Fanon's rather disheartening conclusion: "The tragedy of man is that he was once a child."[31] Harris, however, goes beyond the "tragedy" of social conditioning that Fanon confronts. He presents the child, although often marginal to his plots, as a symbol of possibility. At the end of *Carnival*, for instance, an unnamed girl is miraculously gifted to the couple, Jonathan Weyl and his wife, Amaryllis. She is the orphaned progeny of Everyman Masters, who after at least two deaths is released from a purgatorial trial of "soul" that took him back to his childhood in a Guyanese-like plantation location called New Forest to the working-class factories of mid-twentieth-century London. The child's appearance at the end of the novel, therefore, signals an arrival at the possibility of a "new century of mind" on which individual/communal recovery from the tyrannies of a capital-driven, prejudicial and violent world order depends.

As novelists, Anthony and Harris undoubtedly vary vastly at almost every level. Yet *The Year in San Fernando* captures, in a less-complicated design, something of Harris's preoccupation with the need to lay the foundation for fresh ways of seeing and relating. For both, the treatment of "character" plays a seminal role in producing this "vision" of renewal. Evident in Anthony's characterization of Francis is a capacity for that "new" mind of which Harris speaks, but is made possible through what Ramchand describes as the gift of an "open" "consciousness". This facility, he argues, allows the boy's mind to move beyond ways "habituated to seeing" in "disparate" binaries.[32] Interestingly, he chooses to concentrate his analysis on Anthony's substantive metonymic treatment of landscape to suggest the boy's inner growth and recuperation. No mention is made of the binarized social categories related to class, race and gender, yet these are applicable given the tensions of the plot. However, the point not to be missed in this approach is that via metaphoric association, the boy's interaction with the natural world mobilizes an implied interdependence with the sociocultural challenges that face him and the society as a whole.

Perceptual decentring either throws into relief instituted/formalized habits of seeing/knowing or allows present experiences to be assessed in relation to an either enabling or disabling anteriority. Thus, the boy's observations of landscape do, in fact, play a major role. As Francis journeys to San Fernando, for instance, Ramchand draws attention to the way his nostalgia for the lost rural home shifts to excited anticipation of his arrival in the unknown town of San Fernando.[33] It can also be added that on his return journey, the ordinarily familiar landscape awakens in him the experience of encountering the unknown. So on seeing the houses pass by through the window of the bus, he notes that he "could not remember these parts at all" (*Year*, 183). Further, not only does the old appear new, but the recent past also appears to be already receding. When he attempts to look back at the San Fernando Hills, he discovers that the rain and the closed windows of the bus obstruct the view (183). To go back is to move forward to a renewed engagement with the familiar, just as the present is already receding into the past, not to be forgotten but to be critically revisited in light of his newly learned realities.

Working together with the simultaneous pleasant and unsettling experience of disorientation and recognition he undergoes is the shuttle of his thought through time and space. His expanding consciousness of the world this signals is thereby recorded as a process of education and re-education. On his journey home, for instance, Francis's attentiveness to landscape is linked to a series of "thoughts" that preoccupy him. All pivot around his San Fernando experience. He thinks of Linden Chandles, now homeless and committed to a loveless marriage with the socially approved Marva, while his affair with Julia remains unresolved. He thinks also of the aged and dying Mrs Chandles, as well as the dollar note he neglects to give her but hides under the house. In this way, he begins formulating pertinent assessments about the attitudes and behaviour of others, as well as his own. The disrespectful communication between mother and son, for example, is weighted against his experience of family life. His inhibition to speak freely to the Indian bus conductor, Balgobin, in the presence of the class-conscious Mr Chandles is reassessed through the recall of their warm friendship. The "quiet hate [he] felt pouring into [his] head . . . for those two upstairs" at the beginning of his San Fernando stay makes room for compassion for the dying mother and the defeated Linden Chandles (41).

Throughout the plot's evolution, the reader's attention is drawn to the boy's capacity to (re-)evaluate his circumstances and to be refreshed by the ever-renewing potential of experience itself. Responsibility is thereby placed on the individual to begin clearing the ground for greater understanding across differences in which forgiveness is an essential requirement. The narrative gently points to this way forward, not only for Francis as he grows to manhood, but for the entire society as it anticipates independence. This tacit formula for healing embedded in Anthony's narrative has been developed with greater intensity and depth by later Caribbean writers. Apart from Harris's consistent experimentations with harrowing purgatorial sagas of psychospiritual renewal already mentioned in *Carnival*, Earl Lovelace's *Salt* offers a masterly study of the crisis.[34] However, while Anthony makes more of the class prejudices of the colonial status quo the focus of his narrative, leaving the reader to deduce their race- and gender-based corollaries, Lovelace takes on the historical origins of the "them" and "us" politics of the race and class divides that perpetuate stasis and suspicion in Trinidadian society.

But always, there are no guarantees for an immediate recovery, echoed, for instance, in both the failed attempt by Alford George to initiate a new social order and culture based on unity in diversity and the conditionality inlaid in Amaryllis's prediction about the unnamed orphaned daughter of Everyman Masters that, "Should she, this child, survive, into a new century of mind we may all recover."[35] This new order of relations is not so much actualized as individually and communally rehearsed, for instance, by Edwin's proffered handshake and Bango's carnival-like Independence Day parade of children dressed to represent the nation's race and ethnic diversity.[36] Anthony's plot, in a similar vein, avoids romantic foreclosures. The novel sets the stage for social and ideological transition with the society, like Francis, standing at the crossroads of a collapsing colonial framework and the as-yet-uncertain shape of its postcolonial future. This open-endedness is critical to the novel's questioning and searching mode, one that is incompatible with any temptation to think in simplistic absolutes or pseudo-libratory binary categories.

Therefore, it would be erroneous to conclude that Francis's future is predicated on an idealized rural/urban, working-class/middle-class divide or, for that matter, on a complete rejection of the world beyond his Mayaro origins. In fact, such resolutions are interrupted by an often-missed moment of ambivalence towards the end of the text when Francis finds himself on the receiving end of Edwin's perhaps inadvertent linguistic slip-up. During their parting conversation, Edwin asks him if he would return to San Fernando. Francis decisively replies, "I'm not coming back" (*Year*, 179), signalling his intention to make a clean break with the sterile world and value system of the Chandles home. In turn, Edwin delivers the rather strange response, "But in case you don't come back, shake fresh . . . "(179).

That significant reconciliatory handshake is therefore predicated on a misunderstanding that reverses the boy's reply to Edwin's question. Located in the awkward space of departure, the blunder is perhaps understandable. However, it provides a teasing textual knot with at least two interpretative possibilities. First, the error opens the ground for a renewed future relationship with the very city that so rudely awakened him, suggested, for instance, in their reciprocated exchange, "Till we meet again" (179). Second, latent in Edwin's (un)intentional reversal of Francis's response is the subtle persistence of a stubborn "authoritarianism", the colonial malady of an ascendant, educated middle class to which he belongs, if only marginally, as the exiled son, but now legal inheritor of the family house. He is thereby positioned to ensure that either "things will change up there" (178) or remain the same. The scene, therefore, leaves the issue of the boy's return open, as well as renders the promise of "change" questionable. Both characters, in that instant, stand inconclusively on the edge of old and new worlds. Francis thereby simultaneously becomes the same and Other of Carter's child who "ran" but also "wants to run / into the sea, into the horizon" ("Child", 108).

In "Literary Theory and the Caribbean: Theory, Belief and Desire, or Designing Theory", Baugh reminds us that "All theories are designs. The design is that theory is a projection of the theorist's belief, and belief is a function of desire."[37] With so many groups of varied identity locations, it is no wonder that such a range of symbols used to theorize the Caribbean's many-chaptered saga of evolution/revolution exists. Yet as diverse as these imaginings have been and continue to be, Baugh makes an important point about the reconciliatory impetus that characterizes a Caribbean poetics. It is one that witnesses to the effort of writers and theorists to "grapple, in different ways, and perhaps with different degrees of success, with the fact of violence and the challenge of how not to perpetuate it".[38] The literary child is not to be excluded from this tradition, having long served as a primary articulator of our desired Caribbeans of imagination. Anthony's fidelity to what he imagines to be the mind of the child offers a path to national development that avoids the pitfall of recrimination and the reinstitution of exclusive binaries in confronting historical and social injustices.

The child as symbol of change therefore challenges Manichaean theoretical models and methodologies for reading Caribbean cultural productions, inappropriate as these are incompatible with the region's sociocultural and imaginative evolution. The very polemic at the heart of the Ramchand/Wynter confrontation is the need to reorganize and rebalance the old politics of relations. This is the underbelly of the necessary reformation of "mind" for which they both advocate, but as Anthony's narrative intimates cannot be achieved by polarized thinking frames. Francis's gift of "natural recovery" both frees him to move forward unencumbered by the past though not naive of the class, race and gender politics that demarcate his society. In the novel's subtly managed allegorical framework, Anthony presents Francis both as a sign of the chronic psychosocial dislocation of a debilitating colonial order and of the new consciousness/nation he visualizes. Yet, as the walk to the bus stop with the perturbed and defeated Linden Chandles indicates, the future Francis heralds bears a cloud of uncertainty about its incarnation, mirrored by the conflicted weather conditions through which they travel. As sunshine and rain interrupt each other, Francis thinks, "here was the Devil and his Wife again, fighting on Christmas Eve" (179). The novel is open ended and perhaps appropriately so, as the resolution is left with the reader/public: allegory's final destination.

Notes

1. Meenakshi Bharat, *The Ultimate Colony: The Child in Postcolonial Fiction* (New Delhi: Allied Publishers, 2003), 3.
2. See Kenneth Ramchand, "Novels of Childhood", in *The West Indian Novel and Its Background* (London: Faber, 1970), 205–22. All references to Ramchand's analysis of *The Year in San Fernando* are taken from this edition.
3. Austin Clarke, *Amongst Thistles and Thorns* (London: Heinemann, 1965); George Lamming, *In the Castle of My Skin* (Port of Spain: Longman, 1970); Geoffrey Drayton, *Christopher* (London: Collins, 1959); Michael Anthony, *The Year in San Fernando* (London: Heinemann, 1970).
4. Merle Hodge, *Crick Crack, Monkey* (London: André Deutsch, 1970); Zee Edgell,

Beka Lamb (London: Heinemann, 1982); Jamaica Kincaid, *Annie John* (New York: Farrar, Straus and Giroux, 1985).

5. Lakshmi Persaud, *Butterfly in the Wind* (Leeds: Peepal Tree Press, 1990); Joanne Haynes, *Walking* (Hong Kong: Macmillan, 2007).

6. Merle Hodge, *For the Life of Laetitia* (New York: Farrar, Straus and Giroux, 1993); Nalo Hopkinson, *Midnight Robber* (New York: Warner Books, 2000); Oonya Kempadoo, *Buxton Spice* (London: Phoenix House, 1998); Oonya Kempadoo, *Tide Running* (New York: Farrar, Straus and Giroux, 2001).

7. Shani Mootoo, *Cereus Blooms at Night* (Toronto: McClelland and Stewart, 1996); Lawrence Scott, *Aelred's Sin* (London: Allison and Busby, 1998); Lawrence Scott, *Night Calypso* (London: Allison and Busby, 2004); Jamaica Kincaid, *Mr. Potter* (New York: Farrar, Straus and Giroux, 2002).

8. Edward Baugh, "Literary Theory and the Caribbean: Theory, Belief and Desire, or Designing Theory", *Shibboleths: Journal of Comparative Theory* 1, no. 1 (2006): 58.

9. Ibid.

10. Martin Carter, "The Child Ran into the Sea" (1974), in *Poems of Succession* (London and Port of Spain: New Beacon Books, 1977), 108.

11. Baugh, "Literary Theory", 58. Norval Edwards ably consolidates the thinking in Wynter's early essays in his " 'Talking About a Little Culture': Sylvia Wynter's Early Essays", *Journal of West Indian Literature* 10, nos. 1 and 2 (November 2001): 12–38. See pages 18–20. I draw on his discussion of Wynter's "challenging criticism" and the debate that ensued between her and Ramchand. See also Sylvia Wynter's essays "We Must Learn to Sit Down Together and Talk about a Little Culture: Reflections on West Indian Writing and Criticism", *Jamaica Journal* 2 (December 1968): 23–32 and 3 (March 1969): 27–42 and "Creole Criticism: A Critique", *New World Quarterly* 5, no. 4 (1973): 12–36; and Kenneth Ramchand's "Concern for Criticism", *Caribbean Quarterly* 16, no. 2 (1970): 51–60.

12. Wynter, "We Must Learn", 31.

13. Edwards, "Talking", 31.

14. Ibid., 31–33, for a discussion of this debate.

15. Fredric Jameson, "Third-World Literature in the Era of Multinational Capital", *Social Text* 15 (1986): 69. See Aijaz Ahamad's essay, "Jameson's Rhetoric of Otherness and the 'National Allegory' ", *Social Text* 17 (1987): 3–25. Ahamad is the first to comprehensively deconstruct Jameson's argument. He points to the reductive assumptions that reside in a sweeping category like "third-world literature", since it conflates "fundamental issues: of periodization, social and linguistic formations, and political and ideological struggles within the field of literary production" (p. 4).

16. Doris Sommer, "Allegory and Dialectics: A Match Made in Romance", *Boundary 2* 18, no. 1 (1991): 73.
17. Ibid. Sommer draws on Walter Benjamin, whose dispute with the privilege Romantics gave to symbol over allegory' resulted in his development of the notion of a "dialectical allegory". It opposes the hierarchy of value the Romantics established between them. See pp. 63-66.
18. Ibid., 74.
19. Ramchand, *West Indian Novel*, 206.
20. Ibid., 222.
21. Lamming, *Castle*; Kincaid, *Annie John*.
22. Ramchand, *West Indian Novel*, 209.
23. See Sommer, "Allegory", 75. She writes: "The two levels of desire are different, which allows us to remark on an allegorical structure, but they are not discrete. Desire weaves between the individual and public family in a way that shows the terms to be contiguous – coextensive as opposed to merely analogous."
24. Ramchand, *West Indian Novel*, 221.
25. Ramchand compares the rejuvenating ability Anthony sees in landscape to the Romantic poet, William Wordsworth. He therefore draws attention to the author's focus on the "natural recovery" of the protagonist's mind as it shifts from "nostalgia" to "anticipation" (ibid., 210).
26. Ramchand, Preface to *Palace of the Peacock* (London: Faber, 1960), n.p.
27. Ibid.
28. Wilson Harris, "Creoleness? Crossroads of a Civilization?", in *The Unfinished Genesis of the Imagination*, ed. Andrew Bundy (London: Routledge, 1999), 238, 239.
29. Wilson Harris, *Carnival* (London: Faber, 1985), 86.
30. Frantz Fanon, *Black Skin, White Masks*, trans. C.L. Markmann (New York: Grove Press, 1967), 231.
31. Ibid.
32. Ramchand, *West Indian Novel*, 212. Ramchand names binaries such as, "nostalgia-anticipation, town-country, pure-sordid".
33. Ibid., 210.
34. Earl Lovelace, *Salt* (London: Faber, 1996).
35. Harris, *Carnival*, 171.
36. Lovelace, *Salt*, 257.
37. Baugh, "Literary Theory and the Caribbean", 57.
38. Ibid., 60.

3.

"The Thing Without a Name"
The Child as Narrative Strategy in *Miguel Street*

» RYAN DURGASINGH

THE UNNAMED NARRATOR OF V.S. Naipaul's *Miguel Street* relates the picaresque exploits of his neighbours to the reader while his past self, the child who has ostensibly experienced these events, remains peripheral throughout most of the narrative. The child's own development follows an anachronous path and complicates notions of the Bildungsroman as his life is often overshadowed by the colourful characters with whom he associates. Because of this, the child is frequently withdrawn, hovering around the fringes of the narrative, his actions serving to highlight others' characters. This chapter analyses the child as narrative strategy in *Miguel Street* and as a character who is not allowed to be central to his own novel of development until he becomes an adult.

Miguel Street details the stories of the eccentric neighbours among whom the child grows up during Trinidad and Tobago's late colonial period on the eponymous street in the country's capital of Port of Spain. The book explores the colourful exploits of the boy's neighbours as related by his adult self's recollections and past experiences. It is broken up into a series of vignettes concerning different characters and tracing some important development in their lives. Although the boy's own story is infrequently hinted at in the numerous stories of his neighbours' adventures, the reader notes his growing disillusionment with them and the society in general towards the end of the book. At the end of what is his own Bildungsroman, the boy – an adult at novel's end – leaves Trinidad and Tobago for England.

Whether or not *Miguel Street* is a conventional Bildungsroman may be a matter for some debate. A Bildungsroman is defined as a "novel of development"; the term seems to apply to *Miguel Street* since the young boy matures during the course of the narrative and is schooled into adulthood by his experiences. However, the discourse does not explicitly focus in its entirety on the child as the story's protagonist. Not until the book's final chapter does he become the story's protagonist. Most of the narrative is in vignettes, each concerning a different character, with the discourse maintaining its coherence through the frame-like backdrop of the narrator's evaluation of life on Miguel Street and his backgrounded maturation. Moreover, this overarching coherence demands that *Miguel Street* be classified as a novel and not as a series of short stories, as has been posited by some critics;[1] the child's story is a linking device used to maintain the coherence of a disjointed discourse.

As stated previously, while other elements of the Bildungsroman apply (such as the child's movement from a rural to an urban setting, necessitated by his father's death and his growing disillusionment with his society as he matures), his adolescent development is often shoved into the background or elided over. With the exception of the child character's centrality to the story, most of the thematic and formal concerns that Marianne Hirsch identifies as part of the Bildungsroman in "From Great Expectations to Lost Illusions: The Novel of Formation as Genre", apply to *Miguel Street*.

One of the most important features that Hirsch identifies is the "development of selfhood".[2] According to Hirsch, the Bildungsroman's "projected resolution is an accommodation to the existing society. While each protagonist has the choice of accepting or rejecting this projected resolution, each novel ends with a precise stand on his part, with his assessment of himself and his place in society."[3] *Miguel Street*, like Jamaica Kincaid's *Annie John* and Merle Hodge's *Crick Crack, Monkey*, ends with its protagonist leaving his West Indian society for an ostensibly better one, having come to a negative assessment of that society. The propensity of Bildungsromane from the West Indian canon to portray the rejection of West Indian society suggests that some of these Bildungsromane may choose to encode the differences inherent in the growth and development of the West Indian child as distinct from that of the European child's.[4] This propensity also alerts us to the fact that these Bildungsromane may complicate the traditional form of the novel itself, perhaps even allowing the central child figure to be so passive that he is not allowed to be the story's protagonist for its entirety, as happens in *Miguel Street*.[5]

For these reasons, this chapter argues that *Miguel Street* is indeed a Bildungsroman, although one that is complicated by relegating the child to the periphery of the narrative.

One of the main reasons that the child's development in *Miguel Street* is so effectively backgrounded is that the writer uses an anachronous plot in the telling of his story. Anachrony, according to Gerard Genette, deals with deviations within the chronology of a story, a distinction most related to plot, which is the rendering of events or the telling of a story versus the story itself, mostly related to a strict chronological ordering of those events.[6] Anachrony complicates the story by telling it out of sequential order, thereby hiding or emphasizing certain aspects of the discourse. There are three types of anachrony: *analepsis* (flashback), *prolepsis* (flash forward) and *ellipsis* (omission).[7]

Miguel Street uses retrospective narration; the narrator is the grown-up child looking back on his formative years on Miguel Street, actively reconstructing his experiences there. His retrospective narrative, however, does not follow a simple beginning-to-end mode, but a complex shifting timeline involving numerous analepses, prolepses and ellipses sometimes embedded in a single vignette. The reason for this complexity lies at the heart of the narrator's intent; he deliberately shifts the story in each vignette to focus exclusively on one of Miguel Street's inhabitants. For some of the vignettes, this structure effectively places the child character in the background, making it difficult to say who has experienced these events and calling the first-person narration into question.

Evidence of this complex timeline and questionable narration can be seen with reference to "Bogart", the first vignette in the novel, which begins with Hat and the eponymous Bogart playing out their morning exchange of salutations:

> Every morning when he got up Hat would sit on the banister of his back verandah and shout across, "What happening there, Bogart?"
> Bogart would turn in his bed and mumble softly, so that no one heard, "What happening there, Hat?"[8]

The narrator's assertion that "no one heard" Bogart's response raises issues with his first-person narration. If no one heard it, how then does the child (the one who has experienced all of this) grow into the narrator who relates it? Such markers (which can be found throughout the discourse) suggest some sort of omniscience that is obviously at odds with the limited perspective of a first-person narrative. This evidence leads one to question the reliability of the narration of the child's experiences, perhaps also alerting one to the possibility that what is being put forth as a child's perspective is, in fact, an adult's constructed one, a matter of psychological perspective in the narrative.

Psychological perspective concerns who the narrator of a text is, that is, who observes the events that take place and the types of discourse that are used by the narrative voice.9 In speaking about psychological perspective, it is useful to make the distinction between *homodiegetic* narratives (ones in which the narrator is a character in the story) and *heterodiegetic* narratives (ones in which the narrator operates outside the story). In *Miguel Street*, there is a stated "I" character who has experienced these events, leading us to conclude that this is a homodiegetic narrative. Yet the narrator's knowledge throughout the novel constantly questions his limited perspective since it bears markers of heterodiegetic narration. The first-person narrator's foregrounded perspective may, in turn, raise the question of whether or not a subtle *metalepsis* (or transgression of narrative levels) is occurring throughout the narrative.

From a beginning that immediately calls the reliability of its witness into account, the first vignette complicates its story further with anachrony. From *story-now* (the time during which the events of the story are assumed to have taken place),10 the narrator uses analepsis to explore how Bogart came by his name (from *Casablanca* and the movie's popularity in Port of Spain). From this analepsis, we move to another in which we explore Bogart's first nickname (Patience) and get his physical description as well as his failed attempt at being a tailor, finally ending with the narrator's musings on how a man such as Bogart became so popular. This analepsis then ends with a return to story-now, in which Bogart fails to respond to Hat's salutation and disappears. Thereafter, another analepsis occurs, one that concerns how Bogart came to Miguel Street. The plot finally winds its way back to story-now and finishes Bogart's vignette without further analepsis.

This complex shift through time, in which the retrospective narration deals with events in the more remote past while using the more recent past as a link, sets the stage for the rest of the novel. Each vignette plays with time, moving between episodes in each character's life or eliding over particulars, so as to show the relatedness of certain scenes. Each vignette mainly uses ellipsis, which jumps from significant and related scenes to others in each character's life, and which is of central importance to anachrony in the novel. Analepsis and, to a smaller extent, prolepsis are certainly involved.

The immediate effect of all of this anachrony is a disjointed timeline in which all of the vignettes are either occurring concurrently or overlapping, as can be seen when Bogart appears in the third chapter, "George and the Pink House". He draws circles on the pavement (*Miguel Street*, 19), an affectation he was said to have before he disappeared for the first time, suggesting that he has yet to leave by the time that Elias's mother dies. Thus, the timeline is fractured and fragmentary, pieced together to focus on a specific character's (and not the child's) development. Therefore, events and people who have had their stories already told are encountered before major actions have taken place in their lives, in other characters' vignettes. The implications for the child, who is the only character to appear in all of the sketches, are far reaching.

Because the timeline is pieced together to examine a particular character's development (following Labov's model of natural narrative), the narrative perspective of the child is often a complex amalgam of different maturational stages.[11] While he is assumed to be present for each vignette (although, as we have noticed, the first-person narration is questionable), he is often not the focus of the narrative voice (the adult narrator). The child, therefore, becomes a reactionary subject; his actions are predicated upon the adult characters' actions. In "Bogart", he paints the sign as requested of him and then silently watches the story unfold.[12] In "The Thing Without a Name", he is the recipient of Popo's philosophical musings; in "George and the Pink House", he is terrified by George. This pattern continues with the child's story being backgrounded in every vignette. Yet, clearly because of the numerous leaps through time that the story makes, he must be at different stages in his development. The penultimate chapter, "Hat", begins when the child is young and ends with him as an adult, suggesting that his sketch of Hat has spanned not just the entire narrative, but his entire adolescence, as well.

Even when we do learn about the child's life, it is in relation to one of the other characters. Although the child is present from the novel's beginning, we do not get the story of how he came to live on Miguel Street until the ninth vignette ("Titus Hoyt, I.A."), in which we learn that his father has died, and he has come to live with his mother. This information is shared because the narrator wishes to focus on Titus Hoyt: "Titus Hoyt was the first man I met when I came to Port of Spain, a year of two before the war" (72). An analepsis, which details his arrival and subsequent first meeting with Titus Hoyt, follows.

Thus, the anachronous plot makes it clear that the child is the discourse's canvas. He functions as a background against which the colourful characters (made all the more colourful by his lack of colour) can be emphasized. The discourse maintains its coherence because of the implied story of his life behind the others' stories, although we are rarely given any hints of that story until they are necessary to enhance another character's story. Bruce King alludes to the Bildungsroman going on behind the scenes: "The various stories are linked subsections of a larger story concerning the narrator and his relationship with Hat, which comes to a conclusion in the next-to-last story of the volume and which is followed by the narrator's disillusionment and departure for England."[13] King's assertion suggests that the child is far more central than he really is. The child's development happens in the interstices, away from the main action of the narrative.

This evidence relates directly to issues of power in the novel. Children's-literature theorists argue that the child in literature is always at "the mercy of adult power and authority".[14] Childhood and the child, therefore, are created and characterized through a host of socio-historical value systems that are embedded in the discourse. Constructions of childhood have long been subjected to the inconsistencies of adult memory and perception. Adult narrators who relate past experiences of their childhoods seek to recapture and retell past stories based on subjective memory, known for often creating, emphasizing, deemphasizing or wholly eliding over, moments in time. The instability of past memories obviously also pertains to authors who may draw inspiration for their child characters from either societal constructions of the child or from their own recollected past experiences.

Because memory is subjective, and since time places distance between childhood and adulthood, the very process of remembering events as an adult means that the controlling perspective is that of an adult, and one that can only represent an idea of the child. Because of this controlling perspective, Karin Lesnik-Oberstein, as well as many other children's-literature theorists, argues that in literature "the child does not exist".[15] The immediate effect on our discussion is to highlight how little the child is allowed to be central to his novel of development. The implications of adult power for the child and childhood are twofold in *Miguel Street*: on the level of narration and as a discursive strategy.

First, on the level of the narrative itself, we see that the child character and childhood companions are often subjected to adult power. While the children in the story are relegated to the sidelines of the narrative, no boundaries are placed on their being physically present during the action of that narrative, a feature that certainly speaks to the ambivalent place of the child in the West Indies. Power in *Miguel Street* is rigidly maintained in terms of patriarchal hegemony, so when the children, who are boys, transgress the boundaries of "child" and attempt to take up masculine roles as markers of power, they are swiftly chastised. In the novel, the child is always allowed to be Miguel Street's subject, but never its agent. When the central child figure decides to emulate Eddoes's role of "sweet-man" by wearing a toothbrush, his mother is quick to re-establish the power dynamic:

> My mother said, "You playing man? But why you don't wait until your pee make froth?"
> That made me miserable for days.
> But it didn't prevent me taking the tooth-brush to school and wearing it there. It caused quite a stir. But I quickly realised that only a man like Eddoes could have worn a tooth-brush and carried it off. (93)

The obvious implication of "only a man like Eddoes" (other than that Eddoes is a particular kind of man) is that other men can do certain things that the child cannot or is not allowed to do. Characters in the novel rely heavily on the attainment of adult male power to achieve agency; the child, however, is always precluded from doing so.

Sexual knowledge is not frowned upon such that topics are deemed too taboo to talk about in front of the children. But when they themselves make reference to sexual relationships, the adult wastes no time in reinforcing the child's subservient status. When Eddoes brings news of his impending fatherhood, Boyee tries to console him after Hat has disparaged the woman whom Eddoes thinks is bearing his child:

> Boyee said, "Don't worry, Eddoes. Wait and see if it is your baby. Wait and see."
> Hat said, "Boyee, ain't you too damn small to be meddling with talk like this?" (100)

The adult's ambivalent treatment of the child smacks of control. Hat's response to Boyee's statement alerts us that the boy is allowed to be present but not opinionated, a contradiction that Jacqueline Rose alludes to when she argues that there "is a need within Western society to capture, define, control and release and protect the 'child' ".[16]

The children grow up in an adult society filled with adult structures of power. The newspaper is one such model of adult power, reinforcing belief through assumed objectivity and wide circulation. Things are given extra truth value if read in the papers, as Fawzia Mustafa states: "By understanding that the newspaper performs a novelistic function of creating the means whereby a community can conceive of itself, Naipaul's habit of obsessively quoting, or creating, headlines, articles, reports, and newspaper competitions in his first four books helps locate an important conceptual pulse that his fiction depends upon."[17] It follows that one of the reasons that the child is impressed with Hat is because he "always read the papers. He read them from about ten in the morning until about six in the evening" (14).

Part of the *conceptual perspective* (the mental attitude of the speaker towards the thing expressed) of the characters in the novel is certainly the emphasis placed on adult authority and the newspaper as an agent of that authority.[18] When the group tries to puzzle out Mrs Hereira's reasons for staying on Miguel Street, the following exchange occurs:

> Boyee had an idea.
>
> He said, "Hat, you know the advertisements people does put out when their wife or husband leave them?"
>
> Hat said, "Boyee, you know you getting too damn big too damn fast. How the hell a little boy like you know about a thing like that?"
>
> Boyee took this as a compliment.
>
> Hat said, "How you know anyway that Mrs Hereira leave she husband? How you know that she ain't married to Toni?"
>
> Boyee said, "I telling you, Hat. I used to see that woman up Mucurapo way when I was delivering milk. I telling you so, man."
>
> Hat said, "White people don't do that sort of thing, putting advertisement in the paper and thing like that."
>
> Eddoes said, "You ain't know what you talking about, Hat. How much white people you know?"
>
> In the end Hat promised to read the paper more carefully. (110–11)

The child is immediately chastised for his knowledge of both the nature of adult relationships (that women often leave their men is recurrent in the narrative) and for citing the adult authority of the newspaper. That he should feel complimented by Hat's response to his precociousness suggests his yearning to be equal with men in terms of adult power. Also, his use of strongly modalized epistemological verbs such as "tell" and "see" (which establish his absolute faith in what he says) do nothing to sway Hat, who assumes that, because he is a child, he simply cannot understand or know these things. Eddoes finally convinces Hat that "white people" might operate in the same sphere as the poor black commoner, also leading us to realize that Hat's unwillingness to accept Boyee's idea is based on a belief that the boy does not and cannot understand social stratification at his age.

The void created by the central child's lack of power leads him to look to Hat as the adult male power figure in the novel. Recurrently, we are told that Hat's opinions are shared by the group in general, and it is often Hat's beliefs that are accepted by the child as truth. Hat's power in the street is seen in his ability to name those around him, as when he names both Bogart and Passion, Eddoes's child. Hat becomes the child's source for truth and philosophy, so much so that the child refuses to believe ill of him when someone tells him that Hat is using him and the other boys to beg for candy while selling it at a much higher price than he is paying them (52).

The only vignette in which Hat does not appear is "B. Wordsworth". As we have seen before, the vignettes depend on anachrony to maintain their focus on a particular individual; the narrator deliberately backgrounds or foregrounds events to sketch a certain character. That Hat should not appear in "B. Wordsworth" is compelling when one considers that Wordsworth is the only other character in the novel who competes for the role of adult male figure in the child's life. The child's frequent beatings from his mother (which establish his powerlessness) send him reeling to Wordsworth, in whose company he finds peace in an appreciation of beauty. After a severe beating, he runs to Wordsworth, who gives him both psychic healing and an intellectual awakening:

> B. Wordsworth said, "Now let us lie on the grass and look up at the sky, and I want you to think how far those stars are from us."
>
> I did as he told me, and I saw what he meant. I felt like nothing, and at the same time I had never felt so big and great in all my life. I forgot all about my anger and all my tears and all the blows. (44)

"B. Wordsworth" is divorced from the rest of the novel in that only the mother, the child and the eponymous Wordsworth appear in it; there are no other characters or hints of other stories so there is no way of situating it in the discourse's fractured chronology. The narrator deliberately focuses on an essential part of his early experience while backgrounding the rest of the discourse entirely. Wordsworth even lives on Alberto Street (44), away from the novel's main *story space* ("the spatial environment . . . of the story's action episodes").[19]

Wordsworth's appearance in this vignette and no other, then, affords the individual attention and affection that neither Hat's posse nor the boy's mother can provide. When Hat speaks in the story, it is mostly using the plural pronouns "us" or "we", but because the child is allowed individuality and, therefore, a measure of power by Wordsworth, the pronouns are singular: "I" or "me". This power is fleeting, though, for when Wordsworth's health fails, he sends the boy away, once more highlighting the child's lack of power.

The role that size plays in the determination of power relations in the narrative is another important point. In the excerpts in which Boyee's precociousness angers Hat, Hat frequently mentions size as a determiner of adult power: Boyee is "getting too damn big too damn fast" (111), he is too much of a "little boy" (111) to understand the adult world and he is "too damn small to be meddling" (100) in adult conversations. Phil Graham observes that, on the important narrative level of evaluation, special mention should be made of *significance* (what the narrator deems important).[20] In *Miguel Street*, both the narrator and characters repeatedly equate significance and size. However, size is not simply used literally. The conceptual perspective that it portrays is metaphorical: The attainment of experiential knowledge (that of sex and gender roles) is equated to the body's physical growth.[21] This is readily apparent in the formation of collocations in the discourse: "big" and "man" co-occur while "small" and "little" collocate with "boy" or "child". Thus, when Boyee shows that he has experiential knowledge, he transgresses the boundary of child and adult since, in Hat's view, his physical stature as child does not allow him the right to adult experience.

Being "big", therefore, is not simply about being an adult, it is about "knowing" like one. For this reason, many of the men in the story do not feel like men until they can show that they are not "small", that they have attained experiential knowledge. Desire to be "big" is what forces Bogart to want so badly to have a child, what makes Morgan boast of his ten children while ranting about being "better" (68) than all of the other men, what makes Popo give up his dreams of making "the thing without a name" to win back his wife, and what makes Edward leave Miguel Street when his marriage fails. Thus, to be small is to be relegated to the fringes and to be a child, but to be big is to have power and "to be a man, among we men" (7).

When the central child character shows one of the markers of adult male power, smoking, Hat recognizes his status as a man, even though he has also physically matured:

> I offered Hat a cigarette and he took it mechanically.
> Then he shouted, "But eh-eh, what is this? You come a big man now! When I leave you wasn't smoking. Was a long time now, though." (172)

This excerpt occurs at the end of the penultimate vignette, "Hat", and serves as a prologue to the final one, the only vignette that focuses on the central figure. Significantly, this occurs only when the central figure is no longer a child. He is sidelined, both by other characters and his older narrating self, until he has attained adult male power.

Thus, we see that the narrator exercises control over the child (himself). As Rampaul states, "to write the child is therefore to exercise power over the child – it involves defining the child, constructing the child according to the individual's idea of what constitutes childhood even in those texts that adopt a child narrator and claim to write from the perspective of a child – a clearly impossible thing to do".[22] This exercise of control explains why metaleptic heterodiegetic markers of omniscience appear in the discourse. The child's knowledge/perspective is also a construct of adult power, a power that allows the homodiegetic adult narrator to stretch beyond the bounds of his knowledge and to say and assume things that the child could not have experienced.

As stated previously, the implications of adult power are twofold for the child in *Miguel Street*. On the second level, that of discursive strategy, the child is used to reinforce authorial intent in the narrative. There is an autobiographical element to *Miguel Street*, since Naipaul lived in Port of Spain as a child and described it as an idyllic part of his life. In any case, Naipaul's work tends towards autobiography, as King notes: "Naipaul's fiction often has subtexts: the novels can be understood as autobiographical in the sense that they are projections of his own life and anxieties of homelessness, of living in more than one culture, of needing to find a narrative order for experience, of needing to achieve, of needing to create, of having to build a monument to his own existence through his writing."[23]

Numerous critics have pointed out Naipaul's overarching satirical vision in *Miguel Street*, which is in keeping with his critical commentary on the nature of colonial society. In her paper on *The Mystic Masseur*, Barbara Lalla examines the discursive construction of "nothing" in relation to Naipaul's ideological beliefs. She especially highlights fraudulence as a main marker of nothingness in that novel: "Not only is there no identity to discover from the shattered past but even the construction of identity . . . is denied. Instead, the novel deconstructs identity through revelation of fragmentation and fraudulence. The failure of identity construction (ethnic, intellectual and so forth) at [the] individual level mirrors a failure of national construction."[24]

Fraudulence plays a major role in *Miguel Street* as well; it is at the heart of the mimicry present throughout the narrative and suggests Naipaul's vision of a colonial society in which nothing is what is created. The comedic tone of *Miguel Street* is constructed by underscoring such fraudulence through irony and uses the child as its main instrument to accentuate this element in the discourse. The effect is to create a satirical vision of *Miguel Street*'s society, thereby allowing Naipaul to proffer his ideology.

As highlighted earlier, the child is a background upon which other characters can be emphasized. Since the child carries the sociocultural burden of implied innocence, he is used to underscore satire by accepting his community's ideals uncritically.[25] Indeed, Gordon Rohlehr argues that "the boy narrator is not Naipaul, but a device exploited by Naipaul the artist who operates in detachment. If these stories are autobiography, they are autobiography set at a distance through irony."[26] Thus, the child is integral to constructing Naipaul's ideological stance, which creates satire by juxtaposing the narrative perspective of the child with the narrative voice of the adult narrator.

The incongruence that this creates forms the backbone of comic irony. On one level, we accept that the child's perspective is valid for him and his community, but on another level, the evaluative voice of the adult narrator highlights the fraudulent nature of this perspective by showing it to be farcical. The clash between narrative voice and narrative perspective is what makes comic irony work as negative evaluation in the discourse, leading to the novel's satire. Peggy Nightingale states that "while the perspective is most often that of a boy, uncritical and easily impressed, the narrator frequently offers a more mature judgment as a comment on his own youthful simplicity which he is recreating".[27] This recontextualization of past events also ties into the Bildungsroman tradition: "The narrative point of view and voice, whether it be the first or the third person, is characterized by irony toward the inexperienced protagonist, rather than nostalgia for youth. There is always a distance between the perspective of the narrator and that of the protagonist."[28] Thus, on the narrative level of evaluation, the narrator comments on the spiritual bankruptcy of the society through the boy's acceptance of it, highlighting the fact that the characters must create and adopt personas that will shield them from the realities of their existence.

What happens in "Man-man" is just one of the examples of comic irony that we notice throughout the novel. When Man-man proclaims that he has seen God (after the inauspicious occasion of taking a bath), the narrator states that "this didn't surprise any of us. Seeing God was quite common in Port of Spain, and, indeed, in Trinidad at that time. . . . and I suppose it was natural that since God was in the area Man-man should see Him" (37). While the child's perspective is that of the community at large, Trinidad's naive acceptance of Man-man as a prophet, and then as a messiah, is constantly criticized by the narrative voice.

The Miguel Street inhabitants are, however, ambivalent about Man-man's claims. Because they remember his antics before his prophetic vision, they "tried to comfort themselves by saying that Man-man was really mad, but, like me, I think they weren't sure that Man-man wasn't really right" (38). But while they share some belief or hope that Man-man might be what he says, they also have inklings that he might be a fraud. Part of Naipaul's satire, though, hinges on the community's respect for fraudulence and mimicry as markers of style, which is why the narrator stresses that Hat (who later voices suspicion that the cross that Man-man must bear is in fact light) is proud that "they sending some police" (38) to Man-man's crucifixion. The presence of governmental authority adds a layer of sensationalism to the proceedings, which emphasizes their farcical nature. Here, Naipaul shows the misplaced values of colonial society, hoping for salvation but willing to settle all too readily for a minstrel show.

Rohlehr posits a compelling theory on Naipaul's satirical vision: "In a society which is seen as having no true standards irony is bound to operate in reverse, the ironist starting with an abnormal situation and hinting at a sanity which is absent from his world."[29] Naipaul's use of this reverse irony can clearly be seen in "The Thing Without a Name", the vignette that focuses on the cuckolded Popo. To regain his wife's affections, Popo steals furniture, redecorates his home and then sells the remaining furniture, leading to his arrest. The group is critical of his stupidity: "Hat spoke for all of us when he said, 'That man too foolish. Why he had to sell what he thief? Just tell me that. Why?' " (14). That they should lament that Popo was stupid enough to get caught, and not that he committed illegal acts in the first place, speaks of a dangerously corrupt value system. The child is once again party to this absurd exchange and is uncritical of it, even going so far, as the narrator points out, as to identify himself firmly with the group's belief by using the inclusive proximal deictic pronoun "us".

Miguel Street is a complex discourse that uses the child figure as a narrative strategy throughout. The child's narrating adult self uses his backgrounded novel of development to hold the discourse together while highlighting the adult characters around him, adults who invariably wield power over his development. He is then used to reinforce the ideological underpinnings of the discourse by reinforcing Naipaul's satire through his uncritical complicity. These characteristics allude to the powerlessness of the child in the narrative discourse, leading us to realize that, in *Miguel Street*, he has been crafted into the "thing without a name" in order to carry out everyone's agenda but his own.

Notes

1. This is an argument that has been put forward by numerous critics. Jeremy Poynting, in "The Caribbean Short Story", states that (along with other significant works) *Miguel Street* "signalled the centrality of the short story to the second generation of Anglophone Caribbean writing". Interestingly enough, Poynting also alludes to a greater controlling narrative at work in the novel: "VS Naipaul's *Miguel Street* has been a significant model . . . in which the relationship between the individual focus of each story and the associative coherence of the collection as a whole mirrors Naipaul's vision that 'Everyone was an individual, fighting for his place in the community . . . we had somehow found ourselves on the same small island.' " The "associative coherence" of which he speaks is not the only factor holding the narrative together, though, for one must consider the child protagonist's presence as the seeing "I" in all the vignettes as the major contributor to coherence in the novel. Poynting's views point to an ambiguity surrounding the genre to which *Miguel Street* belongs, an ambiguity that I hope to clarify by positing its status as a Bildungsroman in this chapter. Jeremy Poynting, "The Caribbean Short Story", 22 March 2003, http://www.peepaltreepress.com/feature_display.asp?id=1.
2. Marianne Hirsch, "From Great Expectations to Lost Illusions: The Novel of Formation as Genre", *Genre* 12, no. 3 (1979): 298.
3. Ibid.
4. Ibid., 300. Hirsch refers to the Bildungsroman genre as "one of the major fictional types of European realism", which suggests that some West Indian Bildungsromane, like the ones cited, depict a particular facet of West Indian reality in their treatment of the growth and development of the West Indian child. The endings of these three novels especially highlight West Indian migratory practice.

5. Ibid., 297. While making her point about the focus on the central figure, Hirsch also remarks upon his passivity.
6. Gerard Genette, *Narrative Discourse*, trans. Jane E. Lewin (Oxford: Blackwell, 1980), 35–85.
7. Manfred Jahn, *Narratology: A Guide to the Theory of Narrative* (Cologne: University of Cologne, 2005), http://www.uni-koeln.de/~ame02/pppn.htm.
8. V.S. Naipaul, *Miguel Street* (London: Picador, 2002), 1. All subsequent references are taken from this edition and appear parenthetically in the text.
9. Roger Fowler, *Linguistic Criticism* (Oxford: Oxford University Press, 1986), 134.
10. Suzanne Fleischman, *Tense and Narrativity: From Medieval Performance to Modern Fiction* (Austin: University of Texas Press, 1990), 125.
11. Labov's narrative model details six key elements found in narrative discourse: abstraction, orientation, complicating action, resolution, evaluation (which may occur at all levels of the narrative) and coda. See William Labov, *Socioloinguistic Patterns* (Philadelphia: University of Pennsylvania Press, 1972).
12. There is no dialogue in the first vignette attributed to him, save for a line that concerns Popo, referring to a discourse yet to be examined by the narrative voice.
13. Bruce King, *V.S. Naipaul* (Hampshire: Macmillan, 1993), 24.
14. Giselle Rampaul, "The West Indian Child as Subject/Object: Interrogating Notions of Power in *Annie John*" (forthcoming in *Journal of Caribbean Literatures*), 1.
15. Karin Lesnik-Oberstein, *Children's Literature: Criticism and the Fictional Child* (Oxford: Clarendon Press, 1994), 9.
16. Jacqueline Rose, *The Case of Peter Pan or the Impossibility of Children's Fiction* (Philadelphia: University of Pennsylvania Press, 1984), 8.
17. Fawzia Mustafa, *V.S. Naipaul* (Cambridge: Cambridge University Press, 1995), 40.
18. Bolo's loss of faith in the newspapers heralds a downward spiral that sees him slowly withdrawing from his community, thus suggesting that the shared belief in authority helps to maintain and reinforce the community through a belief in common experience and knowledge.
19. Jahn, *Narratology*.
20. Phil Graham, "Critical Discourse Analysis and Evaluative Meaning: Interdisciplinarity as a Critical Turn", in *Critical Discourse Analysis: Theory and Interdisciplinarity*, ed. Gilbert Weiss and Ruth Wodak (New York: Palgrave Macmillan, 2003), 115.
21. This particular *conceptual metaphor* (one in which a target domain is under-

stood in terms of a more familiar one, or source domain) is of course not unique to *Miguel Street*. Andreas Demetriou and Athanassios Raftopoulos, *Cognitive Developmental Change: Theories, Models and Measurement* (Cambridge: Cambridge University Press, 2004), 174, state that "the metaphor 'bigger is better' is a powerful reminder of one of the mapping relations that people observe in many situations in life".

22. Rampaul, "The West Indian Child as Subject/Object", 3.
23. King, *V.S. Naipaul*, 3.
24. Barbara Lalla, "Signifying Nothing: Writing about not Writing in *The Mystic Masseur*", *Anthurium* 5, no. 2 (Fall 2007), 7, http://anthurium.miami.edu/volume_5/issue_2/lalla-signifying.html.
25. Lesnik-Oberstein, "Children's Literature", 9–10, argues that "the 'child' is a construction, constructed and described in different, often clashing terms . . . I am in no sense disputing the visible presence of new-born or young human beings. Rather, I am arguing that these creatures have ascribed to them – become 'carriers' for – a load of emotional and moral meanings." It follows that "innocence" (an unstable and difficult concept at best) is just one of these "meanings" that has been attributed to children.
26. Gordon Rohlehr, "The Ironic Approach: The Novels of V.S. Naipaul", in *Critical Perspectives on V.S. Naipaul*, ed. Robert D. Hamner (Washington: Three Continents Press, 1977), 181.
27. Peggy Nightingale, *Journey through Darkness: The Writing of V.S. Naipaul* (New York: University of Queensland Press, 1987), 20.
28. Hirsch, "From Great Expectations to Lost Illusions", 298.
29. Rohlehr, "The Ironic Approach", 182.

Part 2.

UNSTABLE IDENTITIES

4.

Child's "I" and Other in Olive Senior's Narratives of Self-Invention

» BARBARA LALLA

> Look now the child
> facing death. Who
> will commute this sentence to life?
> –Olive Senior, "Children's Hospital"

THIS CHAPTER CONSIDERS OLIVE SENIOR'S exploration of the extent to which a child or others can commute her sentence through the opportunities that discourse presents for imposing coherence; the brilliant puns on "life" and "sentence" in the epigraph above are an example. Crucial sentences that Senior's characters utter include Ascot's poignant and ambiguous assertion, "I haffe leave"; the groping, unanswered concern of the girl with two grandmothers "Is dark really bad, Mummy?"; and the howl of denial of "The Lizardy Man and His Lady", "Is not my mother."[1] In a range of short stories and narrative poems, Senior conveys the displaced child's attempts at self-construction or self-retrieval, as well as the possibilities of adult intervention, through discourse itself.

Narrative discourse is a logical tool for self-construction because narration is a means of imposing order; of exerting control over events by defining their sequence, relationship and significance in accordance with the speaker's own values and interests. Through a range of discursive strategies, Senior explores dissociation and loss of control during female maturation both in childhood and in young womanhood, moving sometimes towards personally contrived coherence (as in "The Tenantry of Birds") but also often towards ultimate psychological collapse (as in "You Tink a Mad Miss?" and "See the Tiki Tiki Scatter").[2]

In third-person narratives like "The Tenantry of Birds", the central consciousness recalls her childhood experience of dissociation as "a dream, feeling that she had not yet entered into life but was just waiting" ("Tenantry", 53). She recalls assessing herself in comparison to her wilder country cousins and feeling "restricted, as if she were not a person in herself but a creation, an extension of her mother" ("Tenantry", 50), a mother who has consistently silenced her along the way to organizing her into a dysfunctional marriage. Ultimately she frees herself by bursting into sound, employing a folk expression ("Green bush! Green bush!") to drive off her tormentors. Another third-person narrative, "Lily Lily", ends in harmony only through maternal intervention in the trauma of abused childhood. Lily's true mother inscribes the authentic version of events and lays down the acceptable pattern for the future.3 Order may be imposed by an adult character who recalls, sorts and properly relates events and experiences.

Other children are not so fortunate. No such character comes forward. The third-person account of a nameless child in "Tears of the Sea" includes grandparents who are caring as long as the child remains desperately ill but who are otherwise dismissive, omitting her from their worlds and leaving her to devise dialogues with seashells.4 "Where are your mother and father?" asks the shell ("Tears", 79), and nothing commutes this child's sentence. Motherlessness is similarly toxic in "Country of the One-Eye God", a vacuum in communication producing a youth prepared to kill his own grandmother, the (harsh) surrogate mother of his childhood.

Far more directly in first-person narratives, like "The Two Grandmothers" and Shelley-Ann's accounts in "The Lizardy Man and His Lady", the child narrator's "I" comprises an eye into the embattled consciousness of the child in search of coherence. In "The Two Grandmothers", the first-person child narrator addresses her mother in a mixture of report and request, demonstrating increasing materialism in her value system as she reflects on her experience of country and town grandmothers.5 The account flows from a single but evolving, increasingly demanding, speaker. It remains a monologue distributed over years, during which she puts herself together superficially, her growing self-indulgence and self-importance eroded from beneath by doubts of self-worth ("Mummy, am I really a nigger?", in "The Two Grandmothers", 73). Despite the potential for schizophrenia, the addressee, her mother, never responds so as to meaningfully assemble the disconnected selves of the developing girl child.

Indeed, because of the healing, even empowering potential of the act of narrating, narrative itself constitutes an important theme in Caribbean discourse, and the effort to impose coherence interlaces topics of individual and community development and of maturation in the nation. Senior's "A Meditation on Yellow" thus retraces the journey towards a people's self-awareness and insistence on their own account of this journey:

> You cannot tear my song
> from my throat
> you cannot erase the memory
> of my story . . .[6]

This interlacing of individual, national or regional stories is characteristic of Senior and other writers of her generation.[7] Senior, in particular, links coherence in narrative with sustainable living.

Now, coherence in narrative is achieved through the organization of temporal order to make sense of experience by forging chronological links between events or circumstances, and and by connecting comparable ideas or concepts through parallelism. The selection of a protagonist around whom events will be organized is another means of inducing coherence. Causality is less straightforward a link because of its connection with logic, simply because it is debatable whether narrative is constructed through logic or whether narrative is a mechanism for achieving logic. Whatever the mechanisms used for producing coherence, mechanisms are repeatable and, normally (at least to some degree) familiar to an audience so that as a narrative is being unfolded, both audience and narrator make links on the basis of their experience of narrative. So, in narrative, achievement of understanding is thus collaborative. Senior's connections between coherent living and coherent narrative tap into all these dimensions of coherence.

Because all narrative operates from an angle of viewing, it necessarily implicates location or can convey dislocation, and these effects too contribute to or reduce coherence. A consistent, unequivocal presentation of location, of orientation in space and time, contributes to our sense of a narrator's stability. And Senior persistently and poignantly evokes the Caribbean, and Jamaica in particular, as the location of her narrators. A sense of locatedness, of being *baan ya* ("born/belonging here"), sites child protagonist, adult narrator and adult author in the Caribbean, a setting that Senior evokes through local rather than imported epistemes: exile across the seas, a background of slavery, sugar cane, mountain fastness, marronage, gourd and womb, balmyard, madwoman and lizard. Arguments such as those of Silvio Torres-Saillant sometimes enable an author to elide emplacement, forego location in actual and real space.[8] Some definitions of the Caribbean expand Caribbeanness to proportions that eventually strip the term of meaning, and some critics go so far as to propose that the Caribbean is so dispersed geographically and diasporically that it hardly exists.[9] However, the Caribbean is impossible to define out of existence in Senior's portrayals.

Senior evokes the Caribbean by highlighting oral rather than literary culture, by representing the Creole voice and by conveying a social as well as a geographical location, and she does so with greater specificity than a vague regional frame of reference. The Snake Woman's routings and re-rootings are definitively Jamaican, first through the bay and then (more permanently) in the mountainous interior, where the Ganges recedes to an almost imaginary landscape of the exotic past. The Snake Woman, a girl barely past childhood, awakens in the boy who is the central consciousness a fascination with the Other, yet (although her own otherness persists) her son roots in the community as surely as the boy protagonist evolves from it. The protagonist's development, however, is enabled only because she inserts her discourse into his. She intervenes in the unravelling of that future he constructed in his mind and promotes the coherent development of his story.[10]

The Caribbean is not the sum of the spaces that Senior's child characters inhabit. Senior's children are sharply delineated in relation, not only to their outer, but also their inner locations. The child's emplacement in some dimension of Jamaican society enables her to mirror that society in displaying the challenges of development, as in the case of Sadie's struggle for local epistemes in the Kingdom of the Water Hyacinths in "Zigzag"[11] or the boy narrator's dilemma regarding education and religion in "Arrival of the Snake Woman". The child's consciousness thus illuminates and unmasks the adult world of class and race confrontation. In particular, as the child struggles to forge herself in the clash of colliding worlds that constitutes social reality in Jamaica, she may be faced with gaps that arise through a vacuum of parenting. The setting is a Caribbean (and more specifically a Jamaican) one in which crucial landmarks in the psychological terrain are shifting or ambiguous.[12] In "See the Tiki Tiki Scatter" and in "The Lizardy Man and His Lady", disconnection from the mother and related dislocations are conveyed even as the child is clearly located in a realistic landscape.

The disconnected self is evoked not only in terms of spatial dislocation from the pivotal source of nurture but also in terms of ambivalent temporality. For a child, the past is not yet developed and the present is, essentially, all there is for inferring the future. In Senior's dislocated child, even the limited past that may be available is tattered and the present discontinuous. The perspectival dynamics of childhood are fraught with the child's transitionality in time, and some of Senior's child narrators experience this transitionality in a vacuum, leaving them floating in the in-between, unfastening other dimensions of orientation, in particular conceptual orientation (psychological as well as attitudinal): "She floated aimlessly in rooms of dark corners and silences" ("Tiki Tiki", 83). The trauma of being in-between is social and racial as well, represented in brownness, wild tangled hair and mesolect, an experience of "yellow" in which self-development labours between mimicry and invention (see "Meditation on Yellow").

Pickney business (the proper occupation for a growing child) is maturation, in the process of which the child may lean towards "force ripe" but although such precociousness is viewed with disapproval the child must nevertheless at all times press towards adulthood (as far as adulthood can possibly be understood in all its contradictory manifestations). In the process, the child experiments with identities, seeks to order her existence through alternative accounts, to narrate a story for her life, to forge an advance biography.[13]

When "there is no Other to take the place of Mother", what is at stake in the child's narration is nothing less than survival. In such circumstances, Senior's landscape normally contains a grandmother, as in "See the Tiki Tiki Scatter", and in narrative poems like "Hurricane Story 1903" and "Hurricane Story 1951", or a surrogate mother, like Gatha, the nurse in "The Lizardy Man and His Lady".[14] These figures present opportunities for intervention in the child's construction of self. If the mother-substitute figure is unsuccessful, the unmothered child is caught in colliding worlds in which game and reality horrifyingly intersect to induce psychological crisis.

As we consider the circumstances of Senior's child narrators, it is helpful to bear in mind that mechanisms employed in dealing with a crisis are similar to narrative. According to Karen Taylor, Rita Durant, and David Boje, "Crisis by its very nature asks us to find new ways to imagine meaning in our worlds, to engage in the intersubjective process that draws upon the work of many."[15] The first-person child narrators most directly display their responses to crisis, the I-magining of ways to seek meaning in their worlds, the assembling of fragments of information to coherence.

In circumstances of dissociation, then, Senior characteristically identifies potential for adult intervention, but this needful alignment of vision may never be achieved in the narrative, even as narration becomes the crucial mechanism for imposing coherence on a shattering consciousness. Performance, role playing and fictionalizing of self in "See the Tiki Tiki Scatter" do not end in a commuted sentence. The most direct betrayals of such engagements with crisis are first person, and to examine the operation of narrative in a child narrator's search for coherence, I focus on "The Lizardy Man and His Lady", where the narrative takes shattered form: a series of dialogues, each a performance, each an argumentative encounter.

"The Lizardy Man" opens with an exchange between children, Shelley-Ann (the focal character), and Roger, a boy with whom she plays while her nurse visits a friend employed at his mother's home. This exchange is one of an imaginary shoot-out, an invention of violent, indeed fatal, gunfire, followed by mutual accusation and blame – a game perhaps learned from television, glamourized on television dramas, established as reality on television news – an exchange of fire that gathers reality by the end of the tale.

Gatha interrupts the opening game by rebuking Shelley-Ann and invoking the holy family, then moves into an account of abortive family relationships. Her intention is to protect and guide Shelley-Ann, but her method is constraining. She locates blame, she silences, she fixes. The children must sit in front of the television without another peep out of them. She recognizes noise from Shelley-Ann, rather than communication, and she suppresses it in between delivering her own monologue, in contrast to Shelley-Ann's interactivity.

In shifting address to her friend, Miss Ernsie, Gatha adjusts her tone from hectoring to chatty, while she narrates the unravelling family relationships of Shelley-Ann's mother. In a narrative imbued with gossip and embedded with rumour, she relays various accounts of not-talking, from the silence that grows between Miss Ella and her mother to Gatha's claim to her own silence: "mi swallow mi tongue". Gatha's is an account of degradation in relationships that result in *turn down*, a social lowering from association with riff-raff of the sort that spoil a young woman. *Walla-walla* of course bestializes Ella's relationships (pigs wallow), even as references to "eat[ing] with the devil" demonize them. Gatha's selection, assembly and evaluation of events comprise an account of Miss Ella's decline from human relationships: an account that unfolds in front of Ella's daughter, Shelley-Ann.

The exchange that follows, between Shelley-Ann and Roger, concretizes the bestial and demonic that occupy the space Shelley-Ann cannot conceive of as home. The man to whom her mother is currently attached is a sum of fragmented and troubling images. He is faceless, recognizable by his shoes (lizard skin, as she says). His movements, his noises are other than human. He is non-talking. He is *turn-skin*, has a reptilian capacity to change his skin. He is not-daddy. He is the Lizardy Man. The child's imagination operates through an image of the absolute Other.[16] Metonym and metaphor convey the inversion of the Holy Family through comparison and contiguity with the reptilian skin of the thing lounging at the heart of what should be home. The Lizardy Man is metonymic, associated through contiguity, through connection within a single domain, because his shoes are made of what appears to be lizard skin; but he is also metaphoric, associated through comparison, through connection across two conceptual domains, because he is a man who is lizard-like.[17] In Jamaica, the lizard typically induces revulsion and, as the lizard constitutes the absolute Other, so the mother associated with the Lizardy Man must be Othered also.

Against this troubled psychological landscape the child's role playing draws on personal experience of flawed human interaction and on social reality, so that violence and game interconnect. The guns introduced as childish imagining mirror social reality and mimic cultural models (from television) but are also projected from personal experience (part of the Lizardy Man's equipment), growing in power from the handgun to the M16. At the same time, the nurse's strictures, meant to prevent Shelley-Ann from growing wild, parallel the child's revelations of the raw-meat-eating dogs, and these animal references intensify and nuance dehumanization in her circumstances. The narrative (at this point simultaneous on Shelley-Ann's side and retrospective on Gatha's) becomes embedded with forecasting, made explicit in the prophetic "something had to happen" ("Lizardy Man", 106).

While the children's talk shifts between game, lie and wild speculation, Gatha (again invoking the Holy Family and silencing the children) invests more and more in metadiscourse as she addresses Miss Ernsie: a claim of not lying, an account of not talking between Shelley-Ann and her mother. Gatha's attempt to comfort the child takes the form of silencing. (In Jamaica, *hush* means "don't cry" as well as "be quiet".) Concerned and faithful as she is, Gatha addresses Shelley-Ann's concerns with such advice as, "Don't say that you have no mother" and "Don't ask questions." So a critical dimension of the tale is this metadiscursive thrust, Gatha devoting much attention to talking about talking, talking about not talking, talking about expression that is proper to childhood and, eventually, proposing writing as the ultimate effort for restoring order, as authenticating the circumstances she is so far relaying only orally.

When Shelley-Ann and Roger resume their exchange of rumour, secret and speculation *cum* prophecy, they convey to the reader the reality behind the game: Shelley-Ann's existence in a context of guns, Dobermans and electric gates. However, Shelley-Ann flags her constructions of alternative identities and relationships in her home as possibly not serious, by accompanying her speculations with "ha ha", and Roger immediately censors her more outlandish ideas.

The reader/audience never encounters either the Lizardy Man or his Lady; we are merely provided with two accounts and arrive at their gate with Shelley-Ann and Gatha – a scene relayed in fragments through Gatha's outburst, which comprises impressions of shock ("Lawd have mercy"), inferences regarding disaster ("autoclaps"), instructions connoting caution ("Don't go in") and expressions of panic ("run"). Not a peep emerges from Shelley-Ann until her return to Roger, beginning with denial ("I don't know"), both with regard to actual reality (what happened) and with regard to performance (what game to play). In response to a proposed game in which "police going shoot [Shelley-Ann] dead", she offers Roger a secret: "something happen". Her denial of what she knows or thinks alternates with fragmented information: the open gate, the dead dogs. The impossibility of the reality ("Doberman can't dead") opens the way to speculation on the unthinkable (the possible shooting both of the Lizardy Man and of Ella), which even Roger identifies as unspeakable ("Stop joking Shelley-Ann") ("Lizardy Man", 103–5). In the growing consciousness of undeniable circumstances, the child rejects the most crucial of relationships ("She's not my mother", then "she not my mother", in "Lizardy Man", 97) and begins to break things, against Gatha's wailing invocation (yet again) of the Holy Family. The thrice-given denial ("Is not my mother", in "Lizardy Man", 105) has moved from Standard English towards Creole.

In all of this, a number of narrative strategies deserve attention. First, the child shuffles trial identities around alongside the nurse's attempts to impose order, each aiming at a viable account of events. To recount these events, the narrative form selected includes co-articulation and simultaneity. Events are recounted both by knowing and by unknowing participants, who produce a performance text, one that unfolds as it is told.[18] Gatha mostly recounts events retrospectively but increasingly speculates on events to come, an (inferred) prospective dimension to the narrative. The child's consciousness, however, operates mainly on simultaneity, ordering events "on a time line that has the moment of speech as the anchoring point", as described by Ayhan Aksu-Koç and Christiane von Stutterheim, who distinguish between simultaneity and two other basic concepts of time, before and after.[19] So the child's simultaneous narrative unfolds alongside the retrospective account (and evaluations) of the nurse.

Episodic unfolding of memories in the nurse's narrative reconstructs events on which she places importance and which she produces in contexts she selects. On the other hand, the child's generic or implicit memories seem more random, a reflection of the way things happen, inadvertent self-revelation.[20] The result is an episodic structure of accumulating accounts. Alexandra Georgakopoulou notes that "small stories" (as of recent or still unfolding events) called *breaking news* involve anticipation of events, disruptions and participants jointly drafting scenarios – a collusive activity.[21] At the end of the tale, Gatha and Shelley Ann produce breaking news, anticipation and projection, and Shelley-Ann involves Roger in an attempt to negotiate or co-author details.

The narrative's disorderliness is crucial. The alternating voices of Shelley-Ann and Gatha recount different sets of events moving at different paces and in different directions through time and follow dual plot lines of different durations. Besides, in addition to challenging conventional temporality, the alternating I-narrators collude to produce the cacophony of voices that concludes the short story. Brian Richardson identifies as dangerous poetics "one that lays bare and demystifies the artifactuality of fiction-making" and Senior may be said to engage in such dangerous poetics as she lays bare procedures by which Shelley-Ann and Gatha undertake their constructions of the child's circumstances, even as the discourse itself fractures.[22] Indeed, this short story approaches the "garden path" type of narrative as the adult's observation of the child is dispersed by the child's observation of the adult disordered world in which (as game and reality interact) the human family is revealed as monstrous. Domestic disorder is indistinct from social confusion, and these shatter into psychological fragmentation.[23]

How is this disorder conveyed? Order is based on stability and stateability of pattern, ability to classify, predictability, identifiability of causes, clear chronology and periodicity. In this short story, however, the narrative foregrounds *metalepsis* (a crossing of boundaries between narrator and narrated), as one narrator gives an account of the other, and both attempt to account for the dysfunctional mother, cumulatively producing a form that is non-linear, unpredictable, lacking in causality. The narrators produce conflicting versions of events or situations (is her mother/is not my mother) in a chronology that the alternation of the simultaneous and retrospective narrations scramble.[24] In the course of these alternating accounts, the narrative passes through a variety of discourse types with all the connotations of these types: proverb and folk wisdom; gossip and its implications of community; rumour and its associations of unreliability; riddle and its association with mystery and interrogation; kas-kas and its suggestion of hostility, challenge or competition; and game, lie and trickery, with their attendant risk and instability.

The alternating voices that convey the action remain clearly distinct through the use of direct speech, and for the course of the tale the child resists all attempts to silence her. Shelley-Ann's voice rises above the forces that suppress expression, recalling Senior's explanation of her own intentions as a writer: "What I think I'm doing is engaging 'The Other' in a dialogue. I'm providing the means by which people who have been voiceless in the pages of history can now engage in dialogue with those people who formerly had control of the world."[25] Orality is foregrounded through the employment of direct speech in a performance-type narrative. Orality is further foregrounded through the code choices of that speech varying along the continuum according to personal and social circumstances (children at play, a nurse unburdening her heart to a friend, a nurse rebuking her charge). This oral quality achieved in the written discourse promotes our awareness of tellership and reinforces our sense of the narrative as emerging through interaction of participants who have varying extents of knowledge about the events they convey.[25]

Narrative in "The Lizardy Man and His Lady" is pluralized, variable, fragmented, "hinged on a view of narrative as consisting of a multitude of genres" such as Georgakopoulou discerns in small stories, which may be co-articulate when applied to making sense of self-identities.[27] In noting "that children, like adults, discursively construct and experiment with identities", Lori Montalbano-Phelps and L. Cynthia Gordon note that their plots and dialogues "derive from children's sociocultural knowledge as well as their individual experiences".[28] Thus, even as the nurse, Gatha, provides a biography for Shelley-Ann, the child is experimenting with an alternative autobiography for dealing with circumstances that are unacceptable ("is not my mother"), for Shelley-Ann's identity is unfixed, something she is trying to work out in relation to other people through categorization and through marking and testing of boundaries.[29] Reinforcing this is her history of repeated uprooting, likely enough to have promoted in her something of a migrant sensibility.[30]

A location becomes embodied when it becomes intrinsically linked with personal histories and geographies, but Shelley-Ann's history is one of repeated dislocation.[31] Physically she is clearly emplaced in the Caribbean, in Jamaican society, but psychologically she becomes increasingly dislocated. Her experiences "take place" in territory presided over by alien presences, defined (indeed guarded) by the savage and demonic and her map comprises dividing lines that delineate her exclusion. Shelley-Ann therefore constructs and comes to mentally inhabit alternative spaces in the cartographic experiments in her head. In games with Roger she is a participant – in street fights, for example, and shoot outs – and the games appear to become real in the end; but in her real life she walks to and from restricted areas, areas inhabited by a monstrosity to which only a woman who is not her mother could have exposed her. In the end, coherence completely breaks down. No one can commute the sentence, "is not my mother". The child's voice is silenced, and the other voices reveal that she is shattering her surroundings.

Until this final denouement, the child's narration has constituted discursive interventions in the adult account. The child's dispersed discourse constitutes part of a cumulative narrative that assembles alternative identities in the child's desperate and uncoordinated attempts to impose order on her life. For her own part, Shelley-Ann (like others of Senior's child protagonists) appears to be reaching out for a sustainable story for going forward.

Notes

1. Olive Senior, "Country of the One-Eye God", in *Summer Lightning and Other Stories* (London: Longman Caribbean, 1986), 16–25; Senior, "The Two Grandmothers", in *The Arrival of the Snake Woman and Other Stories* (Burnt Mill, Harlow: Longman, 1989), 62–75; Senior, "The Lizardy Man and His Lady", in *Discerner of Hearts and Other Stories* (Toronto: McClelland and Stewart, 1995), 92–105.
2. Senior, "The Tenantry of Birds", in *The Arrival of the Snake Woman and Other Stories*, 46–61; "You Tink a Mad Miss", in *Discerner of Hearts and Other Stories*, 75–82; "See the Tiki Tiki Scatter", in *The Arrival of the Snake Woman*, 83–89.
3. Senior, "Lily, Lily", in *The Arrival of the Snake Woman*, 112–45.
4. Senior, "Tears of the Sea", in *The Arrival of the Snake Woman*, 62–75.

5. Senior, "The Two Grandmothers", in *The Arrival of the Snake Woman*, 62–75.
6. Olive Senior, "A Meditation on Yellow", in *Gardening in the Tropics* (Toronto: Insomniac Press, 2005).
7. Elsewhere I have investigated this, as in Barbara Lalla, "Registering Woman: Senior's Zig-Zag Discourse and Code-Switching in Jamaican Narrative", *A Review of International English Literature* 29:4 (1998), 83–98; "Gender, Identity and Nationhood in Diaspora Literature: The Novels of Merle Hodge" (paper presented at the Centre for Gender and Development Studies Round Table for Fiftieth Anniversary Distinguished Lecture Series, University of the West Indies, Hugh Wooding Law School, 2 April 1998).
8. See Silvio Torres-Saillant, "Caribbean Literature III: Towards a New Caribbean Poetics in the Twenty-first Century", in *Reading the Caribbean: Approaches to Anglophone Caribbean Literature and Culture*, ed. Klaus Stierstorfer (Heidelberg: Universitätsverlag, 2007), 13, 14.
9. Jana Gohrisch, "Literary Literature II: Themes and Narratives", in *Reading the Caribbean: Approaches to Anglophone Caribbean Literature and Culture*, ed. Klaus Stierstorfer (Heidelberg: Universitätsverlag, 2007), 51–72.
10. Senior, "The Arrival of the Snake Woman", in *The Arrival of the Snake Woman*, 1–45.
11. Senior, "Zig zag", in *Discerner of Hearts and Other Stories*.
12. See Richard F. Patteson, "Olive Senior: Country Air and Juggled Worlds", in *Caribbean Passages: A Critical Perspective on New Fiction from the West Indies* (Boulder, CO: Lynne Rienner Publishers, 1998), 19, on negotiating identity in a context of competing cultures.
13. This process, like the finding of a voice on national or regional levels, recalls Eduard Glissant's distinction between a free versus a forced poetics that emerges from local culture and produces self-recognition rather than being stifled by another, dominating poetics. Eduard Glissant, *Caribbean Discourse: Selected Essays*, trans. J. Michael Dash (Charlottesville: University Press of Virginia, 1989), 236.
14. "Hurricane Story 1903" involves a caring and vigilant grandmother, in Senior, *Gardening in the Tropics*.
15. Karen Taylor, Rita Durant and David Boje, "Telling the Story, Hearing the Story: Narrative Co-Construction and Crisis Research", *American Communication Journal* 9, no. 1 (Spring 2007), http://acjournal.org/holdings/vol9/spring/articles/co-construction.html.
16. The shifting viewpoints from which the narrative unfolds include numerous

17. Dan Fass, *Processing Metonymy and Metaphor* (Greenwich and London: Ablex, 1979). Elsewhere, Senior notes the image of the lizard as a spiritual form in African mythology but records the fear and revulsion in Jamaican lore (especially among women). This devaluing conforms to the pattern in colonial revisioning of world views, of demonizing spiritual forces in Other religions. Like all metaphors, the lizard metaphor is influenced not only by general physical experience of life but by individual experience in our personal history and by our sociocultural context. Indeed Zoltan Kövecses asks whether metaphor only reflects or whether it also constitutes cultural models in *Metaphor in Culture: Universality and Variation* (Cambridge: Cambridge University Press, 2005), 79, 193, 264.

indications of distance and of decline (such as *turn down*) reinforced by references to bestialization, monsterization or demonization.

18. This is a form Senior comments on in an interview with Anna Rutherford, "Interview with Olive Senior", *Kunapipi* 8, no. 2 (1986): 19.
19. Ayhan Aksu-Koç, and Christiane von Stutterheim, "Temporal Relations in Narrative: Simultaneity", in *Relating Events in Narrative: A Crosslinguistic Developmental Study*, ed. Ruth Aronson Berman and Dan Isaac Slobin (Hillsdale, NJ: Lawrence Erlbaum Associates, 1994), 393–455.
20. Hyacinth M. Simpson refers to the crucial function of inadvertent self-revelation by first person narrators, and this takes place in Senior's narrative in an episodic structure that provides a scaffolding of displacement for the child protagonist [" 'Voicing the Text': The Making of an Oral Poetics in Olive Senior's Short Fiction", *Callaloo* 27, no. 3 (2004): 829–44]. Compare Sidonie Smith, "Memory, Narrative, and the Discourses of Identity", in *Postcolonialism and Autobiography: Michelle Cliff, David Dabydeen, Opal Palmer Adisa*, Textxet: Studies in Comparative Literature, no. 19, ed. Alfred Hornung and Ernstpeter Ruhe. (Amsterdam and Atlanta: Rodopi, 1998), 41–42.
21. Alexandra Georgakopoulou, *Small Stories, Interactions and Identities*, Studies in Narrative 8 (Amsterdam and Philadelphia: John Benjamins, 2007).
22. Brian Richardson, "Narrative Poetics and Postmodern Transgression: Theorizing the Collapse of Time, Voice and Frame", *Narrative* 8, no. 1 (January 2008): 25–28, 37.
23. David Herman discusses "garden path" narratives such as that in which an alien narrator turns out to be observing the human, in *Narratologies: New Perspectives on Narrative Analysis* (Columbus: Ohio State University Press, 1999), 167–94.
24. See Jo Alyson Parker, who applies to literary criticism applications of dynamical

systems theory, popularly termed *chaos theory, Narrative Form and Chaos Theory in Sterne, Proust, Woolf and Faulkner* (New York: Palgrave Macmillan, 2007).

25. Kwame Senu and Neville Dawes, *Talk You Talk: Interviews with Caribbean Poets* (Charlottesville: University of Virginia Press, 2001), 73–85.
26. Georgakopoulou, *Small Stories*, 57.
27. Ibid., 86, 119.
28. Lori Montalbano-Phelps, *Taking Narrative Risk: The Empowerment of Abuse Survivors* (Dallas, TX: University Press of America, 2004); Cynthia Gordon, "Repetition and Identity Experimentation", in *Selves and Identities in Narratives and Discourse*, ed. Michael Bamburg, Anna De Fina and Deborah Schriffrin (Amsterdam and Philadelphia: John Benjamins, 2007), 135.
29. Dan Shen remarks on the flexibility of the first-person account through the "coexistence of the retrospective and experiencing perspective", even though the first-person viewpoint is associated with a more restricted angle of vision. Dan Shen, "Difference behind Similarity: Focalization in the First Person Centre-of-Consciousness and First Person Retrospective Narration", in *Acts of Narrative*, ed. Carol Jacobs and Henry Sussman (Palo Alto, CA: Stanford University Press, 2003), 81–92.
30. Compare Michael Krzyzanowski and Ruth Wodak, "Multiple Identities, Migration and Belonging: Voices of Migrants", in *Identity Trouble: Critical Discourse and Contested Identities*, ed. Carmen Rosa Caldas-Coulthard and Rick Iedema (London: Palgrave Macmillan, 2007), 95–119.
31. See Nedra Reynolds, *Geographies of Writing: Inhabiting Places and Encountering Difference* (Carbondale: Southern Illinois University Press, 2004), 2.

5.

"How the Mirror Broke"
Deconstructing Colonial Fairy Tales in "I Remember Pampalam"

» GISELLE RAMPAUL

OLIVE SENIOR'S POEM, "Colonial Girls' School", from which the title of this chapter comes, examines the negative implications of a colonial education on the school children (specifically, girls) of the Caribbean. The narrator of the poem looks forward to these colonial myths being shattered through the image of the breaking mirror, suggesting that Caribbean society was being indoctrinated into reflecting English and European culture by alluding specifically to the mirror that always revealed Snow White to be "the fairest one of all". Joyce Gittens's story, "I Remember Pampalam", published in 1947, also addresses this issue by demonstrating how irrelevant cultural myths and fairy tales (including specifically *Snow White*) contributed to the definition of social norms in colonial societies and to the shaping of the ideological perspective the child character is encouraged to assume.[1] The story, however, also reveals the dangers of this limited and selective perception, which ill equips her for an understanding of the reality of her situation of living in a barrack-yard[2] culture in Trinidad.

"I Remember Pampalam" is the story of a young girl growing up in colonial Trinidad with her parents, who live in a shop overlooking a barrack-yard. Her physical distance from the yard suggests that she is of a higher class than the inhabitants of the yard, and she is attracted to polite manners and beautiful things associated with colonial culture. She fancies herself a fairy-tale princess in her imaginative play, and she is attracted to the bride, whom she compared to a fairy and an angel, at the beginning of the story. The girl is, however, also fascinated by the many colourful characters who live in the yard and especially enjoys the scenes at Carnival time when the yard comes alive with colour and masquerade.

We hear about the yard inhabitants' unconventional familial and sexual relationships, which contrast with the nuclear family to which the child belongs and which establish patriarchy and heterosexuality as normative social performances. However, the child and her adult narrating self do not comment on these relationships, as the narrator seems to try to preserve the "purity" of her childhood experiences.

The child's world changes with the entrance of a new character, Pampalam, to the yard. Pampalam, whom she finds repulsive, represents everything contrary to her fairy-tale ideals, and she is paralysed by her presence. The story ends when Pampalam dies in questionable circumstances, and the child suddenly remembers two significant instances in which Pampalam was very kind to her. No comment is explicitly made on the significance of these sudden memories, but the story implies that they are important to the child's remembering of Pampalam and to the shattering of the colonial mirror that obscured the reality of the situation.

Tales of Childhood: Memory and Ideology

Narratives, like "I Remember Pampalam", which construct childhood memories, are complex in their use of narrative perspective. The narrator is actually an adult whose perspective is retrospective: that is, the adult is looking back through memory at her childhood experiences. According to Evelyne Ender, "childhood memories are always retrospective constructions: we are reading the manifest contents of scenes that are not available to consciousness. . . . Our earliest experiences . . . are only available to us as retrospective constructions – that is, as *memories* whose building blocks belong to our present sensibility, awareness and language."[3] And Seymour Chatman, in his study of narrative structure, points out that the narrator "is looking back at his own earlier perception-as-a-character. But that looking back is a conception, no longer a perception."[4]

In this way, then, the narrator of the childhood memories creates an *idea* of herself as a child, constructs her child self, according to her adult perspective. However, there is a simultaneous suggestion or illusion that the story is from the child's perspective as the information relayed is characteristically defined by a sort of "innocent" reading of events that is constructed from a refusal to evaluate and interpret the significance or meaning of these memories. The narrator, though, seems necessarily to be an adult by virtue of having memories of childhood experiences that she can construct into a coherent narrative. The story therefore constructs a child *character*; it is an *evocation* of childhood – in fact, Ender also speaks about memory being an act of the imagination – and therefore the narrative also constructs a certain ideology that is associated with a certain conception of childhood (that is, as "innocent") but also that is associated with the specific child character's world view.5

This world view or ideological/conceptual perspective and its relationship with memory, subjectivity and identity is the especial concern of this chapter. Many theorists have, of course, commented on the "falseness" of ideology and its tendency to obscure the subject's perception and understanding of objective reality. Ideology, for Marxists like Louis Althusser, meant a "false consciousness", "the system of ideas and representations which dominate the mind of man or a social group".6 For Althusser, ideology is a "pure dream", it is "empty and vain", "an imaginary assemblage", and "represents the imaginary relationship of individuals to their real conditions of existence".7 According to Terry Eagleton, ideology "signifies the way men live out their roles in class-society, the values, ideas and images which tie them by their social functions and so prevent them from a true knowledge of society as a whole".8 It is easy to see how this class-based system of ideology is readily applicable to colonial societies that were founded on Manichaean oppositions and involved the brainwashing of the less powerful subject peoples into accepting systems of thought that ensured the colonizers' political, epistemological and ontological dominance.9 The colonial mirror, as represented by the Snow White fairy tale in the story and into which colonized peoples were encouraged to gaze, did not reflect images of themselves but gave them false representations of their world and of themselves.

The narrator remembers the events of her past and is therefore speaking from a position in which the mirror that fed her colonial ideologies as a child has already been broken. But her story is also about her inability to remember certain events in her childhood because her experiences were so much defined or influenced by those colonial ideologies. Significant experiences are forgotten in a temporary amnesia and can only be narrated later, in retrospect because the child can only see her world from a limited (that is, colonial) perspective, a perspective that does not help her to correctly, or at least fairly, interpret events and people. The story of the narrator's childhood self is therefore about the conceptual perspective of the child who yet stands in front of the unbroken colonial mirror.

The Colonial Child Subject and Lacan's Mirror

The Marxist definition of ideology as a "false consciousness" has invited critique from poststructuralists who interrogate the relationship between ideology and subjectivity. Poststructuralists argue that "subjects – people – make their own ideology at the same time as ideology makes them subjects . . . 'ideology' goes to the heart of personal identity, of how we conceive ourselves as subjects in the world."[10] The idea of subjectivity, therefore, simultaneously suggests agency and passive reception to influences. According to Michel Foucault, "There are two meanings of the word 'subject': subject to someone else by control and dependence, and tied to one's own identity by a conscience or self-knowledge."[11] As Bennett and Royle argue, "an 'I' or 'me' is always *subject* to forces and effects both outside itself (environmental, social, cultural, economic, educational etc.) and 'within' itself (in particular in terms of what is called the unconscious or, in more recent philosophical terms, otherness)".[12] As Karen Coats puts it, "The subject is both active and passive; it has agency and responsibility, but at the same time it is bound by rules and laws outside itself and constrained by its own unconscious processes. . . . It is therefore within the language and images of a specific culture that the subject must *find* and *create* himself."[13]

This ties into Jacques Derrida's famous quotation, "Il n'y a pas de hors-texte" or "There is no outside-text", which points to the idea that texts not only reflect reality, but also actually produce and construct reality.[14] Subjectivity and identity are, therefore, very much determined by the texts we read. The child character in the story is shaped by the colonial fairy tales fed to her and which she adopts into her performance of her subject positions – not only in terms of class, race and gender, but also in her relationships with those around her.

Jacques Lacan's psychoanalytical mirror stage is important to this chapter in its articulation of how reflections of the body become assimilated into the viewer's subjectivity and identity.[15] The mirror stage occurs when a child sees a reflection of herself for the first time in a mirror and perceives the difference between her uncoordinated and fragmented body (as she perceives it) and the coordinated and unified or whole body she sees reflected in the mirror. It is at this point that the child identifies with that "Other" image on which she "hangs" her self. As Coats explains:

> Unlike the traditional view of mirror images as passively accurate reflections of what *is*, Lacan's understanding of the mirror image is that it is an anticipation

that structures a subject. The child looking into a mirror sees an idealized image of his potential. This image, in its specular completeness, is at odds with how he *experiences* his body. His trajectory of becoming is towards the image; he takes its completeness, fantasized as it is, as his goal. Though he may experience himself as fragmented and incomplete, he can imagine himself as whole, and it is towards this imaginary ideal that he moves.[16]

The child comes into recognition of herself therefore only in "a fictional way", that is, "through alienation (knowing oneself through an external image), duality (the result of a deep ambivalence caused by the alienation between the subject and its ideal image) and identification (the attempt to dissolve the subject into the ideal image and say, 'This is me')."[17]

Coats further points out that it is not only an actual mirror that provides the child with an ideal; other people or stories may also provide these ideal images that the child attempts to mirror: "The child [can take] an adult fantasy, manifested in a story, as his ideal image, and undertakes to enact it as his own subjective structure."[18] The child in Gittens's story perceives the representations of the fairy-tale princess as an ideal that she then tries to emulate and perform.

Gail Ching-Liang Low, however, also draws attention to the fact that the mirror stage not only "ushers in a narcissistic moment of idealization" but also a tendency of "aggressivity":

> The mirrored body presents a body of agency and control; the child's libidinal overinvestment in the figure results in frustration and jealousy. . . . The image in the mirror provides a pleasurable and erotic process of self-affirmation [but also an] unpleasurable process of alienation and retroactive nostalgia for wholeness. The reflected image, after all, is not the self but an image of the self as Other; identification is hence both recognition and misrecognition.[19]

Or, according to Wendy Doniger, "true recognition" and "distortion";[20] or, as Homi Bhabha expresses it in terms of his explication of colonial mimicry, "at once resemblance and menace", leading to recognition and disavowal.[21] Even as the child attempts to imitate or perform the ideal that the mirror offers, she is frustrated by the "slippage" that occurs between the self and the Other image of the self. In the colonial child subject, this is manifested in a sort of cultural schizophrenia and ontological insecurity.

Coats further points out that Lacan's focus is on "the way the subject situates itself with respect to the Other in language and the Other as language":

> Much of that "Other" language comes to the subject in the form of stories. Children are especially vulnerable to being structured by stories because they are still in the process of collecting the experiences that will shape and define their relation to the Other. . . . What we get from children's literature are the very patterns and signifiers that define our understanding of and our positions with respect to the Other and, in so doing, structure our sense of self. The literature we encounter as children, then, should be seen as central to the formation of subjectivity.[22]

In this quotation, Coats emphasizes the double vulnerability of the child in her inherent state of becoming and in her being shaped by ideals filtered through stories. Meenakshi Bharat's analysis emphasizes the particular situation of the colonized child subject: "In the child's unsuspecting reception and intake of colonial edicts, not only is the modus operandi of the colonizers highlighted, but by accenting the helpless innocence of children as the site of final control, the ultimate degrading implications of colonization are brought home. . . . [T]he most silent, disempowered, the most marginalized of colonial subjects, the child becomes the location of a major political and ideological battle."[23] But the child character also becomes the ideal symbol of the subaltern in stories about childhood memories because, as already discussed in the previous section, the child is also colonized by her own adult narrating self.[24] Because of the various levels of powerlessness, colonization and subjectivity associated with childhood, the child character becomes an attractive trope for many writers wishing to interrogate the colonial enterprise.

For Henry Jenkins, "Childhood becomes an emblem for anxieties about the passing of time, the destruction of historical formations, or conversely, a vehicle for hopes for the future."[25] And for Bill Ashcroft, the child becomes "a potent sign of post-colonial conceptions of imaginative and cultural possibility".[26] But I wish to argue that the child can only become a symbol of hope for the future when some of these aspects of colonization can be sloughed off – that is, when the child becomes an adult, and has more agency in the forming and negotiations of her subject positions. The possibility of the future is only embodied in the symbolism of the child character through the understanding that she will one day no longer be a child.

"Mirror, Mirror on the Wall"

The memories narrated in the story reveal an ideology strongly influenced by colonial education as the narrator defines her experiences in terms of or in relation to fairy tales and other foreign cultural references that are "far removed from . . . immediate experience".[27] The story itself is narrated in Standard English and is the only voice in the text apart from the direct speech of Pampalam, who speaks in Barbadian Creole. The story opens with the narrator's memory of her first encounter with the dreaded Pampalam, who later comes to live in the barrack-yard her verandah overlooks.

In recalling this first encounter, the narrator describes her excitement at seeing a wedding on her way home from school and the bride whom she describes as a fairy or an angel: "a lovely, radiant fairy thing, her satin dress dazzling my eyes, her billowing veil like a heavenly cloud surrounding an angel!" ("Pampalam", 20). These initial images are important in constructing a sense of the child's world view. Her mention of the fairy, of the heavenly cloud and of the angel all relate to her colonial education; but her fascination with the bride and the wedding also suggests her socialization into heterosexuality and the Western concept of the nuclear family as reinforced by fairy tales such as Snow White, which culminate in marriage. Richard Dyer argues that "weddings are the privileged moment of heterosexuality, . . . and also of women since they are glorified on what is seen as their day".[28] According to Marcia R. Lierberman, "We must consider the possibility that the classical attributes of 'femininity' found in these stories are in fact imprinted in children and reinforced by the stories themselves."[29] She further argues that fairy tales "have been made the repositories of the dreams, hopes, and fantasies of generations of girls" and that "millions of women must surely have formed their psycho-sexual self-concepts . . . in part from their favourite fairy tales".[30]

The positive associations of implied whiteness, richness, elegance the child makes with this beautiful sight are, however, very quickly replaced in the next paragraph with a description of the poor, black, dirty woman, Pampalam, who roughly shoves her out of the way. Whereas she is attracted to the beautiful fairy angel bride, she recoils in fear and disgust from Pampalam, who is described as having "the most unsavoury body", as "oily, frowsy, filthy", as a "foetid ensemble" ("Pampalam", 20); her clothes are torn, grimy and smelly. The juxtaposition of these descriptions significantly introduces the opposition of associations that is sustained throughout the story and that comes about because of her colonial ideology, which has little or nothing to do with reality. It is an opposition, however, that, at the end of the story, is revealed to be quite complicated.

In the first few lines of the story, the narrator tells us that Pampalam's "evil personality kept [her] tremulous with a shadowy, blind though powerful fear from which nothing freed [her]" ("Pampalam", 20). This sentence is very important because it reveals an early and immediate value judgement about Pampalam (she is described as having an "evil personality"; a lasting emotional response ("a shadowy, blind though powerful fear"). The child becomes imprisoned by her perspective (which involves both this value judgement and emotional response) on Pampalam ("from which nothing freed [her]"). The description of this fear as "shadowy" and "blind" also seems important in relation to how these initial responses relate to memory and to perception or ideology. Pampalam affects the child so profoundly because she represents everything opposed to the ideology she is encouraged to assume.

A significant image is, however, presented at the beginning of the story, which prepares us for the dissolution, or at least complication, of this Manichaean binary (as the child sees it) at the end of the story. We are prepared for Pampalam's death as the narrator tells us that five years later, after she first encountered the woman, she would watch "her dead body go out in a cheap coffin". When she first bumps into Pampalam, the latter scolds her: "Weh de hell you goine? Who is you at all to be pushin'? You t'ink because you got a lil bit o' colour, you kin move aside me as you want? You t'ink when Oi deid an' you deid, dey goine put me six foot in de groun' and dey goine put you six foot up in a tree? Eh?" The child reacts thus: "her closing words conjured up hazily the picture of Snow White in her glass coffin, placed safely in a tree by the sorrowing Dwarfs" ("Pampalam", 20).

The mention of the coffin links both the child and Pampalam in the latter's scolding. In the image conjured up in the child's mind, she links herself with Snow White, and the spatial orientation of the coffin up in a tree suggests a dissociation in her perception between Snow White and Pampalam. But the narrative links the image of the coffin to the child, Snow White *and* Pampalam, suggesting that the situation may be more complex than the child first perceives and that the dichotomy she imagines might lead her to the wrong conclusions about people. It does in fact encourage prejudice, to see others as inferior.

So, despite the fact that her encounter with Pampalam sends her, like Snow White, into a sort of sleep and a forgetting, a sort of mental paralysis, this does not make Pampalam the "she-monster" ("Pampalam", 23) she imagines her to be.

And, in fact, Sandra M. Gilbert and Susan Gubar see a close relationship between the mirror and the crystal coffin in the fairy tale, as they both represent "the tools patriarchy suggests that women use to kill themselves into art".[31] The common association of the coffin and the equalizing reality of mortality might also signal a common humanity that the child is yet unable to perceive.

The distorted image of Pampalam as "she-monster" only occurs because the child is enamoured with the vision she sees in the colonial mirror of an ideal self, such that Pampalam appears to her as a grotesque Other. Bruno Bettleheim does indeed see a relationship between the Snow White story and narcissism through the symbol of the mirror: "The queen's consulting the mirror about her worth – i.e., beauty – repeats the ancient theme of Narcissus, who loved only himself, so much that he became swallowed up by his self-love. . . . Narcissism is very much part of the young child's make-up. The child must gradually learn to transcend this dangerous form of self-involvement. The story of Snow White warns of the evil consequences of narcissism."[32]

But the mirror, while it encourages narcissism and the idealization of the self, also reveals a tension between the actual viewing body and its representation – the "misrecognition" that Lacan talks about. And this "misrecognition", which comes from the knowledge that the mirror image is and is not the self, seems to be at the heart of the child's trauma. The vision she has of Pampalam is, in her mind, diametrically opposed to that of the fairy-tale princesses with whom she identifies, but there is "menace" in the possibility that such a vision can also be a reflection of her self as a colonial person. It is a possibility so traumatic with which to come to terms that the child becomes paralysed with fear and revulsion.

It is also not surprising that the child associates herself with Snow White, given that Pampalam also refers to her "lil bit o' colour" ("Pampalam", 20). Dyer points out that whiteness is "a passport to privilege", and Alfred J. Lopez also acknowledges "the privilege and power associated with whiteness" and "the ways in which whiteness has historically used its normative power to suppress and marginalize its others".[33] In the fairy tale, whiteness is also Snow White's most defining feature (as, of course, suggested by her name), which makes her beautiful and therefore powerful.

This, however, is not to say that the child is white. Her family is middle class, as they are shop owners, and Pampalam's "lil bit" suggests that the child is light skinned, although not white. Still, in colonial Trinidad, this light-coloured or "fair" skin (which recalls the mirror's verdict in the fairy tale) was enough to guarantee privileges evident in the child's perception of herself as a sort of fairy princess.34 This distance between the child and the yard characters is also augmented by her imagining Snow White in the coffin *up in a tree*, while she also observes the activities in the yard from her balcony, far removed literally and metaphorically from the yard.

In addition, she admits her habit of "pretending to be a beautiful Eastern princess on [her] ivory balcony with all [her] slaves below. Sometimes, I was held captive by a bad ogre (that was when I was being punished by my father). A prince was to come and serenade me, swarm up my balcony and take me safely away from the terrible ogre!" ("Pampalam", 21). The mention of ivory recalls Snow White and the colour question that separates her from the yard characters, but she also imagines them her slaves, emphasizing the difference ingrained in her mind between them and her, as well as alluding to colonization. The description of the Eastern princess seems an obvious reference to the colonial exoticization of the Orient and is therefore a sort of second-hand or "borrowed image", to use Olive Senior's opening line in "Colonial Girls' School".

The child's conceptions of societal norms about love, sex, gender roles and relationships also seem to be shaped by these reveries and not by the reality of her situation of living in a barrack-yard. Her make-believe games reveal her subscription to a patriarchal society in which the male (her father) is agent of power and punishment but also the key to happiness through courtship and marriage (the prince). No wonder she was also so attracted to the wedding at the beginning of the story. According to Nancy Backes, "The mirror, mirror on the wall inevitably has the voice of a patriarch. . . . 'Snow White' is a tale that instils the virtues of beauty and acquiescence, a girl's guide to a successful life in a patriarchal society."35 Mary Daly also refers to Snow White's "patriarchal plot";36 and Karen E. Rowe, likewise, emphasizes the "significance of romantic tales in forming female attitudes towards the self, men, marriage and society" and their "awesome imaginative power over the female psyche".37 According to Donald Haase, "there has long been a tacit awareness of the fairy tale's role in the cultural discourse on gender", but the text reveals these norms to be mostly irrelevant to the child's lived experience, and they emerge as simply childhood romantic illusions.38 The intrusion of Pampalam on that occasion and the intrusion of the ping ping of the steel pan that the narrator says was "the only serenade [she] ever had from that slumyard" ("Pampalam", 21) reveal a sort of discontinuity between her imagination based on colonial ideology and the actual social reality of the yard.

This ideology is further augmented by the child's own social class and the characters of whom her parents approve and disapprove. The child is afforded the luxury of living in a big house with a front and back verandah, while the inhabitants of the yard live in slums. Her father is a shopkeeper, and although they have moved from the country to the city, his occupation suggests stability and money while the yard characters hardly ever work or do not have steady employment. To compound this separation, the child is encouraged to associate with characters like Miss Fina, whose very name allegorically suggests the finery and delicacy with which she is associated. She is associated with a more polite and civilized way of life, having had the experience of working with rich white people and is neat, clean and speaks "properly", contrasting with Pampalam's use of Creole, and imbues all the (colonial) virtues of which the child's mother is supportive. And although, being a member of the yard, she is associated with Carnival, it is the artistic, delicate bead and needlework with which she is occupied. To the child's mother, she is a "nice" woman worthy of all the nuances of meaning embedded in that adjective and therefore suitable for fostering the child's colonial world view and the fairy-tale persona she assumes.

Tante Zaza is the character who contrasts with Miss Fina and whose room is forbidden to the child by her mother. Tante Zaza is associated with superstition and *obeah*, the folk culture, as opposed to the artificiality and refinement of Miss Fina. Her room is restricted to the child, whose parents try to shield her from these common people and their activities. (Her mother, for example, does not answer when she is asked about the meaning of another character's name, Two Bits, and sends her to bed during a fight that takes place in the yard.)

The narrative provides descriptions of the other characters who live with Tante Zaza, but the reader is expected to glean much more from what is simply stated without judgement. For example, Two Bits is a prostitute, but she also seems to be the keeper of Baggie, Tante Zaza's son who never works;[39] but his powdered face and his association with the Sandal Man, who wears bright red nail polish, also suggest homosexuality and fluid gender identities. These sexual relationships become even more confusing when the two girls who are supposedly Tante Zaza's daughters fight over Baggie. One cannot quite make sense of these relationships, but it is obvious that they are of some sort of alternative sexual nature – contrasting with the description of the bride as an angel and therefore virginal and sexually innocent – and that they do not adhere to the conservative Western heterosexual nuclear family structure of the child's own family.

The Zaza household also takes part in Carnival, and their masquerade costumes only contribute to their subversion of colonial norms even as they, like the child in her make-believe, re-enact colonial stories: "Baggie was Robin Hood and The Sandal Man was Maid Marion – he did look like a girl. Tante Zaza was Friar Tuck. Another year they dressed up as Egyptians. Baggie was Mark Antony and the Sandal Man was Cleopatra. Tante Zaza was Caesar" ("Pampalam", 22). The colour dichotomy becomes even more apparent as the child's attraction to notions of whiteness in her fascination with the bride, the association with Snow White and her imaginary ivory balcony is contrasted with red lipstick, red nail polish, black skin and the myriad lurid colours of the yard characters' Carnival masquerade.

Cross-dressing and role playing play significant parts in these masks, rendering sexual orientation and relationships even more ambiguous and confusing. While the Sandal Man plays the role of a woman in both instances, Tante Zaza also plays a cross-gendered role. The result is the subversion of these stories through an ironic mirroring of the colonial characters and of the societal norms the child and her parents uphold. According to Tony Watkins, "the struggle [in cultural expressions of this kind] is for meaning: dominant groups [in this case the colonial power] attempt to render as 'natural' meanings which serve their interests [that is, by disseminating and perpetuating colonial ideals and values], whereas subordinate groups resist this process in various ways, trying to make meanings that serve their interests".[40]

The donning of the colonial mask in these instances has quite different political implications from the child's adoption of the mask of the fairy-tale princess. Instead of being disturbed by the slippage between the self and its image in the colonial mirror, the yard characters exploit this gap to their advantage, mimicking the colonizers' image but in a parodic way. As Ranjana Khanna argues, "The modern colonized subject has, then, a different ontological makeup than that of the colonizer rendered through the relationship of looking, and not seeing oneself as a mask, but rather, one's gestalt, and one's mask as a self."[41] Their revelry in this subversion at Carnival time therefore shifts the balance of power – even if only temporarily – to their side.

"How the Mirror Broke"

When Pampalam enters the yard, its nature changes dramatically. She enters with violence, beating Two Bits and chasing away the two sisters who lived with Tante

Zaza, and when she leaves, it is because she has been violently and fatally stabbed. The childish fantasies are over for good – "those lovely days were over, there was no longer in me the stuff of which dreams are made, my fear had dried it all up" ("Pampalam", 23). The Carnival activities also cease: there is only "Old Masque on the Monday morning for Jou'vert" ("Pampalam", 23) in which the beautiful, colourful costumes are markedly absent. Quarrels become frequent among the yard members, and the child's consciousness is taken over and paralysed by fear.

It is only when Pampalam dies that the child remembers the kindness displayed during the two horrid incidents in which she met the woman face to face. It is here we see the fragility and the erroneousness of the masks the child has constructed in her understanding and perception of the people around her. According to Lewis A. Kirschner, "the interweaving of psychic and historical 'facts' forms the fabric of a subject who is not a unity but an open system, continually being redefined by new experiences and reinterpretations of the past, which in turn may highlight episodes previously forgotten or disregarded".[42] The child therefore has to re-member the details of her experiences of Pampalam to create a more objective picture of the woman: "That which had been coded as abject in the initial configuring of the body, both individual and social, returns and has to be dealt with all over again."[43]

The first of these encounters occurs when she had fallen over and was picked up gently by Pampalam; the second when she dropped her two pennies, which were about to be coveted by two boys, and Pampalam chased them away, wiped the dirty pennies on her dress and returned them to the child. Her memory is so sudden and vivid at the end of the story that she "sat bolt upright in bed" ("Pampalam", 24). As Fred Inglis argues, "the stories we tell ourselves about ourselves are not just a help to moral education; they comprise the only moral education which can gain purchase on the modern world. . . . They are theories with which to think forwards . . . and understand backwards."[44] It is therefore necessary for the child to remember this significant part of the story of her interaction with Pampalam against the blinding colonial ideology that encouraged her to dissociate herself from these memories that give her a truer understanding of the situation and of Pampalam.

After the death of Pampalam, there is the return to fancy-mas Carnival in which the costumes are pretty and ornamental but significantly the choice of costumes denotes something morbid, forbidding and dark: "Baggie was Macbeth, and The Sandal Man was Lady Macbeth; he had red stuff just like blood, dripping from his right hand. Tante Zaza was Banquo's Ghost" ("Pampalam", 24). As Bettleheim notices, the Snow White fairy tale involves the colours white and red from the beginning of the story as Snow White's mother pricks her finger, and three drops of red blood fall on the snow. He argues that the colours are important: "Here the problems the story sets out to solve are intimated: sexual innocence, whiteness, is contrasted with sexual desire, symbolized by the red blood."[45] This use of these colours in "I Remember Pampalam" encourages a similar reading. The white fairy angel bride with whom the child identifies at the beginning of the story makes way for the characters, who are associated with lurid red make-up and red blood and who present the child with alternative ways of being. The masquerade costumes in the choice of *Macbeth* again refer to colonial education, but they also suggest the culpability of Tante Zaza's group in the murder of Pampalam. Although the child gives no judgement or analysis of this final image, the ambivalence of the colonial masks becomes apparent.

The story takes us through three main phases in its deconstruction of colonial fairy tales as irrelevant and blinding. It presents the child's ideology, which is shaped by these colonial stories; it complicates these stories by presenting them as Carnival masks and therefore removed from reality; and it shows that the characters are more complex than the child perceives based on her limited and limiting colonial ideology. The Zaza household is involved in murder, the prissy Miss Fina's morality is subtly questioned as she seems to be involved in some dubious dealings, and the child herself is revealed to be prejudiced in her belief that she is superior to the yard characters. Pampalam is the only character in the story who does not don a mask of some sort, and she is the most genuine character despite her grotesque and gross appearance. The mask of "she-monster" comes from the child's perception only and, specifically, from her indoctrination into colonial ideologies. As Haase argues, "fairy tales act as broken mirrors for women who use them to construct incoherent and unknowable images of themselves, thereby confirming the complex and problematic relation between the classic tales and constructions of female subjectivity".[46] But these fairy tales do not only encourage "incoherent and unknowable images" of the child protagonist. They also encourage such images of others so that she cannot form objective opinions about herself or others. Her fascination with and performance of these colonial stories only limit her understanding of and divorce her from the real world.

Only at the end of the story is she able to recall other pertinent information necessary for constructing a more complete picture of the events, although the narrator, still faithful to her evocation of an ideology of childhood, refrains from interpreting this information. According to Barbara Lalla, "perspective may sometimes be revealed *after* an event, suggesting or enabling re-appraisal or recontextualization".47 As Coats elaborates, "The subject must abject, that is, define and exclude, those things which threaten it and must build strong defences against their return. She must take up a position with respect to difference and must learn what her culture values as ideal in terms of bodies and behaviours."48 In this sense the narrative also becomes dialogical; according to Jefferson Singer and Pavel Blagov, it "invokes a response from the self and others that have 'read' or 'listened' to [it]".49 The end of the story becomes a sort of beginning, encouraging the reader to re-evaluate all the previously narrated information and therefore encouraging the reader himself or herself to re-member Pampalam. The re-membering of Pampalam for the child entails also a re-membering or re-definition of the self; according to Tony Watkins, because "subjectivity is a social construction, it is always open to change".50

Memory is therefore shown to be shaped by ideology in the short story and determines one's subjectivity and identity, but it is also revealed to be something beyond ideology – that is, not limited by ideology – and can be the key to more profound understanding and a consequent reshaping of identity. It is with the shattering of the colonial mirror, in other words, that the colonized people can begin to take control of their own subjectivity and begin to articulate their own identity on their own terms. As Jack Zipes, writing about the way enchantment works within fairy tales, puts it, "Enchantment equals petrification. Breaking the spell equals emancipation."51

Notes

1. Joyce Gittens, "I Remember Pampalam", *Bim* 2, no. 8 (1947): 20–24. All references to "I Remember Pampalam" are taken from this edition, and subsequent references to the story appear parenthetically in the text.
2. A courtyard surrounded by modest dwelling-houses, found usually in poor urban areas.
3. Evelyn Ender, *Architexts of Memory: Literature, Science and Autobiography* (Ann Arbor: University of Michigan Press, 2008), 71, 73.

4. Seymour Chatman, *Story and Discourse: Narrative Structure in Fiction and Film* (Ithaca: Cornell University Press, 1980), 155.
5. Ender, *Architexts of Memory*, 64.
6. Louis Althusser, "Ideology and Ideological State Apparatuses", in *Lenin and Philosophy and Other Essays*, trans. Ben Brewster (London: New Left Books, 1977), 149.
7. Ibid., 155, 153.
8. Terry Eagleton, *Marxism and Literary Criticism* (London: Routledge, 1976), 16–17.
9. See, for example, Abdul R. JanMohammed, "The Economy of Manichean Allegory: The Function of Racial Difference", *Critical Enquiry* 12(1) 1985: 59–87; Edward Said, *Orientalism* (New York: Vintage, 1979); and Gayatri Chakravorty Spivak, "Can the Subaltern Speak?", in *Marxism and the Interpretation of Culture*, eds. Cary Nelson and Lawrence Grossberg (Urbana: University of Illinois Press, 1988), 271–313.
10. Andrew Bennett and Nicholas Royle, *Introduction to Literature, Criticism and Theory* (London and New York: Pearson, Longman, 2004), 173.
11. Michel Foucault, "The Subject and Power", in *Michel Foucault: Beyond Structuralism and Hermeneutics*, eds. Hubert L. Dreyfus and Paul Rabinow (Chicago: University of Chicago Press, 1983), 212.
12. Bennett and Royle, *Introduction to Literature*, 125.
13. Karen Coats, *Looking Glasses and Neverlands: Lacan, Desire and Subjectivity in Children's Literature* (Iowa City: University of Iowa Press, 2004), 3.
14. Jacques Derrida, *Of Grammatology*, trans. Gayatri Chakravorty Spivak (Baltimore: Johns Hopkins University Press, 1976), 158.
15. See Jacques Lacan, "The Mirror Stage as Formative of the I Function as Revealed in Psychoanalytical Experience", trans. Bruce Fink, *Ecrit: The First Complete Translation in English* (New York: Norton, 2005), 75–81.
16. Coats, *Looking Glasses*, 6.
17. Ibid., 19.
18. Ibid., 7.
19. Gail Ching-Liang Low, *White Skins/Black Masks: Representation and Colonialism* (London and New York: Routledge, 1996), 194.
20. Wendy Doniger, *The Bedtrick: Tales of Sex and Masquerade* (Chicago: University of Chicago Press, 2000), 103.
21. Homi Bhabha, "Of Mimicry and Man: The Ambivalence of Colonial Discourse", in *The Location of Culture* (London and New York: Routledge, 1994), 85–92.
22. Coats, *Looking Glasses*, 4.

23. Meenakshi Bharat, *The Ultimate Colony: The Child in Postcolonial Fiction* (Mumbai: Allied Publishers, 2003), 101. Other critics have also written about the construction of the colonized person as "child". See, for example, Jo-Ann Wallace, "De-Scribing *The Water Babies*: 'The Child' in Post-colonial Theory", in *De-Scribing Empire: Postcolonialism and Textuality*, eds. Chris Tiffin and Alan Lawson (London: Routledge, 1994), 171–84; Catherine Hall, "Histories, Empires and the Post-Colonial Moment" in *The Post-colonial Question*, eds. Iain Chambers and Lidia Curti (London: Routledge, 1996), 65–77; and Bill Ashcroft, *On Post-colonial Futures: Transformations of Colonial Culture* (London: Continuum, 2001).
24. See, for example, Roderick McGillis, "Postcolonialism, Children and Their Literature", *Ariel* 2, no. 1 (January, 1997): 7–15; Jacqueline Rose, *The Case of Peter Pan: or The Impossibility of Children's Literature* (London: Macmillan, 1984); and Perry Nodelman, "The Other: Orientalism, Colonialism, and Children's Literature", *Children's Literature Association Quarterly* 17 (1992): 29–35.
25. Henry Jenkins, "Childhood Innocence and Other Modern Myths", in *The Children's Culture Reader*, ed. Henry Jenkins (New York: New York University Press, 1998), 5.
26. Ashcroft, *On Post-colonial Futures*, 54.
27. J. Thompson and G. Woodard, "Black Perspective in Books for Children", in *The Black American in Books for Children: Readings in Racism*, eds. D. MacCann and G. Woodard (Metuchen, NJ: Scarecrow Press, 1972), 23.
28. Richard Dyer, *White* (London: Routledge, 1997), 124.
29. Marcia R. Lierberman, "'Some Day My Prince Will Come': Female Acculturation through the Fairy Tale", *College English* 34, no. 3 (1972): 395.
30. Ibid., 385.
31. Sandra M. Gilbert and Susan Gubar, "Snow White and Her Wicked Stepmother", in *The Classical Fairy Tales: Texts, Criticism*, ed. Maria Tatar (New York and London: W.W. Norton, 1999), 292.
32. Bruno Bettleheim, *The Uses of Enchantment: The Meaning and Importance of Fairy Tales* (New York: Vintage Books, 1989), 202–3.
33. Dyer, *White*, 44; Alfred J. Lopez, "Introduction: Whiteness after Empire", in *Postcolonial Whiteness: A Critical Reader on Race and Empire*, ed. Alfred J. Lopez (Albany: State University of New York Press, 2005), 2.
34. The word "fair" in the fairy tale means "beautiful". However, in colonial and postcolonial Trinidad, the word took on other nuances of meaning, referring to light-coloured skin and equating "fair" skin with beauty.

35. Nancy Backes, "Growing Up Desperately: The Adolescent 'Other' in the Novels of Paule Marshall, Toni Morrison, and Michelle Cliff", in *Women of Colour: Defining the Issues, Hearing the Voices*, eds. Diane Long Hoeveler and Janet K. Boles (Westport, CT: Greenwood Press, 2001), 151.
36. Mary Daly, *Gyn/Ecology: The Metaethics of Radical Feminism* (Boston: Beacon Press, 1990), 44.
37. Karen E. Rowe, "Feminism and Fairy Tales", *Women's Studies: An Interdisciplinary Journal* 6 (1979): 222, 218.
38. Donald Haase, "Feminist Fairy-Tale Scholarship", in *Fairy Tales and Feminism: New Approaches*, ed. Donald Haase (Detroit, MI: Wayne State University Press, 2004), viii.
39. In *yard literature*, a keeper was usually a woman who provided for and took care of the financial and other domestic needs of her lover.
40. Tony Watkins, "The Setting of Childen's Literature: History and Culture", in *Understanding Children's Literature*, ed. Peter Hunt (London and New York: Routledge, 1999), 35.
41. Ranjana Khanna, *Dark Continents: Psychoanalysis and Colonialism* (Durham, NC: Duke University Press, 2003), 187.
42. Lewis A. Kirschner, "Concepts of Reality and Psychic Reality in Psychoanalysis as Illustrated by the Disagreement between Freud and Ferenczi", *International Journal of Psychoanalysis* 74 (1993): 228.
43. Coats, *Looking Glasses*, 10.
44. Fred Inglis, *Cultural Studies* (Oxford: Blackwell, 1993), 214.
45. Bettleheim, *The Uses of Enchantment*, 202.
46. Haase, "Feminist Fairy-Tale Scholarship", in *Fairy Tales and Feminism*, 25.
47. Barbara Lalla, "Signifying Nothing: Writing about Not Writing in *The Mystic Masseur*", *Anthurium* 5, no. 1 (Fall 2007), http://anthurium.miami.edu/volume_5/issue_2/lalla-signifying.html.
48. Coats, *Looking Glasses*, 8.
49. Jefferson Singer and Pavel Blagov, "The Integrative Function of Narrative Processing: Autobiographical Memory, Self-Defining Memories and the Life Story of Identity", in *The Self and Memory*, eds. Denise R. Beike, James M. Lampinen and Douglas A. Behrend (New York: Psychology Press, 2004), 133.
50. Watkins, "The Setting of Childen's Literature: History and Culture", in *Understanding Children's Literature*, 35.
51. Jack Zipes, *When Dreams Came True: Classical Fairy Tales and Their Tradition* (New York: Routledge, 2007), 6.

6.

"What Child Is This?"
Same-Sex Desire among Children in the Anglophone Caribbean Short Story

» GERALDINE ELIZABETH SKEETE

GROWING-UP STORIES HAVE long been a staple in anglophone Caribbean literature, but emphasis was previously given to heterosexual characters. The internal, peer and societal pressures gay and lesbian youths endure as they struggle to conform to or go against the status quo, including instances of their joys and acceptance of their sexuality, are poignantly portrayed in the contemporary Bildungsroman unlike in the past. This recent literature shows that the gay youth faces extreme pressure to adhere to a compulsory masculinity in preparation for manhood, whereas his female counterpart faces less censure, since she has greater freedom to indulge in lesbian eroticism within friendship circles and in the idolization of women. Focus will be given here to the short story and its practitioners, such as Lawrence Scott, Dionne Brand, Shani Mootoo, Ayiah Jahan and Desoto Wong, with a brief mention of Michelle Cliff. Some literary critics have described the short story form as, in part, being peopled with characters that are "non-hegemonic", "peripheral" and "at odds with the dominant culture"; these descriptors also fit the subject position of the non-heterosexual. Therefore, it is of interest in this essay to analyse through close readings and a literary linguistics approach how the aforementioned writers skilfully use this genre to explore the alternative experiences of gay and lesbian children in the literary discourse.

Helmut Bonheim explains, in the way of a definition, that a short story "is a narrative too short to be published by itself". Also, a short story has a limited length which affects "a limited cast of characters, a restricted time scheme, a single action or at least only a few separate actions, and a unity of technique and tone".[1] Nevertheless, a *collection* of short stories, such as those to be discussed in this chapter, offers myriad plots, themes and perspectives that can together give voice to lesbian and gay experiences. Katie Wales notes how genre is an intertextual concept, with the conventions of particular traditions being adopted by writers and their contemporaries.[2] Despite the short story's paradoxical tightness and open-endedness, the themes the writers who also use this form are able to explore are nonetheless plentiful.

Female authors like Cliff, Brand and Mootoo, for example, treat with similar explorations of lesbian love and desire in the short story as they do in their novels. Mary Eagleton's observation about what has been said of the short story genre is incidentally equivalent to the position gays, lesbians, bisexuals and transgendered persons are relegated to in the society. She notes that critics have, for example, considered the short story as holding "a marginal and ambiguous position in literary culture, and is peopled with characters who are in some way at odds with the dominant culture . . ."; it "[according to Frank O'Connor in *The Lonely Voice*] deals with 'submerged population groups'"; and the "image they [the critics] offer of the short story writer and character [is] non-hegemonic, peripheral, contradictory".[3] Similarly, Axel Nissen introduces his discussion on "The Queer Short Story" by outlining the oppositional and dialectical positioning of the short story and the novel, which like other binary constructions with regard to race, gender and sexuality, he opines, is "not innocent". Also, he states in part:

> While the short story is often seen to be minor, fragmented, underdeveloped, superficial, immature and simple, the novel is considered major, whole, fully developed, exhaustive, mature, and complex. The short story is the "other" of fictional prose narrative. As the other it must continually justify its existence, worry about the circumstances of its being and becoming, agonize about its value and identity. Not unlike homosexuality, the short story was born into the world as a generic problem, a problem that required a solution or at least a definition. It is a curious coincidence, then, that the modern homosexual and the modern short story were invented at the same time.[4]

Notwithstanding Nissen's personification of the short story to embellish his point, his description of the *genre* closely resembles those mentioned by Eagleton regarding the types of *character* found in the short story. Mary Louise Pratt observes in her own contrastive analysis of the novel and short story in "The Short

Story: The Long and the Short of It" that, as regards *subject matter*, "the short story is often the genre used to introduce new (and possibly stigmatized) subject matters into the literary arena".[5] Pratt's observation is in keeping with Lawrence Scott's own observation, in a 26 February 2004 interview with this researcher, that "a lot of new gay fiction . . . has come through the short story". Pratt cites the eminent French practitioner of the short story, Henri René Albert Guy de Maupassant, and his use of the form to break down taboos related to class and sexuality.[6] This breaking down of sexual taboos is also undertaken by the Caribbean diasporic short story writers discussed in this paper.

The child as subject is also amenable to the short story form, for as Pratt also notes:

> Obviously, whether a given subject is central or peripheral, established or new in a literature has a great deal to do with what is central and peripheral in the community outside its literature, a great deal to do, that is, with values, and with socioeconomic, political and cultural realities. In some cases at least, there seem to develop dialectical correspondences between minor or marginal genres and what are evaluated as minor or marginal subjects. *So for example, we find the short story used especially often for portraying childhood experience.*[7]

She discusses how novels rarely deal with childhood experiences unless they belong to specialized forms like the picaresque and the Bildungsroman, for which tendency reasons include "length and interest – a child's perspective is too naïve, too thin, too unrevealing to sustain 'full-length' novel treatment"; however, she poses a rhetorical question: "Isn't this really a way of saying that childhood experience is not considered normative or authoritative in the society, or that it is considered an incomplete basis for the supposed totalizing vision of the novel?"[8] Conversely, much of what is known and acclaimed in the literature of the anglophone Caribbean – and some of which have been mainstays in the syllabuses of secondary and tertiary institutions – is its Bildungsroman such as V.S. Naipaul's *A House for Mr Biswas*, George Lamming's *In the Castle of My Skin*, Jamaica Kincaid's *Annie John*, Geoffrey Drayton's *Christopher*, Merle Hodge's *Crick Crack, Monkey*, Michael Anthony's *The Year in San Fernando* and *Green Days by the River*, Ian McDonald's *The Humming Bird Tree*, M. NourbeSe Philip's *Harriet's Daughter* and Zee Edgell's *Beka Lamb*, just to name a few from a significantly long list.[9] Many of these analogize the child as subject with the nation as subject in terms of juxtaposing the one's physical, spiritual, emotional, moral and intellectual growth and development with the other's social, economic, cultural and political transformations.

Pratt's ranging discussion on the compatibility of the short story genre with its different kinds of subject matter is relevant here specifically with regard to taboos surrounding sexuality and childhood experiences, since both aspects combined illustrate this chapter's focus. Although the child protagonists are "not considered normative" because of traits society associates with sexual deviancy, in no way are they presented in the literary discourse as "thin", "unrevealing" or "incomplete", for instance.

Lawrence Scott, the 1986 winner of the Tom-Gallon short story award and a judge of the 2006 Commonwealth Short Story Competition, has been selected as the lone Caribbean male writer because he has most recognizably been the one from the anglophone Caribbean to use the short story form to directly address themes of homosexuality and homoeroticism among children, albeit as characterized by his *male* protagonists. The unifying thread in the works selected here can be garnered from his words in an e-mail message to this researcher on 6 April 2010: "while writing [his short story collection] *Ballad for the New World* I was empowered to write and include two stories, 'Chameleon' and 'I Want to Follow My Friend' which deal with male homosexual childhood relationships and identity through a raised consciousness brought about by feminist and lesbian feminist writing in the 1980s".[10] Scott also indicates that, before he became a published writer, he had an interest in "the psychology of children, their finding of themselves, their sexual identities". As a teacher in London he was engaged in socialist initiatives advocating for the improvement of the rights of marginalized groups, including stemming racism and bullying in schools, and "trying to find appropriate and relevant ways to introduce same-sex themes for teenage groups through literature". His story "I Want to Follow My Friend" provides this chapter, therefore, with an example of the depiction of same-sex desire as experienced by a male child and how it is fraught with issues emanating from the home and school. Despite the short story's tightness and open-endedness, Scott is able, as he does in his novel, *Aelred's Sin*, to use plot, narrative perspective, literary tropes and characterization, for example, to subvert and invert heterosexuality.

Most representations of childhood and alternative sexuality, however, have been undertaken by women writers and this is what this essay reflects by those selected for the discussion. Eagleton's prime focus in her essay is on the various issues surrounding the woman writer's approach in using the short story form.

She notes that one reason for the interest in this form is the "hope that the flexible, open-ended qualities of the short story may offer a transforming potential, an ability to ask the unspoken question, to raise new subject matter".[11] In this regard, in the context of anglophone Caribbean women's writing, the short stories written by Cliff, Mootoo and Brand, among others, seem to offer vignettes and unveil perspectives about what it means to be a Caribbean lesbian at home or abroad. The brevity and tightness of the form – despite the flexibility Eagleton speaks of – inevitably allow the writer and reader to engage with particular issues with respect to the lesbian experience.

As it is in most other cultures, in the anglophone Caribbean the sexualization of children by adults is extremely taboo and in particular circumstances is even criminalized. Whether or not children can experience and articulate sexual desire has also been debated and contested, stemming from conflicting ideologies and findings regarding the matter. For example, Stevi Jackson notes, as regards childhood experience, that the only "aspect of pre-adolescent development that has greatest relevance for sexuality is the learning of gender roles".[12] She, therefore, counters and debunks Freud's psychosexual theories on infantile sexuality, drawing on and agreeing with findings by William Simon and John H. Gagnon who state that "[s]exual behaviour is socially scripted behaviour and not the . . . expression of some primordial drive";[13] and she argues that children cannot possess the linguistic competence to express erotic feelings:

> If sexuality lies not in the quality of an act but in the meaning given to it, then a child's behaviour or responses cannot be interpreted as being sexual when the child has not yet learnt the vocabulary of motives through which sexual activity is mediated . . . What is sexual depends on culturally defined and socially learnt meanings. . . . In what sense can a child be said to have desire when the concept of desire and, indeed, all knowledge through which she could make sense of her experience as sexual, is not available to her? . . . . a child cannot be experiencing sexual desire in the sense that an adult would, since she cannot make sense of her feelings in those terms. . . . how can a child who cannot name desire be said to experience it?[14]

The title of this chapter, therefore, may be contentious on three fronts: because it conveys the idea that children do experience *desire* as well as, and more problematically, because it is so taboo, that they can experience such a troubling transgression as *same-sex* desire. The controversy about whether this same-sex desire may not only be *learned*, but that it may also be *innate*, also arises. The paramount objective of this chapter, though, is to discuss and interrogate what is being portrayed by writers as regards alternative sexuality among juvenile characters in the literary discourse.

Jackson is referring to the infant child. The child protagonists in the selected short stories to be discussed here are, however, in – or on the cusp of – their adolescent years. The only exception cited is Shani Mootoo's real-life recollection of being seven years old and attracted to someone of the same sex. In addition, the words *child* and *children* are being used here in their definitions of a son or daughter and of being young and not as yet fully physically developed.[15] That the protagonists are generally of high school age is significant, though, because as Jackson notes: "Adolescence is the period of life when conscious sexual learning begins. At this time children make discoveries concerning the facts of sex and reproduction, experience changes in their bodies, and begin to learn the socio-sexual scripts that govern adult sexual behaviour."[16] In the short stories cited in this chapter, one of those scripts is non-heterosexual.

One of the environments in which this script is learned is in the classroom, and in Dionne Brand's short story, it is the teacher who, unwittingly, is the subject *and* the object of that learning. Brand's "Madame Alaird's Breasts" is the only one in *Sans Souci and Other Stories* – her collection of eleven short stories – that deals exclusively with female-female desire. In some cases, it is difficult to say with much certainty whether some of the characters are definitely lesbian. Some may instead be partaking in what Adrienne Rich calls "woman-identified experience[s]" that include "many more forms of primary intensity between and among women" and not just those that have to do with women who have had or have "consciously desired genital sexual experience" with other women, what Rich defines as a "lesbian continuum".[17] This continuum includes females who identify as lesbian as well as those who do not.[18] Paula C. Rust notes that Rich's concept of woman-identification, which is a woman's political and social commitment to other women, as being at the heart of lesbianism, "made it theoretically possible for any woman to call herself a lesbian".[19]

Some have criticized the continuum as one that desexualizes lesbianism and downplays women's many ethnic, class and sexual differences, or, put in another way by Sara Mills and Christine A. White, that "result[s] in the erasure of the specificity of lesbianism, and mask[s] much of the discrimination suffered by lesbians".[20] However, the concept seems quite applicable here, where the literature also depicts non-sexual, sometimes intense, friendships between women and girls.

If some readers have deduced sexual undertones in the friendship between Annie and the "red girl" in Jamaica Kincaid's *Annie John*, then Brand's short story, "Madame Alaird's Breasts", approaches the female adolescent's attraction for another female, in this case an older woman, on another plane.[21] One may argue that this short story is less about lesbianism than about secondary schoolgirls' exuberant fascination with the French teacher's overly large breasts, objects that encourage humour, persiflage and jest among them. As budding women themselves, it may not surprise that they would have a natural interest in that particular part of the female anatomy, which is somewhat more visible as regards its growth, size and shape, and would wonder about their own prospects. For example, one girl asks the others during their habitual Tuesday and Thursday walking-home-from-school conversations about Madame Alaird's breasts – their French class takes place on those days – "You think I go have breasts like Madame Alaird?" ("Mme Alaird", 80). Genital development and other physiological changes, as well as body image on the whole, are concerns for both adolescent girls and boys. Jackson, acquiescing with Simon and Gagnon's observation, explains that adolescent girls "learn to enact sexual scripts within the milieu of their peer group, an environment which may be characterized as homo-social and heterosexual. . . . So, although their sexual interest is focused on the opposite sex, it is primarily to their same-sex peers that adolescents will look for validation of their sexual attitudes and accomplishments."[22]

However, the author herself, who is openly lesbian, debunks what could be an innocent interpretation of the story by her remarks in the non-fiction *Bread Out of Stone*, in the chapter "This Body for Itself".[23] After apologizing for "bringing sex up" and then reading the story for participants at the First Caribbean Women Writers' Conference in Massachusetts, where she feels that discussion of the body, especially the female body, was being avoided, there is "Outrage" and "indignation" for her "indiscretion", and she declares that

> Only the feminists and the lesbians talk to me after that. I'm late and I hear that the next session is charged with questions about lesbianism and homosexuality. The lesbian *double entendre* has just dawned on some. . . . When I come near, people stop talking; friends look glazed, as if they do not want to show me the least recognition lest they be associated with my travesty, or they whisper behind my back.[24]

Various lexical items, including adjectives, and the use of figurative language, such as metaphor and simile, and *verba sentiendi* (what Boris Uspensky describes as the "words denoting feelings, thoughts, and perceptions, primary signals of a subjective point of view" – also keys to a character's inscape) are dispersed throughout the story, betraying a lesbian erotic among the thirteen-year-old girls in this all-female school.[25] Expressions include "Lustful and unrepentent [sic]" ("Mme Alaird", 84); "We loved Madame Alaird's breasts" (79); "sharpened by the excitement of Madame Alaird's breasts" (79); "Madame Alaird's breasts drove us to extremes" (83); "Madame Alaird was almost naked as far as we were concerned. It did not matter that she was always fully clothed" (81); "we lapped our tongues over her breasts once again" (83), in reference to their French pronunciations and drills; and, "Our renewed obsession with Madame Alaird's breasts, our passion for their snug bounciness, their warm purpleness, their juicy fruitedness" (83). In addition, it may be said that the narrator presents this teacher as someone who, for the girls, acts as an initiator into the world where women love other women. This is, of course, unknown to Madame Alaird. One can glean this from the following lines:

> Madame Alaird's breasts gave us imagination beyond our years or possibilities, of burgundy velvet rooms with big-legged women and rum and calypso music. Next to Madame Alaird's breasts, we loved Madame Alaird's lips. They made water spring to our mouths just like when the skin bursts eating a purple fat mammy sipote fruit . . . In the wooden and musty paper smell of our thirteen-year-old girl lives, in the stifling, uniformed, Presbyterian hush of our days, in the bone and stick of our youngness, Madame Alaird was a vision, a promise of the dark-red fleshiness of real life. (80, 82)

In *Bread Out of Stone*, Brand affirms that "I think that women learn about sexual pleasure from women" (*Bread*, 97). This epistemic expression refers to women who are either lesbian or straight. She goes on to recount memories and images of ordinary women who helped form her own sensibility as a lesbian (*Bread*, 98). "Madame Alaird's Breasts" undoubtedly demonstrates the author's perspective in this regard for it shows how, albeit in an all-female environment, young girls experience desire by admiring one of their own sex. As Brand notes: "The strict code of heterosexuality would have us think that we come upon sexual pleasure when we notice men or that we should" (*Bread*, 97). The reader can certainly accept this as only one view of female sexuality, for indeed it can be attested that many young or pubescent girls' knowledge and awareness of sexual pleasure do not begin with the admiration of other women in this way. The short story in question, however, provides a glimpse into instances in which the opposite sex is not initially responsible for sexual awakening in the female body.

Shani Mootoo's "Last Day Pandemonium and Heart Beats" is one of the stories in her collection, *Out on Main Street and Other Stories*, that cannot be strictly classified as lesbian fiction, although there is a hint of same-sex attraction in the closing paragraphs.[26] The story smacks of what we see being represented in Brand's "Madame Alaird's Breasts", insofar as there is a depiction of exuberant admiration of one female for another. In Mootoo's story, however, there is no teenaged girl being attracted to an older woman, but there is an adolescent-girl-swooning-over-another-adolescent-girl final scene as the "I" protagonist remembers last-day-of-the-term activities at the convent school she attended. As was noted with respect to Brand's story, the reaction of this form 1 student to the presence of and attention given her by her form 6 schoolmate, Althea, may not at all suggest that the former is of a lesbian orientation. Yet, the fact that this piece is contained within a collection that is written by a lesbian author, again – as with Brand and her story – begs the question as to whether lesbian eroticism is implied.

The author's own personal context is also brought to mind because she penned a testimony in the volume of women's writing entitled, *Desire: in Seven Voices*, in which she recounts her "nervousness and confusion", her "unspeakable, confusing attraction to that girl", Marilyn, who attended an all-female secondary school when she, Mootoo, was seven years old.[27] Like Marilyn, Althea is white; and like the seven-year-old Mootoo, the "I" protagonist wants to show off her skill to impress the older girl. Mootoo remembers her shock, her grin and how her "face stung" when Marilyn notices her wild show of athleticism, while the "I" character talks about how she becomes wide-eyed, her heart races and her "cheeks burn", how she is "thrilled to the point of being squeaky-voiced" inside her head, and how she grins widely ("Last Day", 93) when Althea shows acknowledgement of her artistic ability and she is presented with a lost chance to display that ability.[28] Although the first-person narrator indicates that the events in the story took place that morning (of the "story now" time frame), there is a level of ambiguity in the text because there is the sense that the narrator/protagonist is also an older person in the "speaker now" time frame because of what is stated in the last sentence of the story: "Even now, just thinking about it, I still have what you might call a silly smile right across my face" ("Last Day", 93).

This final pronouncement and the similarity between the actual and the literary accounts of one girl's attraction for another – with the former by the author who ultimately turns out to be lesbian – conveys an implicature that the narrator's reaction towards Althea may be more than just girlhood fancy.

In the real-life testimonials offered in the anthology, *Tongues on Fire: Caribbean Lesbian Lives and Stories*, edited by Rosamund Elwin, Caribbean diasporic writers who were originally from English-speaking islands such as Barbados, Dominica, Jamaica, St Lucia, and Trinidad and Tobago address various issues relating to lesbian relationships and lifestyles. Ayiah Jahan's "Best Friends" and Desoto Wong's "Sister", two short stories found in the fictional section of *Tongues on Fire*, look at the lesbian teenager and child, respectively, as they struggle with the realization of their sexual orientation.[29]

Jahan's story deals with the issue of revealing one's lesbian identity and the fear of the reactions that might be meted out by family, friends and society. Free indirect thought (FIT) is used: The narrator's voice and the protagonist's consciousness merge, so, although Miranda does not speak to us directly via a first-person narration, we get insight into her anxiety, hurt and fear that she may lose her best friend and that her family, church and school may punish her because of her lesbianism.[30] Jahan's use of free indirect discourse (FID) does what Katie Wales says of the FID mode: It foregrounds Miranda's viewpoint and manipulates our degree of sympathy for her.[31] In the midst of her anguish there is much negativity, evidenced by the number of questions she asks herself because she is unsure of what the future will hold. The storyline is somewhat predictable and contrived since, after much haranguing and emotional distress, both friends turn out to be lesbian. Miranda reveals her true orientation by kissing Gayle, but, after having directed much scorn at her best friend, Gayle turns out to be a lesbian herself, despite having had a boyfriend, and therefore seems to have been in denial of her own lesbian identity.

Wong's is a retrospective, autodiegetic narrative: It is narrated in first-person perspective by its protagonist. The narrator-protagonist is the "speaker now", looking back at when she was seven years old, the "story now", at a time when she was enamoured with her favourite teacher, Sister Alethia, and with her schoolmate, Lola Eng, about whom she has sexual fantasies. The story may indeed be autobiographical, since the nun calls the "I" character "Desoto" towards the close of the story.

Even at this age, Wong realizes that her desires are considered sinful, and she seeks atonement in the confessional. She confesses to the priest that she thinks she is a homosexual; his response, in part, is: "Try not to think those thoughts anymore. You will grow out of it and the Lord will forgive you, if you really try" ("Sister", 223). In addition, she has only to deal with "the light penance of two Hail Marys and one Our Father" ("Sister", 223). Homosexuality in a child is thus dismissed as an innocuous phase. Ironically, the implicature is that Sister, too, is of a lesbian orientation. After she returns to her Scottish homeland, she corresponds with Desoto and sends her a photograph of herself and another nun. The story ends suggestively with the description of their pose: "Her hand is resting on the shoulder of another, unnamed nun whose lips are parted, shyly. They look into each other's eyes and smile" ("Sister", 224). Therefore, by using language that is both verbal and non-verbal, these two members of the cloth – the priest and the nun – relay conflicting impressions of homosexuality to the child: one that denies it and the other that affirms it. The story suggests that the non-verbal message had a more lasting impression.

As suggested earlier, there may be more obloquy and sanctions targeted against homoeroticism and homosexuality among boys than girls. This treatment mirrors what gay men endure in comparison to lesbians. Cliff's title story, "The Store of a Million Items", portrays, but does not focus on, *effeminophobia*, which can be defined as the disliking of males who exhibit feminine traits and behaviour.[32] An effeminate boy rescues a girl who is being raped, to the surprise and puzzlement of his father who considers him to be a "pansy". Although Gerard is not overtly depicted as gay, he is nonetheless considered more feminine than masculine because of his actions, dress and tastes. There is ultimately a subtle irony and subversion in the story because he intrudes on the rapist who is in a business suit, a signifier of power and maleness; and rape, as Stevi Jackson explains, is a manifestation of male dominance and aggression.[33]

In Lawrence Scott's "I Want to Follow My Friend", sports and gang membership are here the defining features of masculinity.[34] These are among the socio-sexual scripts that young males are taught at home and in school. "Sports, plenty of sports, young man . . . Make a man of you", Christopher's father insists ("Follow My Friend", 84). However, Christopher is afraid of the dangerous power and speed of the cork ball and is keenly aware of the heaviness and awkwardness of the bat that his father gives him ("Follow My Friend", 84). Christopher seems happy to be immersed in a world of play and games and is uneasy with the things that would eventually make him a "man". Even now that he is a pre-teenager, his father calls him "my man" and "young man", and his mother arranges for his new school uniform to be a few sizes larger so that he can "grow into them" ("Follow My Friend", 85). The reader infers Christopher's unease by the third-person narrator's repetition of:

> Christopher heard his mother and father.
> Make a man of you.
> He'll grow into them. ("Follow My Friend", 85, 86)

Paul Simpson defines *transitivity* as "how speakers encode in language their mental picture of reality and how they account for their experience of the world around them".35 In the transitivity model, within the clause, the verb phrase expresses the process, noun phrases identify the participants, and adverbial and prepositional phrases depict the circumstances related to the process. The *senser* (the "conscious being that is perceiving, reacting or thinking") and the *phenomenon* ("that which is perceived, reacted to or thought about") are the participant roles in the mental processes. The mental processes, one of the internalized processes within the transitivity model, include the process of perception that involves the senses of seeing and hearing. In Scott's story, at least three times the narrator repeats, and thereby emphasizes and foregrounds the fact that Christopher "heard" his mother and father's expectations of what manhood means and how he is expected to fulfil these expectations – in other words, how he internalizes these messages and also how they bother him are stressed.

Stephen M. Whitehead observes that "one area of leisure-time activities wherein masculinities become particularly vivid is sport" where perceived masculine behaviours of aggression and competitiveness are highly valued, even though these may be unattainable and have emotionally damaging consequences.36 Christopher's lack of readiness for approaching manhood and for adopting a masculinist ethos is symbolized in his lack of enthusiasm for his "father's game" of teaching him to play cricket, in the distress and anger that arise whenever he and David play "adult" games with their toy cars and those that involve the brokering for power, and in his inability to join the gangs at his new boys' school. Juxtaposed with Mr and Mrs Wainwright's expectations is a marked contrast in what occurs when Christopher goes to boarding school: There he is called a "sissy" because he does not fit into any of the gangs and is told by an older boy that "I want to kiss you like if you were a girl" ("Follow My Friend", 87). Even before he goes off to school, he enjoys dressing in a butterfly costume and indulges in secretive, erotic games with his friend, David. The opening sentence of the story, "Mrs Wainwright kept an eye on the two boys", is, therefore, full of irony, because neither she nor her husband ever realize the nature of the closeness between her son and his friend, which is Christopher's real reason for wanting to go to the same institution David attends ("Follow My Friend", 81).

This story is ultimately about the homoerotic play and eventual lost friendship that occur between the two friends, as well as the pain of the separation Christopher endures. To reiterate, another kind of maleness depicted in this story is the one that a boy acquires by being a gang member. While David is "chosen by other boys" and becomes part of the school's gang culture, Christopher finds himself on the fringes, since he does not like the boys with whom David associates. Christopher realizes and ponders that "It was not safe to be on your own, or to be with a single friend. There were loyalties and rivalries . . . Why did some boys belong to one gang and others to another? Why couldn't he belong to David's gang? Why couldn't he be alone with David?" ("Follow My Friend", 87). Unlike the all-female school environment in Brand's story, where the girls openly indulge in eroticizing their own sex, albeit an adult, in Scott's story, Christopher must guard against revealing his feelings for and former intimate physical contact with David. He knows that in an all-male environment such as this, their secret games "were definitely not to be spoken about. In a way, what they did was a secret from themselves. They avoided each other when other boys were around" ("Follow My Friend", 87). Yet, in the open-ended conclusion to the story, the reader leaves Christopher waiting in hopeful expectation for the return of the boy who wanted to kiss him as though he were a girl, which is an indication of his willingness to eschew and resist the bonds of masculinism imposed by parents and schoolmates.

The contrast between the girls and boys in Brand's and Scott's stories, respectively, illustrates in part that the "ways in which [socio-sexual] scripts are learnt is profoundly affected by the gender-role learning of childhood, so that girls and boys learn to be sexual in different ways. These diverging lines of development are not the result of repression or accession of libido, but of differential learning experiences built on to a firmly established sense of gender identity."[37] The overarching message in all of the selected short stories, though, is the eventual acceptance of an alternative sexuality by these lesbian and gay youth, whether society approves or not. Some stories are told in the first person, whereas in others it is as though the narrator, through the FID mode, is speaking for and at the same time, *along with* the protagonist, since most of these writers are of an alternative sexuality themselves. The short story may entail a cast of few characters and may be of limited length and focus, but it nonetheless can cover topics and themes that have a wide resonance for how we view transgressive discourses.

Notes

1. Helmut Bonheim, *The Narrative Modes: Techniques of the Short Story* (Cambridge: D.S. Brewer, c.1982), 166.
2. Katie Wales, *A Dictionary of Stylistics* (Essex: Pearson, 2001), 221. Wales notes that intertextuality can basically be defined as: "UTTERANCES/TEXTS [sic] in relation to other utterances/texts. So even within a single text there can be, as it were, a continual 'dialogue' between the text given and other texts/utterances that exist outside it, literary and non-literary: either within that same period of composition, or in previous centuries. Kristeva [who coined the term 'intertextuality' in the 1960s] argues, in fact, that no text is 'free' of other texts or truly original" (220–21).
3. Mary Eagleton, "Genre and Gender", in *Modern Genre Theory*, ed. David Duff (Essex: Pearson, 2000), 256; Eagleton cites Frank O'Connor's well-known phrase from his influential book, *The Lonely Voice: A Sketch of the Short Story* (Cleveland: The World Publishing Co., 1962), 18–19.
4. Axel Nissen, "The Queer Short Story", in *The Art of Brevity: Excursions in Short Fiction Theory and Analysis*, ed. Per Winther, Jakob Lothe and Hans H. Skei (Columbia: University of South Carolina Press, 2004), 181.
5. Mary Louise Pratt, "The Short Story: The Long and the Short of It", in *The New Short Story Theories*, ed. Charles E. May (Athens: Ohio University Press, 1994), 105.
6. Ibid., 104.
7. Ibid., 105–6; my emphasis.
8. Ibid., 106.
9. V.S. Naipaul, *A House for Mr Biswas* (London: André Deutsch, 1961); George Lamming, *In the Castle of My Skin* (Essex: Longman, 1953); Jamaica Kincaid, *Annie John* (London: Vintage, 1985); Geoffrey Drayton, *Christopher* (London: Collins, 1959); Merle Hodge, *Crick Crack, Monkey* (Oxford: Heinemann, 1970); Michael Anthony, *The Year in San Fernando* (London: Heinemann, 1965); Michael Anthony, *Green Days by the River* (London: André Deutsch, 1967); Ian

McDonald, *The Humming Bird Tree* (Oxford: Heinemann, 1969); M. NourbeSe Philip, *Harriet's Daughter* (Oxford and Portsmouth: Heinemann, 1988); Zee Edgell, *Beka Lamb* (Essex: Heinemann, 1982).

10. Lawrence Scott, "Chameleon", in *Ballad for the New World and Other Stories* (Oxford and Portsmouth: Heinemann, 1994), 3–39; "I Want to Follow My Friend", in *Ballad for the New World and Other Stories* (Oxford and Portsmouth: Heinemann, 1994), 81–89.
11. Eagleton, "Genre and Gender", 259.
12. Stevi Jackson, *Heterosexuality in Question* (Londoni: Sage, 1999), 36.
13. Jackson, *Heterosexuality in Question*, 38; William Simon and John H. Gagnon, "On Psychosexual Development", in *Handbook of Socialization Theory and Research*, ed. David A. Goslin (Chicago: Rand McNally, 1969), 736.
14. Jackson, *Heterosexuality in Question*, 39, 89, 90.
15. Judy Pearsall, ed., *Concise Oxford Dictionary* (New York: Oxford University Press, 1999), 245.
16. Jackson, *Heterosexuality in Question*, 39.
17. Adrienne Rich, "Compulsory Heterosexuality and Lesbian Existence", in *The Signs Reader*, ed. E. Abel and E.K. Abel (Chicago: University of Chicago Press, 1983), 156.
18. Ibid., 159.
19. Paula C. Rust, quoted in Bonnie Zimmerman, ed. *Lesbian Histories and Cultures: An Encyclopaedia* (New York: Garland, 2000), 383.
20. AnnLouise Keating, "Gender", *glbtq: An Encyclopaedia of Gay, Lesbian, Bisexual, Transgender and Queer Culture*, http://www.glbtq.com/literature/gender.html; Sara Mills and Christine A. White, "Discursive Categories and Desire: Feminists Negotiating Relationships", in *Language and Desire: Encoding Sex, Romance and Intimacy*, ed. Keith Harvey and Celia Shalom (London and New York: Routledge, 1997), 227.
21. Jamaica Kincaid, *Annie John* (London: Vintage, 1983); Dionne Brand, "Madame Alaird's Breasts", in *Sans Souci and Other Stories* (New York: Firebrand Books, 1989), 79–84. Subsequent references to "Madame Alaird's Breasts" appear parenthetically in the text.
22. Jackson, *Heterosexuality in Question*, 41.
23. Dionne Brand, "This Body for Itself", in *Bread Out of Stone: Recollections, Sex, Race, Dreaming, Politics* (Toronto: Vintage, 1994). Subsequent references to *Bread Out of Stone* appear parenthetically in the text.
24. Dionne Brand, *Bread Out of Stone*, 94–95. Brand refers to "Poetry and Politics",

a paper she presented at the first Caribbean Women Writers' Conference in Massachusetts at Wellesley College, 8–10 April 1988.
25. Boris Uspensky quoted in Roger Fowler, *Linguistic Criticism* (Oxford: Oxford University Press, 1996), 136.
26. Shani Mootoo, "Last Day Pandemonium and Heart Beats", in *Out on Main Street and Other Stories* (Vancouver: Press Gang, 1993), 85–93. All references are taken from this edition, and subsequent references appear parenthetically in the text.
27. Shani Mootoo, "Photo Parentheses", in *Desire: in Seven Voices*, ed. Lorna Crozier (Vancouver and Toronto: Douglas and McIntyre, 1999), 107–24.
28. Ibid., 113.
29. Rosamund Elwin, ed. *Tongues on Fire: Caribbean Lesbian Lives and Stories* (Toronto: Women's Press, 1997); Ayiah Jahan, "Best Friends", in *Tongues on Fire*, 197–212; Desoto Wong, "Sister", in *Tongues on Fire*, 217–24.
30. In *free indirect thought* (FIT), there is a blend of the narrator's voice and the character's point of view without a break in the flow of the narrative, the use of past tenses and third- (in the place of first- and second-) person pronouns and a direct or "present" deictic orientation. FIT maintains some of the subjectivity of direct thought; is associated with stream-of-consciousness technique; and is exploited mainly for major, rather than minor, characters. See Wales, *Dictionary of Stylistics*, 166, 263.
31. Wales, *Dictionary of Stylistics*, 169.
32. Michelle Cliff, "The Store of a Million Items", in *The Store of a Million Items: Stories* (Boston and New York: Mariner, 1998), 42–54.
33. Jackson, *Heterosexuality in Question*, 48.
34. Lawrence Scott, "I Want to Follow My Friend", in *Ballad for the New World and Other Stories* (Oxford and Portsmouth: Heinemann, 1994), 81–89.
35. Paul Simpson, *Language, Ideology and Point of View* (London and New York: Routledge, 1993), 88.
36. Stephen M. Whitehead, *Men and Masculinities* (Cambridge: Polity, 2002), 142, 127.
37. Jackson, *Heterosexuality in Question*, 40.

Part 3.

LANGUAGE DEVELOPMENT

7.

The Child and the Structure of Creoles, Pidgins and Signed Languages

» BEN BRAITHWAITE

Introduction

LANGUAGE AND CULTURE ARE inextricably linked: The death of a language is rightly seen as a catastrophic cultural loss, and membership in certain cultural communities is dependent on some degree of linguistic competence.[1] This chapter argues that children play a crucial role in at least one characteristic feature of the creole and signed languages of the Caribbean.

It is well known that creole languages display a striking degree of cross-linguistic similarity. Jamaican Creole shares properties with Saramaccan in Suriname, with Haitian Creole and Hawaiian Creole, with Berbice Dutch and Cape Verdean Creole. These similarities go beyond what can be straightforwardly explained in terms of common ancestry. Signed languages also display striking cross-linguistic patterns. American Sign Language, British Sign Language and Japanese Sign Language have quite different histories and are mutually unintelligible, and yet they also have much more in common than might be expected. Furthermore, many of the linguistic features that crop up time and again in signed languages are exactly the same ones that are repeatedly found in creoles. Why is this? One answer found in the literature argues that what creoles and signed languages have in common is, at least in part, a consequence of the special role of children in their development.

Most deaf children are not born to deaf parents, so the acquisition of their native sign language does not follow the usual course.[2] In many cases, their first exposure to sign language may be from parents who are not themselves native signers, but who may have started learning some signs when they found out that their child was deaf. Despite this, such children routinely acquire at least a near-native level of competence in the sign language, which inevitably exceeds that of their parents. Researchers have pointed out that these circumstances resemble a situation often thought to have existed during the development of creole languages.[3] In this account of creole genesis, children were born to parents who were using a simplified pidgin, but despite this impoverished input, the children ended up speaking a full-fledged language. Much debate has raged within the literature in creole linguistics around the historical accuracy of such hypothesized circumstances.[4] It is not necessary to accept this view of creole genesis, however, to believe that children might be responsible for some of the intriguing structural similarities between creoles and signed languages.

This chapter, therefore, addresses whether there are linguistic features common to creoles and signed languages, which we can confidently link to the crucial influence of children. It argues that one such feature, productive reduplication, may be plausibly attributed to the analogous role that child language acquisition has had in the formation of creoles and signed languages. This chapter also tackles the question of when a certain linguistic feature can best be explained as a result of the influence of children on language development.

Terminological Preliminaries

Before proceeding any further, it seems prudent to make clear the senses in which some key terms will be used here, since they may differ from uses of the same terms elsewhere.

The definition of *child* is biological/developmental. Children are capable of linguistic feats that are beyond most adults. A major focus of much work in linguistics over the past five decades has been on trying to explain how it is that children acquire their native language so quickly and completely and on the basis of limited input, while adults frequently struggle to achieve native-like competence in second languages. The *end of childhood* for current purposes is defined as the end of the hypothesized critical period for language acquisition.[5] If a child has not acquired a language by puberty, usually as a result of lack of exposure to linguistic input, then that child will never reach a state of normal native competence (as in the famous case of Genie, who had almost no exposure to language until thirteen, as reported by Curtiss in 1977).[6] Of course, adopting this definition is not intended to deny the existence or importance of other definitions. As Singler mentions, the social role of children in language change and development is also an important and understudied topic.[7]

Creole has been notoriously difficult to define.[8] While McWhorter argues that creole languages constitute a typological class and can be defined in terms of a certain array of linguistic features, many others have argued that no such definition of creole languages is possible (for example, DeGraff).[9] Caribbean creoles have their origins in the colonial plantations of the seventeenth and eighteenth centuries, in which there was contact between a large number of "substrate" African languages and a European "superstrate" language. In this chapter, some illustrative examples are taken from the Surinamese creoles Sranan, Saramaccan and Ndyuka, and from Berbice Dutch, Jamaican Creole and Haitian Creole. These were chosen because they represent a fairly mixed group in terms of their histories, lexifier languages and linguistic properties.[10]

Pidgin is less debated in the literature, although not without its problems. Pidgins emerge in situations of contact between speakers of different languages as a medium of communication. They are typically thought to be less than "full-fledged" languages, being used often in pragmatically restricted contexts and displaying a high level of syntactic variability. Pidgins lack native speakers and emerge from contact between adults. As DeGraff puts it: "early pidgin creators, then, were typically adults with their own native tongues and with limited practice in the evolving pidgin, initially using it in limited (and limiting) interaction".[11] An example of a Caribbean pidgin is Trio-Ndyuka Pidgin, which developed as a mode of communication in trade contact between Amerindian Trio speakers and speakers of the Surinamese creole Ndyuka.

Signed languages are the native languages of deaf people. Contrary to popular misconceptions, they are fully articulated, structurally complex and expressively powerful natural languages, not mere "pantomime".[12] They are distinguished from the various other signing systems based on spoken languages, which have been used for educational and other purposes, such as Signing Exact English, which uses signs to represent the structure of English. Such codes are not acquired natively by children and often have structural features that are otherwise rather unusual in natural signed languages, such as linear prefixes and suffixes.[13]

Unfortunately, linguists have published very little work on the signed languages used in the Caribbean. Nicaraguan Sign Language, which has been reported on by Judy Kegl, Ann Senghas and their collaborators, is an exception.[14] This research is well known and widely cited and will be discussed further later in this chapter. David Dolman discussed the sign languages used in Jamaica, including Jamaican Country Sign, an indigenous village sign language. The sign language of the Deaf community of Kingston, Jamaica, is the subject of a forthcoming PhD dissertation by Keren Cumberbatch.[15] In this chapter, some evidence comes from the author's observation of deaf (near-)native signers in Trinidad. The language that these signers use is now usually called Trinidad and Tobago Sign Language (TTSL),[16] although in all relevant respects, the facts mentioned in this chapter are identical for American Sign Language (ASL), and TTSL and ASL have much in common. While a dictionary of TTSL was published in 2007, there is no detailed published account of the linguistic situation among the deaf communities of Trinidad and Tobago. Much work needs to be done mapping out the extent of sociolinguistic variation and the degree to which TTSL diverges from ASL.[17]

While the examples referred to in this chapter all come from languages used in the Caribbean region, as far as I know, the generalizations hold beyond, for creoles, pidgins and sign languages around the world.

Patterns and Explanations

Linguists spend much of their time looking for patterns within and across languages and then trying to provide explanations for these patterns. Since the pioneering work of Joseph Greenberg, one powerful tool for learning about linguistic regularities has been to compare large numbers of historically unrelated languages and look for cross-linguistic patterns.[18] Greenberg and his successors have found many striking generalizations that hold across groups of languages or across all known languages, and theories have been developed to explain why these generalizations hold.

Both creoles and signed languages have been observed to form typologically homogeneous groups. Moreover, many of the regularities found across creoles are also found across signed languages.[19] It is important to distinguish between absolute universals and strong tendencies. Ian Robertson, for example, has shown that many of the properties taken to be nearly universal in creoles are not found in Berbice Dutch, so that generalizations such as "creoles lack inflectional morphology" are not absolute, but represent strong tendencies.[20]

One must be cautious about making claims of universals on the basis of a limited set of data. Research into the structure of signed languages has only really taken off in the last forty years, after the pioneering work of William Stokoe.[21] Since then, most of the research has concentrated on a relatively small number of signed languages, those in western Europe, as well as ASL. Only in the last decade has there been a concerted effort to study a broader range of signed languages from around the world.[22] Any statements about sign-language universals must, therefore, be regarded as tentative and may prove to be less robust as our data set expands.

We are lucky now that there is a larger body of work on geographically and historically diverse creoles, making claims of universal creole features somewhat easier to assess. In particular, J. Holm and P. Patrick provide descriptions of grammatical features typical of eighteen creole languages. Their work is the source of the data on creole pronoun systems presented in this chapter.[23] Nonetheless, there exist very few comprehensive grammatical descriptions of Caribbean creole languages, and the caveat that was raised in regard to signed languages must apply also to creoles.

Once cross-linguistic patterns have been established, theoretical accounts have been developed to explain them. Debate over the different theoretical accounts for cross-linguistic patterns in creoles has been particularly lively. The following sections provide sketches of some of the most influential theories. While competing theorists have sometimes taken strong positions, I see no reason why different patterns might not, in principle, be explained in terms of different theoretical accounts. For present purposes, I have divided these accounts into those in which the role of children is crucial to the explanation, those in which adults are central, and those in which neither of these positions is taken.[24]

Children and Adults

Differences between the linguistic behaviour of children and adults have been central to many theoretical debates across the field of linguistics. Much attention has been devoted to studying the differences between the ways in which children acquire their native languages and the ways in which adults learn second languages. Linguists interested in accounting for the ways in which languages change over time have debated the roles played by children and adults in this process. Linguists argue about the relative importance of the roles of children and adults in the origins of creole languages. The chapters in DeGraff discuss at length whether and to what extent the forces underlying these three areas are in fact the same.[25]

For some theorists, most famously D. Bickerton, the child's role is crucial in accounting for cross-linguistic patterns in creoles and signed languages.[26] For Bickerton, the recurrent structural features represent the basic settings of a universal Language Bioprogram (LB), which forms part of the unique genetically encoded biological endowment of all human beings.[27] According to this theory, children exposed to structurally impoverished pidgins had to fill in gaps to come up with a fully articulated language. Because the LB, which allows them to fill in the gaps, is the same for all children, the emergent linguistic features will also be the same. Likewise, because deaf children are also typically exposed to impoverished input, they too have gaps to fill in, and the same basic settings emerge.

One of the most striking demonstrations of the creative power of children comes from research on Nicaraguan Sign Language (LSN), which emerged over a period of a few years after the establishment of the first residential school for the deaf in Managua in the late 1970s. The new language was clearly created, not by the conscious design of teachers, but naturally and organically by the community of deaf children. The language has, furthermore, been shown to possess all the expressive power and linguistic complexity of any other natural language. These facts appear to strengthen the case for some kind of innate linguistic endowment that might have guided the children.[28]

Other creolists have argued that Bickerton's account greatly underestimates the role that adults play in creole formation. Rather than being the creations of children, Caribbean creoles may have been created largely by speakers of West African languages, who learned the vocabulary of their European enslavers but fitted it into the grammatical systems of the African "substrate" languages. For John Lumsden, for example, Haitian Creole is basically Fongbe relexified with French.[29] According to this "substratist" account, adult Fongbe speakers are the principal force behind creole formation.

It is not my intention here to argue for either of these positions. Instead of trying to find an overarching theory of creole genesis, I am interested in taking particular linguistic features and trying to ascertain whether their presence in a group of languages is best accounted for in terms of the influence of children. Wherever one stands on these larger debates, there are certain generalizations about the differences between adult and child language that will be useful in helping us to diagnose child influence. Studies of language acquisition have shown that children and adults produce different kinds of output, even when exposed to identical inputs. As C.L. Hudson-Kam and E.L. Newport summarize, "the variation present in second language (L2) productions is largely unpredictable . . . unlike the variation present in native speech".[30]

Anyone who has spent time with young children will be familiar with the tendency to regularize: A child learning English might talk about "two mans" or say "he goed", applying the regular plural and past tense markers in cases in which the correct form is irregular. Within discussions of language change, a similar finding has been reported: "adults innovate, children regularize".[31] Whether this difference is connected to children's possession of a specifically linguistic faculty that adults lack, like Bickerton's LB, or whether their acquisition is guided by more general, non-language-specific principles is still up for debate. There is broad consensus on this difference between adults and children, and we can therefore use this as a diagnostic: We should expect regularization to be a hallmark of child influence on language structure.

Modality

Within the tradition of sign-language linguistics, certain properties common to signed languages have been accounted for because they use the visual, rather than auditory modality. Signed languages make far greater use of iconicity than spoken languages do. The signs for "tree" in ASL, Danish Sign Language and Chinese Sign Language all correspond recognizably to the shapes of trees, whereas the English word has a purely arbitrary relationship to what it signifies.[32] The main reason why signed languages, make greater use of iconic signs seems fairly obvious: because they can. It is far easier to represent a tree iconically in a signed language than it is to do so in a spoken language.

Sam Supalla has argued that the non-linear morphology typical of signed languages is another modality effect.[33] While, as David Lightfoot points out, sign languages such as ASL do exhibit some linear morphology, and the morphology of the (spoken) Semitic languages is non-linear, Supalla's remains important.[34] When seeking explanations for cross-linguistic commonalities in signed languages, then, we must consider the possibility that they are a consequence of the modality.

Choosing between Explanations

There is no shortage of theories to account for linguistic similarities between creoles and signed languages. And while the strongest versions of certain accounts may be somewhat at odds with one another, it seems likely that different linguistic features may be best explained by different accounts. Adults may be responsible for certain linguistic patterns and children for others. We need diagnostic tests to determine, on a case-by-case basis, which explanation is appropriate. We have already identified one: Regularization is a plausible effect of child influence.

Another strategy is to compare data from the three different language groups. Comparisons between signed languages and creoles can help to rule out certain kinds of explanations. If a linguistic feature is shared by both groups, then it is less likely to be accounted for in terms of substrate influence: Sign languages do not generally have substrates, certainly not the same substrates as creoles.[35] Likewise, features of signed languages that are also features of creoles are less likely to be modality effects.[36]

Comparisons between signed languages and creoles on the one hand and pidgins on the other can help us to check whether certain features can confidently be attributed to the influence of children. Since pidgins do not have child speakers, we would not expect to find features for which children are uniquely responsible in pidgins, so such a feature common to creoles and signed languages ought to be absent in pidgins.

Typological Comparisons

We are now ready to look a little closer at some of the properties that signed languages and creoles have in common. Lillo-Martin and Sandler identify the following features as common to signed languages and creoles:[37]

- use of the verb meaning "finish" as a perfective marker, indicating an event as a bounded whole
- use of word order, rather than bound morphemes (for example, suffixes), to indicate case relations
- frequent use of topicalization and intonation for organizing information structure
- use of reduplication to mark various kinds of intensification, iteration and distribution.[38]

The remainder of the chapter will focus on two features in particular: pronoun systems and the use of productive reduplication, and I will argue that the latter can plausibly be linked to the influence of child language. Examples are provided from a range of Caribbean languages. I stress that it is unlikely that the creole-like properties of TTSL are primarily the result of contact with the Trinidadian and Tobagonian creoles, which are the vernacular languages of most hearing people in Trinidad and Tobago, since, in all relevant respects, TTSL is identical to American Sign Language.

Pronoun Systems

Pronoun systems in Caribbean creoles (CCs) typically differ from those in the lexifier languages in certain respects. Examples are taken from Holm and Patrick.[39] None of these languages distinguishes gender in the third person, nor do they have separate forms to systematically mark nominative versus accusative case distinctions, unlike the lexifier languages, English and French.

(7.1) Haitian Creole

	Singular	Plural
1	mwen	nou
2	ou/wou	zot
3	li	yo

(7.2) Jamaican Creole

	Singular	Plural
1	mi	wi
2	yu	unu
3	im	dem

These features are also typical of signed languages. The TTSL pronoun system, which is representative of systems in signed languages generally, also fails to mark gender or nominative/accusative case distinctions.[40] So, for example, the signs for a first-person singular subject pronoun and a first-person singular object pronoun are identical, and the sign for a third-person singular masculine pronoun is identical to the one for a third-person singular feminine pronoun. The same is true in Jamaican Sign Language.[41] Given this cross-linguistic parallel, we might ask whether it is possible to attribute the pattern to child influence. At first glance, this seems quite plausible.

The idea that gender is, in some sense, a less basic category than number and person is supported by the findings of linguistic typologists. Joseph Greenberg first observed that, "if a language has a category of gender, it always has the category of number".[42] Recently, theoretical linguists have attempted to provide explanations for this fact in terms of our innate linguistic endowment, or Universal Grammar (UG). H. Harley and E. Ritter, for example, argue that UG provides a structured hierarchy of pronoun features.[43] Because the gender features are subordinate to number features, it follows that a language cannot have gender without also having number. These kinds of relationships between features are described in terms of relative *markedness*: Gender is more marked than number (and person).[44] The notion of markedness is very widely used in linguistics. If a certain linguistic feature is more marked, then it should be rarer in the world's languages and less likely to emerge.

Some notion of markedness also plays an important role in many theories of language change, acquisition and creole genesis. Whether markedness hierarchies are predetermined by UG in the way that Harley and Ritter envisage and as Bickerton, for example, also believes, or emerge from other considerations, is not necessarily crucial.[45] If we can show that this markedness hierarchy is available to children, but not to adults, then we could plausibly account for the observed similarities between creoles and signed languages in terms of children's influence.

Crucially, however, data from pidgins challenges such an approach. Pronoun systems in pidgins also typically lack case and gender distinctions, even when these are present in substrate and superstrate languages. For example, C. Jourdan and R. Keesing discuss the development of Solomon Islands Pijin.[46] Pijin remains a second, rather than native language, but it has developed recently in a manner reminiscent of creolization. For Jourdan and Keesing, the principal creolizers here are adults who have moved to the urban centre, Honiara, from rural areas, and learned Pijin as a second language. One of the changes that Jourdan and Keesing report is a simplification of the pronoun system with respect to case marking.[47] Again, this simplification suggests that this tendency is not a special property of child language. Since pidgins have no child speakers, children cannot be responsible for this pattern.

Markedness of some sort does play a role here. Indeed, it would still be possible to understand the facts in terms of recourse to unmarked settings of UG, although we would have to allow that this aspect of UG is available to adults as well as children. Whatever the right analysis of this particular cross-linguistic pattern might be, it is difficult to see how an account that placed the responsibility for it on children would work.

Reduplication

Reduplication is defined as the repetition of some or all of a word to mark a grammatical distinction. Although reduplication is less widely employed in English than in many other languages, patterns like so-called shm-reduplication ("Oedipus shmoedipus") constitute one example.[48] The collection of essays in *Twice as Meaningful: Reduplication in Pidgins, Creoles and Other Contact Languages* provides a thorough cross-linguistic perspective on reduplication in pidgins and creoles.[49] Two intriguing facts that emerge from this survey are that almost all creoles have productive reduplication and almost no pidgin has productive reduplication.[50] Here are examples of reduplication in CCs:

(7.3) Saramaccan
"...-like"
baafu "soup"   baafu-baafu "soup-like"

(7.4) Papiamentu
deverbal nouns
chupa "suck"   chupa-chupa "bloodsucker"

(7.5) Ndyuka
deverbal adjectives
bai "to buy"   bai-bai "bought"

(7.6) Berbice Dutch
plural
inga "thorn"   inga-inga "thorns"

(7.7) Sranan
deverbal nouns
koso "to cough"   koso-koso "cough" (n.)
djompo   djompo-djompo "grasshopper"

Reduplication is also a typological feature of signed languages. In TTSL, for example, the sign meaning "everyone sit down" involves repetition of the sign meaning "sit", and the sign meaning "a comb" involves repetition of the sign meaning "to comb".[51]

However, P. Bakker reports that pidgins appear to systematically lack productive reduplication.[52] This fact is surprising. Trio-Ndyuka, for example, lacks productive reduplication, although both contact languages from which this pidgin emerged, as well as other languages spoken in the area of contact, do have productive reduplication.[53] "Productive" must be stressed here. Some pidgins exhibit reduplication-like patterns, but these patterns never seem to constitute regular rules of these languages.

How best should we account for these patterns? Often, reduplication in Caribbean creoles can be traced to similar rules in substrate West African languages. This finding may adequately explain the presence of some of reduplication in creoles,[54] but it cannot be the entire answer. While it is often impossible to know whether a reduplicative pattern in a creole has a corresponding substrate precursor, the recurrence of reduplication to mark the same types of categories suggests there is something more going on. Indeed, Kouwenburg's *Twice as Meaningful: Reduplication in Pidgins, Creoles and Other Contact Languages* clarifies that, in some cases, reduplication marks a distinction in a creole language for which there is no matching pattern in the substrate.[55] Furthermore, if the creole patterns were purely substrate retentions, why do signed languages also exhibit reduplication, often marking exactly the same grammatical distinctions as in creoles?

The pidgin facts are highly suggestive. If productive reduplication is a result of children's influence, then things fall nicely into place: Pidgins lack productive reduplication because pidgins lack child speakers. But what is the link between child language and productive reduplication? Recall that a distinctive feature of child speech is regularization, which pidgins lack. While individual words with reduplication-like patterns may make it into a pidgin, without the involvement of children, these patterns are not generalized into rules. So, we may attribute the productivity of reduplication in creoles and signed languages to children's influence.

Two other questions must be answered. All languages apart from pidgins have child speakers. Why then do all languages not have productive reduplication? We still need to explain why children have had this special and distinctive influence in this area of the grammars of creoles and signed languages. Second, while children may be accountable for the *productivity* of reduplication in these languages, where did the reduplication come from in the first place? Substrate influence will account for some of the reduplicative patterns found in creoles but not for all, and certainly not for the pervasive use of reduplication in signed languages.

On the second question, reduplication is special because it is frequently iconic, that is, there is a non-arbitrary correspondence between form and meaning, comparable to the similarity, mentioned earlier, between the various signs used to refer to trees in Chinese, Danish and American Sign Languages, and the general shape of trees. It is no coincidence that reduplication is frequently used to mark plurality across languages. "More of the same form" corresponds to "more of the same" meaning.[56] Likewise, many of reduplication's functions in signed languages and in creoles are clearly iconic.

Earlier, I wrote that signed languages generally make more use of iconicity than spoken language just "because they can": that it is a modality effect. But iconicity could also be seen as a particularly useful strategy for languages with a shortage of vocabulary. Signed languages have typically emerged recently and often without much contact with other languages; the Nicaraguan situation discussed earlier is one particularly striking example. As a consequence, it is hardly surprising that they have relatively small, but quickly expanding, vocabularies. Similarly, creole languages have arisen out of situations that involved severe communicative pressures. Adults were the principal creolizers, and this situation involved second-language learning of superstrate vocabulary. If we believe children to be the principal creolizers, the linguistic input is assumed to be pidgins, again likely to have had limited vocabularies. Either way, early creole speakers might well need to find creative ways of increasing their lexical resources. Iconic strategies like reduplication are particularly useful because they provide language users with a way of creating new forms easily understood by other speakers/signers. While spoken languages frequently borrow words from surrounding languages, this is not so easy for signed languages, since the languages spoken by the surrounding community may be inaccessible to members of a deaf community.

The presence of reduplication in signed languages and creoles can therefore be a combination of substrate influence and the communicative pressures faced by early users of these languages. Reduplication has become a regular, productive feature of these languages, while in pidgins it is not. We can put this down to the role of children.

To return, finally, to the first question, we might suppose that the non-universality of productive reduplication reflects the fact that, as languages age, they tend to become less transparent, especially if they have relatively little contact with other languages, and reduplicative patterns that were once productive might become fossilized and even disappear altogether. Likewise, creole languages that appear to lack productive reduplication need not overly concern us.

Summary

In this chapter, I have attempted to do two things. First, I have argued that the productivity of reduplication in creoles and signed languages can plausibly be linked to children's influence. Because pidgins lack child speakers, they may have traces of reduplication, but such reduplication is never productive. Second, I have outlined a fruitful approach to addressing the question of whether any particular feature of a creole or signed language is a result of children's language influence. This approach involves cross-linguistic comparisons between creoles and signed languages and then, if universals emerge, between these and pidgins. This method can help rule out certain kinds of competing explanations for cross-linguistic patterns, including substratist accounts of creole universals and modality-based accounts of sign language universals.

Notes

1. Deaf communities typically define themselves primarily as linguistic communities; thus a hearing person who is a native signer may be considered part of a Deaf community (where capitalization of Deaf is used to indicate a cultural designation).
2. Only around 5 per cent of deaf children have two deaf parents. See J. Schein and M. Delk, *The Deaf Population of the United States* (Silver Springs, MD: National Association of the Deaf, 1974).
3. See, for example, Wendy Sandler and Diane Lillo-Martin, *Sign Language and Linguistic Universals* (Cambridge: Cambridge University Press, 2006), 503–4. A famous case study demonstrating the ability of deaf children to surpass their hearing parents is reported in E.L. Newport, "Reduced Input in the Acquisition of Signed Languages: Contributions to the Study of Creolization", in *Language*

Creation and Language Change: Creolization, Diachrony, and Development, ed. M. DeGraff (Cambridge, MA: MIT Press, 1999).

4. M.C. Alleyne in "Acculturation and the Cultural Matrix of Creolization", in *Pidginization and Creolization of Languages*, ed. D. Hymes (Cambridge: Cambridge University Press, 1971), 169–86; and in M.C. Alleyne, *Comparatiäe Afro-American: An Historical-Comparatiäe Study of English-Based Afro-American Dialects of the New World* (Ann Arbor, MI: Karoma Publishers, 1980). Several others since have presented arguments against such an account.
5. E.H. Lenneberg, *Biological Foundations of Language* (New York: Wiley, 1967).
6. S. Curtiss, *Genie: A Psycholinguistic Study of a Modern-Day "Wild Child"* (Boston: Academic Press, 1977). Among hearing children, such cases usually involve abusive treatment. Deaf children are at particular risk, since they are unable to perceive spoken language and, for various reasons, may not be exposed to a sign language at a young age. Oliver Sacks, in *Seeing Voices* (London: Picador, 1989), 41–42, sees similarities between the development of a deaf child who had no exposure to sign language and that of a hearing child who was locked up and deprived of human contact until after puberty.
7. John Singler, "Children and Creole Genesis", *Journal of Pidgin and Creole Languages* 21, no. 1 (2006): 157–73.
8. Ian Robertson, "Challenging the Definition of Creole", in *Exploring the Boundaries of Caribbean Creole Languages*, ed. Hazel Simmons-McDonald and Ian Robertson (Kingston: University of the West Indies Press, 2006), 3–20.
9. John McWhorter, "Identifying the Creole Prototype: Vindicating a Typological Class", *Language* 74, no. 4 (1998): 788–818; Michel DeGraff, "Linguists' Most Dangerous Myth: The Fallacy of Creole Exceptionalism", *Language in Society* 34, no. 4 (2005): 533–91.
10. Berbice Dutch, for example, is somewhat atypical in having more inflectional morphology than is usually found in other creole languages. See Robertson, "Challenging the Definition of Creole", 16–17.
11. Michel DeGraff, ed., *Language Creation and Language Change: Creolization, Diachrony and Development* (Cambridge, MA: MIT Press, 1999).
12. It is striking that signed languages and creoles have been maligned in many of the same ways as "incomplete", "primitive" or "not proper languages". Indeed, linguists themselves were rather slow to acknowledge that both types have all the characteristics of full languages. Part of the confusion may derive from the existence in both cases of superficially similar pidgins, which are not fully articulated languages.

13. Karen Emmorey, *Language, Cognition, and the Brain: Insights from Sign Language Research* (Mahwah, NJ: Lawrence Erlbaum, 2002), 11.
14. Of course, whether this is to be considered a Caribbean language depends on how we define the Caribbean. Nicaragua has a Caribbean Sea coast, so it qualifies at least under some definitions. Similar comments could be made about Suriname. Judith Kegl, Marie Coppola and Ann Senghas, "Creation through Contact: Sign Language Emergence and Sign Language Change in Nicaragua", in *Language Creation and Language Change: Creolization, Diachrony, and Development*, ed. Michel DeGraff (Cambridge, MA: MIT Press, 1999), 179–237.
15. It is a well-established convention in the literature to distinguish between audiological and cultural deafness typographically: a lower-case "d" is used for the former and upper-case "D" for the latter. Only the lower-case "deaf" is used in this chapter when referring to deaf Trinbagonians. David Dolman, "Sign Languages in Jamaica", *Sign Language Studies* 52 (1986): 235–42; Keren Cumberbatch, "A Linguistic Description of the Language of the Urban Deaf in Jamaica" (PhD diss., University of the West Indies, forthcoming 2010).
16. Among the Deaf community, the language is also sometimes referred to as TTS.
17. Having been introduced through missionary and education contact, ASL is certainly widely used in the Caribbean and must be included in a list of Caribbean languages.
18. Joseph H. Greenberg, ed., *Universals of Language* (Cambridge, MA: MIT Press, 1966).
19. Susan D. Fischer, "Sign Language and Creoles", in *Understanding Language through Sign Language Research*, ed. Patricia A. Siple (New York: Academic Press, 1978), 309–31.
20. Robertson, "Challenging the Definition of Creole", 3–20.
21. William C. Stokoe, *Sign Language Structure: An Outline of the Visual Communication Systems of the American Deaf*, Studies in Linguistics Occasional Papers 8 (Buffalo, NY: University of Buffalo, 1960).
22. The introduction to P. Perniss, R. Pfau and M. Steinbach, "Sources of Variation in Sign Language Structure", in *Visible Variation: Comparative Studies on Sign Language Structure*, ed. P. Perniss, R. Pfau and M. Steinbach (Berlin: Mouton de Gruyter, 2007), 1–35, has a useful summary of the development of the field of sign-language linguistics.
23. J. Holm and P. Patrick, eds., *Comparative Creole Syntax: Parallel Outlines of 18 Creole Grammars* (London: Battlebridge, 2007).
24. The short sketches serve the purposes of the present chapter. They do not pro-

vide a representative summary of the extensive literature. Michel DeGraff's first chapter in Michel DeGraff, ed., *Language Creation and Language Change*, provides a more detailed overview of some of the major debates in the field of creole linguistics.

25. DeGraff, *Language Creation and Language Change*.
26. For example, D. Bickerton, "The Language Bioprogram Hypothesis", *Behavioral and Brain Sciences* 7 (1984): 173–221.
27. Also known as the Language Acquisition Devise (LAD) and close to Noam Chomsky's notion of Universal Grammar (UG). Bickerton, "The Language Bioprogram Hypothesis", 173–221.
28. Though it should be noted that Kegl, Senghas and Coppola, "Creation through Contact: Sign Language Emergence and Sign Language Change in Nicaragua", 223, explicitly avoid giving a simple Bickertonian account of the genesis of LSN.
29. John Lumsden, "Language Acquisition and Creolization", in *Language Creation and Language Change: Creolization, Diachrony, and Development*, ed. Michel Degraff (Cambridge, MA: MIT Press, 1999), 129–57.
30. C.L. Hudson-Kam and E.L. Newport, "Regularizing Unpredictable Variation: The Roles of Adult and Child Learners in Language Formation and Change", *Language Learning and Development* 1, no. 2 (2005): 153–54.
31. Singler, in "Children and Creole Genesis", discusses the role of children in the formation of creoles at some length. While he notes this general difference between child and adult language, he observes that "I have trouble in seeing how it applies widely to the Caribbean" (161).
32. Sandler and Lillo-Martin, *Sign Language and Linguistic Universals*, 497.
33. Sam Supalla, "Manually Coded English: The Modality Question in Signed Language Development", in *Theoretical Issues in Sign Language Research*, volume 2, *Psychology*, ed. Patricia A. Siple and Susan D. Fischer (Chicago: University of Chicago Press, 1991), 85–109.
34. David Lightfoot, "Creoles and Cues", in *Language Creation and Change: Creolization, Diachrony and Development*, ed. Michel DeGraff (Cambridge, MA: MIT Press, 1999), 431–52.
35. The sign language of Martha's Vineyard might plausibly be considered a substrate of ASL.
36. Of course, it is conceivable that a particular pattern found in both signed languages and in creoles may have two different explanations, one for each group.
37. Of course, these features are not unique to signed languages and creoles and are found in many languages that belong to neither group.

38. Sandler and Lillo-Martin, *Sign Language and Linguistic Universals*, 504.
39. Holm and Patrick, *Comparative Creole Syntax*.
40. Some signers in Trinidad use initialized signs to distinguish between nominative and accusative pronouns. For example, some signers use an "I" hand shape when signing a first-person singular subject pronoun and an "M" hand shape when signing a first-person singular object pronoun. Clearly this is a consequence of contact with English. M. Plumlee, "Pronouns in Mexican Sign Language", in *Working Papers of the Summer Institute of Linguistics*, University of North Dakota Session 39 (1995): 81–92, observes analogous patterns in Mexican Sign Language. I consider these forms in the language of Trinidadian signers as markers of Signed English rather than TSL and therefore disregard them for present purposes. In fact, Japanese Sign Language is unusual because it distinguishes gender in pronouns, though not case.
41. Keren Cumberbatch, "A Linguistic Description of the Language of the Urban Deaf in Jamaica".
42. Joseph H. Greenberg, "Some Universals of Grammar with Particular Reference to the Order of Meaningful Elements", in *Universals of Language*, ed. Joseph H. Greenberg (Cambridge, MA: MIT Press, 1966), 95.
43. H. Harley and E. Ritter, "Structuring the Bundle: A Universal Morphosyntactic Feature Geometry", in *Pronouns: Grammar and Representation*, ed. H. Weise and H. Simon (Amsterdam: John Benjamins, 2002), 23–39.
44. The syncretism of second-person singular and plural forms in Modern Standard English (you, you), but not in Caribbean English Lexicon Creoles (compare Jamaican Creole *yu*, "second-person singular" and *unu*, "second person plural"), might be said to be marked in the sense that the Jamaican Creole system is more symmetrical and regular. The same is true for most varieties of non-standard English.
45. See S.S. Mufwene, *The Ecology of Language Evolution* (Cambridge: Cambridge University Press, 2001); and especially DeGraff's *Language Creation and Language Change*, 513–24, discussion of markedness for an overview of the different positions.
46. C. Jourdan and R. Keesing, "From Fisin to Pijin: Creolization in Process in the Solomon Islands", *Language in Society* 26 (1997): 401–20.
47. Ibid., 414.
48. Bert Vaux and Andrew Nevins, "Metalinguistic Shmetalinguistic: The Phonology of Shm-Reduplication", in *CLS 39–1: The Main Session: Papers from the 39th Annual Meeting of the Chicago Linguistic Society*, ed. J. Cihlar, A. Franklin,

D. Kaiser and I. Kimbara (Chicago: Authorhouse, 2007), 702–21.
49. Silvia Kouwenberg, ed., *Twice as Meaningful: Reduplication in Pidgins, Creoles and Other Contact Languages* (London: Battlebridge, 2003).
50. *Productive* here is used to mean that the process can be used with most or all relevant words in the language, including new words, rather than being restricted to a few fixed examples. "Shm" reduplication is quite productive as demonstrated by its application to new words, as in "Google shmoogle".
51. Again, Cumberbatch, "A Linguistic Description of the Language of the Urban Deaf in Jamaica" (forthcoming), reports that various types of reduplication are found in Jamaican Sign Language.
52. P. Bakker, "The Absence of Reduplication in Pidgins", in *Twice as Meaningful: Reduplication in Pidgins, Creoles, and Other Contact Languages*, ed. Silvia Kouwenberg (London: Battlebridge, 2003), 37–46.
53. Ibid., 39.
54. Silvia Kouwenberg and Darlene La Charité, "'More of the Same': Iconicity in Reduplication and the Evidence for Substrate Transfer in the Genesis of Caribbean Creole Languages", in *Twice as Meaningful: Reduplication in Pidgins, Creoles, and Other Contact Languages*, ed. Silvia Kouwenberg (London: Battlebridge, 2003), 7–18.
55. Kouwenberg, *Twice as Meaningful*.
56. Ibid., 3.

8.

"How Yuh Make a Story?"
Narrative Development in Young Trinidadian Children

» KATHY-ANN DRAYTON

Introduction

CHILDREN GROW UP SURROUNDED by narratives. Narratives are told to them, about them and around them, by parents, siblings, assorted relatives and neighbours as they all go about their daily lives. These narratives of success and failure, illness, humour, anger give the eager listeners an insight into the narrative practices of the community to which they belong. They learn which events are reportable to others, and how to link related events into a discursive framework that can inform, engage or entertain a listener. Infants and toddlers are the favourite topics of their parents and so, from quite early, children are immersed in conversations, jokes and stories, most highly contextualized, providing a scaffold for language learning and helping to define cultural identity. The narratives that children hear in the home, the street, the parlour, the schoolyard, provide models of how to tell a story when their turn comes.[1]

Children begin their lives as disjointed storytellers who do not quite possess the syntactic capability, the vocabulary selection or the discursive mastery needed to tell a story with accuracy, economy and creativity. During ages four to six, children begin the transition from the language-learning phase to using language for learning as they develop more complex language skills. This period involves a change from meandering, disjointed productions involving descriptions and analyses of their daily activities to becoming story makers who provide increasing detail, insight and evaluation of the activities and events that take place in their lives. They evolve into adults who can engage all these aspects into text that talks about emotionally salient events and reflects the cultural framework of the speaker. How do children develop these skills? As one six-year-old boy asked in apparent confusion, "How yuh make a story?" A story to him was something to be crafted, a skill to be learned. The focus of this study seeks to answer this question by showing that the increased facility in producing narratives is a reflection of the child's psychosocial, linguistic and cognitive development.

Narratives

Jerome Bruner suggests that narrative, along with reasoning, are the fundamental modes by which humans order reality and the various ways of being that exist within that complexity. He identified two important components that are crucial for understanding and telling good narratives.[2] These are what Bruner refers to as the *landscape of action* and the *landscape of consciousness*. These reflect the fact that personal stories are projections not only of a character's actions, but also of his thoughts and beliefs. A person's ability to navigate this landscape of consciousness develops over time as humans develop *theory of mind*, the ability to attribute feelings and mental states to self and others.

Narratives are a type of transcultural discourse which, as Roland Barthes describes, are "present in myth, legend, fable, tale, novella, epic, history, tragedy, *drame* [suspense drama], comedy, mime, painting, . . . stained glass windows, cinema, comics, news items, conversations".[3] Narratives, especially as produced by children, are at once literary, cultural and developmental, and can be analysed from these perspectives.[4] These streams of analysis have unfortunately been used quite separately, with literary/cultural foci operating almost separately from developmental/cultural analyses. When viewed within a developmental framework, the act of making a story is a reflection of the child's psychosocial, linguistic and cognitive development. Narratives, when viewed within this framework, are important for three main reasons: (1) they are an important aspect of general language skills, (2) narrative skill is closely related to literacy development and (3) narratives are a marker of personal identity formation. As Peggy Miller et al. describe, "narrative can be said to play a privileged role in the process of self-construction".[5] However, since language, literacy and identity develop within a congruence of complex cultural factors, these must also be considered.

Linguistically, narrative is most common in oral language discourse, a frame in which the language itself is central but in which objects, gestures and paralinguistic features may combine to tell the story. Shirley Brice Heath postulates that these oral narratives fall into four genres. *Recasts* or *recounts* are used to retell events that have already occurred linearly and with consistent point of view. *Event casts* are used to explain activities that are being planned or will occur in the future. *Accounts* involve the sharing or reporting of an experience. The term *story*, although often used interchangeably with *narrative*, is a fourth genre encompassing fictional accounts of people or people and objects with anthropomorphic characteristics.[6] At a basic level, however, *narrative* is a linguistic derivation of mental representations in the speaker's mind, of events and connections between these events, of what Roberto Franzosi labels the "before" and "after" different from the "before".[7]

Labov defines narrative as "one method of recapitulating past experience by matching a verbal sequence of clauses to the sequence of events which (it is inferred) actually occurred".[8] The speaker encapsulates personal experiences within a learned macrostructure, which provides coherence to and evaluation of the actions that have taken place. Thus, narratives are generally decontextualized speech acts, which, as Carole Peterson et al. suggest, "do not describe the here-and-now but rather the there-and-then".[9] The speaker, therefore, goes outside himself to describe himself in a particular place and time or to describe other people as they thought and acted in a particular place and time. Narrative macrostructure provides a way of framing this description to reduce the cognitive and linguistic load on the narrator. This is what R. Berman and D. Slobin identify as narrative *packaging*, or the creation of a hierarchical structure to contain linear events that display complex relations.[10]

Another principle of narrative structure, which has been evident in their extensive cross-linguistic study, is that of narrative *filtering*. The filtering principle highlights that experiences are inevitably filtered by speakers based on factors such as their choice of perspective. Language itself is also filtering, as the formal structures in the language can impact on the information structure and, therefore, indirectly on how events are presented and perceived.

The experience and the sequence of events that make up the experience are reported through different linguistic approaches.[11] One such approach used with children's narratives is a macrostructure known as *story grammar*. Stories move through a reliable progression of beginning, middle and end and contain fairly discrete elements that N. Stein and C. Glenn label as episode, setting, initiating event, internal response, plan, attempt, consequence, reaction and ending.[12] Such a linear structure is, however, biased towards North American narrative cultural norms, setting these norms as the default when they may not work in societies like those in the West Indies. On the other hand, English remains the language of the curriculum in Trinidadian schools, and research has shown that the highly decontextualized language of classroom reading and writing preferences the linear factual narrative mode and can cause problems as children move from oracy to literacy.

Narrative is, however, most linked to language itself, and narrative development is tied to linguistic and cognitive development. Children, for example, must have the necessary vocabulary to accurately describe and identify characters, actions and feelings. They must have acquired the relevant morpho-syntactic structures that allow them to successfully represent the relationships among events in the narrative. They must have discursive skills that allow them to bring disparate parts into a coherent whole, using appropriate linguistic causal and referential elements.

Cognitively the child must, as M. Lahey and L. Bloom describe, "hold in mind a complex model of relations along events while using language to express these relations".[13] To do this, the child narrator must comprehend causal and inferential relationships, which are important aspects of some genres. This is a higher-level activity, since the ability to make inferences, for example, is contingent upon world knowledge stored in long-term memory, information from the present context and the ability to build models to bridge the two.[14]

Narrative and Culture

From a wider sociological or ethnographic perspective, narratives reflect the process of socialization and acculturation children undergo as they learn to be part of a particular community or culture or both. Therefore, narratives can be viewed as a powerful schema used for the encoding of identity. Cross-cultural research into the narrative production of young children has shown a strong cultural indoctrination, however unconscious it may be. Chien-Ju Chang, for example, argues that "the stories children select to remember and tell reflect the framework into which they have been socialized".[15] More explicitly, this means that the analysis of children's narratives can provide a window into understanding the beliefs, values, norms, presumptions and prejudices that children inherit or adopt from their environment and the world view of the community to which they belong.

C. Westby and G. Rouse suggest that what some have labelled *high-* and *low-context cultures* differ in their narrative styles.[16] Cultures with low-context style – for example, mainstream North American culture – are ones in which most information is shared, and learning takes place verbally with a very monochromic concept of time. High-context cultures, like many traditional societies, are ones in which there is a focus on shared knowledge and information that is derived from the physical context and where there is often a polychromic concept of time.

Peggy Miller et al. ("Personal Storytelling") and Q. Wang and M. Leichtman ("Same Beginnings") examined the narratives told by mainstream American children and Chinese children.[17] In both studies, the authors found social, emotional, and cognitive differences in the narratives the two groups produced. The stories the American children told reflected modern Western thought, with a focus on developing autonomy and assertiveness in the midst of complicating events. The narratives the Chinese children produced focused on what the authors claimed were principles based on Confucian teaching, as well as its reliance on didactic narrative.[18] In their stories, these children incorporated aspects of social harmony and moral correctness.

M. Minami and A. McCabe found that while North American families encouraged long, factual narratives about one topic, Japanese families valued short narratives about collections of experiences.[19] In a comparison of two working-class communities in the United States, Heath found that the European-American children typically produced factual, concise stories, while the African-American children emphasized creativity rather than factual, linear narratives.[20] In a later study, Champion described the way in which African-American communities favoured performance and moralizing agents in their narratives. She noted that "storytellers become the words they convey, that is they use both voice and body movement as tools to convey their stories".[21]

One of the problems created in contexts with culturally differing narrative styles occurs when, as several studies have shown, the academic system privileges a particular style, encapsulated in the *Labovian model*, which is detail oriented, highly sequential and involves neat conclusions to the action. Ruth Page describes the unequal value given to Maori narrative styles and that of minority children in this and other cultures: "their full repertoire of narrative styles appears necessarily constrained as the price of academic progress".[22] Miller et al., taking a language socialization perspective, suggest that "the particular version of personal storytelling that is available in the child's culture and the ways in which the child is exposed to that version, together form a culturally organized path of access into storytelling".[23] This path of access must be studied and taken into account when considering the linguistic and social development of the child.

Narrative Style in Trinidad and Tobago

Enculturation of narrative style is certainly present in the Trinidadian and greater Caribbean context. Narratives Trinidadians produce must necessarily be located within the Trinidadian social and cultural milieu. This is a complex task in multicultural Trinidad, which has both a dominant, syncretized Creole culture, and fairly discrete "heritage" cultures drawn from Africa, Asia and Europe. Since narrative is so closely bound to language, and the first and only language of the majority of Trinidadians is Trinidadian English Creole/Trinidadian English (TEC/TrE), it may be fair to assume that the speakers of the language have the same or similar narrative styles.[24]

In Trinidad and Tobago, land of calypso with its traditionally incisive, biting social commentary, and of the Midnight Robber, an extravagantly costumed Carnival character and a braggadocio supreme, narratives must be told with style and flair, to inform but also entertain. Older narrative styles typically included tales about spiritual belief, moral values and cunning, with the Trickster archetype encoded in the character of Anansi. However, Cynthia James argues for the emergence of what she calls "the new orality", in which there is focus on humour and entertainment in the narrative style.[25] Recent generations of Trinidadian children have been acculturated to this style of narrative. If Carnival is considered one of the largest social institutions in Trinidad and Tobago society, then the children of that society will develop practices of entertainment and exhibition.

Yet, there is a curious dichotomy in the minds of many Trinidadian parents when the oral skills of their children are considered. Parents speak with pride of young children who are verbally precocious, mimicking the style and language of those around them. At the same time, there is an almost Victorian style to child rearing, in which the child is to be seen but not heard. Rudeness is discouraged, while ritual politeness is strongly encouraged. Shame falls on the parent whose child does not tread this fine balance.

In this context, narrative plays a particular role and takes on a particular format. James has suggested that the Trinidadian narrators in the manner of traditional West Indian storytellers emphasized "linguistic devices such as double entendre, innuendo and wit" and mixed Creole with Standard English to bring characters to life for the audience.[26] Creativity lay primarily in the words of the stories. The Talk Tents, which emerged in the 1970s, were the epitome of this creativity, aiming to showcase ordinary life through a vivid, comic slant. The narrative style of persons such as Paul Keens-Douglas in his many monologues highlights the narrative style to which many Trinidadians aspire. He is successful as a storyteller, not simply because his stories are funny or nostalgic, but because his style is one that reflects what Trinidadians perhaps unconsciously view as a template of their orality.

Narratives, by their nature, have an essential dichotomy. Narratives are both text and performance, and the innate tension between the two arises out of basic conflict between the form of language and how it is used. David Bloome et al. suggest that this reflects a deep conflict about what language is and how it is to be used.[27] Trinidadian children, like children in other societies, have to learn this answer themselves by learning to use narratives in a way consistent with the narrative practices of the community. To do this, they must learn how to frame their narratives in a particular linguistic structure and to increasingly make this structure more elaborate.

The Study

This chapter investigates the narrative development of Trinidadian children in their early school years, to determine how and when they begin to develop the linguistic skills to formulate a well-developed narrative structure.

Participants

The data for this study were taken from narratives produced by young children from Trinidad and Tobago. Over six hundred four- to six-year-old children throughout the country received speech and language screenings in 2007 as part of a wider project assessing the longitudinal language development of children from primary school entry. Three primary schools in Trinidad were involved in the longitudinal study, with a project intervention group of twenty children receiving speech-language therapy, while their typically developing classmates provided a control group for comparison. For the purpose of this study, the narratives used were those from children who had passed the initial screening and were deemed to have typical language development.

Data Collection

Data were collected at the initial language screening and in approximately three-month intervals over the two-year period. Three main types of narratives were elicited for the project, two of which were used for this study. The first type of elicitation technique, used in the initial speech-language screening, was based on a multi-panel picture stimulus, which is part of the Kindergarten Language Screening Test, 2nd Edition (KLST-2). This instrument uses a three-picture sequence set of children eating at a table, spilling some of their drink on the table and floor and a dog coming in to lick the liquid off the ground. Students were asked to put the pictures in order and then tell the story of what was happening in the pictures. The second type of elicitation technique was the retelling of stories that were familiar to the children or used recently in the classroom as part of a language arts lesson. They were given a prompt during a semi-formal interview, for example, "Tell me about the Gingerbread Man story." These stories were elicited from each child on an individual basis, in a quiet room with minimal distractions. The stories were audiotaped and transcribed for coding of narrative structure and language.

Coding

The narratives were coded using an adaptation of N. Stein and C. Glenn's story grammar method, which has formed the basis for many structured narrative evaluations.[28] The stories were therefore analysed for whether or not they contained the following:

1. Setting: Introduction of main characters
2. Initiating event: An action or a problem that sets up a dilemma for the story
3. Internal response: The protagonist's reactions to the initiating event
4. Plan: Steps that the protagonist intends to take to solve the problem
5. Attempt: An action or a plan by the protagonist to solve the problem
6. Consequence: A response by the protagonist to the consequence

7. Resolution: The protagonist's reaction to the attainment or non-attainment of the goal
8. Ending: A statement that signals the end of the story

The element, *internal state*, is particularly important in perspective building. Several measures of evaluative devices have been suggested in the literature, but the following, based on work by Martha Shiro, were used in this study:[29]

1. Emotion: Expressing affect or emotion (e.g., She was happy)
2. Cognition: Representing thoughts and beliefs (e.g., He thought it was a ghost)
3. Perception: Referring to anything that is perceived through the senses (e.g., He saw the thief)
4. Physical state: Referring to a character's internal state, which is physical not emotional (e.g., The girl was hungry)
5. Intention: Referring to a character's intention of carrying out some action (e.g., She tried to escape)
6. Reported speech: Referring to language representing speech directly or indirectly (e.g., He said "Open the door!", He told him to open the door)

Finally, the narratives were examined in terms of their use of linguistic features including the following:

1. Articles, and anaphoric devices such as pronouns
2. Conjunctions
3. Tense and aspect markers

Analysis and Findings

The narratives the children produced at the beginning of their primary school life had a very basic structure. They were typically made up of short declaratives labelling events and objects within the story. The following was produced by one six-year-old boy who was just entering school:

> (1) Dog and cat was playing. Cat was sleeping. Dog was reaching. Dog was going to chase the cat. And then the cat raise up and throw down the flowers. And then the flowers break.

This story does have a central theme, of the animals cavorting, but consists primarily of labelling the actions using short declarative sentences. There is only a sketchy establishment of *setting* with "Dog and cat was playing", but with no location or time mentioned. There is an *initiating event* and what can be considered an *internal motivation*, in that the dog was reaching because he was going to chase the cat.[30] The young narrator does not directly state a consequence, in this case the non-attainment of the goal. This has to be inferred by the listener. The narrative shows simple sequencing, with an attempt at causality with the reference to the flowers breaking after being thrown down by the cat.

While the child has produced a basic narrative macrostructure, the language that is used is also constrained. The child shows a strong preference for the auxiliary plus progressive verb forms, which are early grammatical morphemes and typical of his age. For the actions requiring completive verb forms, the child uses regular and irregular past tense forms as in "raise up", "throw down" and "break". That these are unmarked can be due either to his status as a predominantly TEC speaker or to the fact that he had not yet acquired these rules, especially for relatively lower-frequency words.[31] This narrator also uses almost none of the linguistic markers that provide cohesion in the discourse. "An" is a very early conjunction in language acquisition and shows up here, but there is little use of the definite article when referring to cat and dog, and there are no pronouns in the narrative.

Another narrative by a five-year-old girl responding to picture stimuli showed similar narrative signs. She too followed the pattern of labelling events around a central setting; with little linkage between the labelled action, the narrative appeared disjointed.

> (2) Dem drinking . . . milk and tea, juice. An playing. An the dog sitting down dey and watching dem. He drinking. She drinking de milk and he. . . . she juice fall out and she juice on de table. Juice on the ground. An the dog licking de juice in the ground. An de dog frighten and de girl get sad.

Once again there is an attempt at establishing setting, but not a good one. Introducing the narrative with a pronoun with no previous reference is confusing to a listener, although the narrator obviously accepts that a pictorial context is adequate enough. There is no description of who the "Dem" are or whether they are to provide background to the story or form a basis for ascribing motivations to the characters. The narrator does introduce an *initiating event* with "she juice fall down". She mentions that the dog was licking the juice off the ground but fails to describe or infer that this may have been a consequence of the children's attempt to solve the problem of the spilled drink. The ending was also not clear, as the final sentence does not signal an end to the story or serve a didactic purpose. Noteworthy in this narrative, though, is the child's attempt to describe the *internal states* of the characters in response to the action "de dog frighten an de girl sad". However, they are not explicitly linked to the narrative, and the listener is left to infer the causes of these feelings.

The narrative includes many hesitations and repetitions, as the child struggles to link the cognitive and linguistic aspects of the discourse. Utterances are again simple declaratives. There is a preponderance of progressive forms, but in this case the child does not use the auxiliary in connection with these. For the discrete action that requires a completive verb form, she does introduce the unmarked past tense "fall". There is frequent use of the conjunction "an" but this child also displays use of different types of pronouns, including the TEC use of subject pronouns as a possessive as in "she juice". The narrator is also using the TEC form of zero marking of the copula before a locative "She juice on the table" and an adjective "the dog frighten". The child is, therefore, clearly using the language of her environment to tell her stories, with the narrative structure that her development allows.

Another child, who claimed his favourite stories were fairy stories, produced a similar narrative structure when asked to recount a story he liked. However, he displayed more narrative elements as well as more complex language:

> (3) Once upon a time there was a boy fairy and a girl fairy. They were practising how to dance and something go wrong. The bad fairy take them away and carry them in prisons. And then he was going to kill them, but they buss out of jail and then they was free and then another good fairy come and rescue them.

This narrative includes an established *setting*, the ubiquitous "Once upon a time", and an introduction of the characters with basic descriptions, "a boy fairy" and "a girl fairy". There is also a clear initiating event, which is described both qualitatively – "something go wrong" – as well as in terms of action, with the bad fairy taking them away. This narrator also ascribes internal motivations to the villain, who is described as wanting to kill the protagonists. Though no reason is given for this plan, it is not unexpected, as in the minds of young children "bad" people are expected to be bad, for badness' sake.[32] There is a successful *attempt* by the protagonists to escape the prison, although there is no description of their feelings at this point. He does, however, describe the *consequence* to the action, that they were free. Thereafter, the child becomes unclear in his resolution to the story, with no final summary. While this narrative has the impressive five story grammar elements, there is little or no evaluative language describing the feelings and cognitions of characters. We know how they act, but we do not learn how they feel and think.

Another narrative was produced by a five-year-old girl retelling a story that was read to her in her classroom:

> (4) De tortoise crawl everywhere an he was tired. He wanted to fly like the ducks. He ask them if he could fly. And they say "let me show you. I will put this stick in your mouth and go on the two end and fly." He bite on the stick. Everybody see a tortoise fly in the sky. They shout, wave at tortoise. He shout out and then he fall off. Tortoise open his mouth and fall, and boong he butt he head.

In this case, the child jumps into the story without establishing the setting. She does, however, provide information on the *internal motivations* of the tortoise, which was tired and wanted to fly. An *initiating event* was projected when the tortoise asked the ducks for help. There was the outlining of a *plan* on how to achieve flight using a stick and one assumes the flying ducks. There is an *attempt*, as the tortoise tries to fly by following the advice the ducks give him; a *consequence*, as the flying works for a while but then fails. However, the tortoise has no reaction to his short flight or subsequent failure, and the ending is not clear.

Still, this narrative did have some interesting linguistic elements. The child imitated direct speech, quoting the ducks and their speech. She also imitated the sound of falling to the ground, using the word "boong". The narrator used unmarked regular and irregular past tense forms throughout the story, with the exception of "He wanted to fly", in which the *-ed* morpheme was added to indicate his state of mind at that particular time, but not necessarily at the present. The child also showed good use of pronouns, alternating reference to the tortoise and the ducks, and with no ambiguity. This helped to pull the discourse together and made the narrative easy to follow.

Later Narratives

As the children grew older, their narratives also developed, growing more sophisticated. By the time the children were at the end of the second year of primary school, with most children aged six to seven, there were more story grammar elements, as well as attempts at producing more complex linguistic elements. The following is produced by a seven-year-old boy who was asked to retell a story that had been read to him and that he was very familiar with:

> (5) In the beginning, Jack was trying to sell he cow to get money cause he was poor. And then Jack went off and he saw a man and the man wanted the cow, and the man gave him beans. That is why they call it beanstalk. And the mommy throw the beans out and it grow a big beanstalk. First the beanstalk was small, then it grow big until it reach to the giant house. That's all I remember. But when the giant was running down Jack from the beanstalk, he cut the beanstalk with . . . What you does call the thing that does go so . . . [*gestures*] . . . An axe. The giant fall with the beanstalk, and the beanstalk hit the giant in he head and the giant died.

The child ascribes a *setting* in the use of the vague "In the beginning" and moves smoothly into describing the *initiating event*, which is Jack trying to sell his cow, and the *internal motivation* behind his actions "because he was poor". This is a general motivation, however, and does not give a specific reason for him choosing to sell the cow at that point. There is some reference to an *attempt* as the child relates that Jack "went off", presumably to some place where he could sell the cow. The reporting of the *consequence* includes the growth of the giant beanstalk. However, at this point the child's attempt at storytelling falters, as he cannot remember exactly what happens next. A second episode in the story, with its own structure, is not given its full expression. The giant is not introduced to the listener, who has no idea from the story who the giant is and what his motivations are. All that is clear is that he is chasing Jack in an *initiating event*, and that Jack engages in an *attempt* to escape him by cutting down the beanstalk. As a *consequence*, the giant falls and dies, but there is no resolution to the larger story at the end of the narrative. Further, although there are increased story grammar elements, the child still does not engage with the feelings of the characters and what they are thinking.

This narrative showed the increasing sophistication of the young narrator who could engage in a story that had more than one episode unit. The child's language also revealed more complexity in sentence structure, with main and subordinate clauses. The narrator continued to use mostly unmarked past-tense forms, and these replaced present progressives as the verb structure of choice. The child did, however, use some past-tense marking, producing "went", "saw", "wanted", "gave" and "died" at different points. There was also use of pronouns to refer to even more items in the story: Jack, the man, the cow, the beans and the giant. The child did this quite well, although there were two instances of potential ambiguity, first with "That is why they call it beanstalk" and later with the potential confusion between Jack and the giant, when he said "when the giant was running down Jack from the beanstalk, he cut the beanstalk".

Another child claimed that his favourite story was Little Red Riding Hood:

> (6) Little Red Riding Hood live in the woods with a mother and a father. And a big, bad wolf live near the woods. He saw Little Red Riding Hood. He said, "I have to eat you all up." She reach by her granny's house, and then she knock on the door. Said the funny voice "Come in" said her grandmother. "What big ears you have" . . . "All the better to see you" said grandmother . . . "What big teeth you have" . . . "All the better so I can eat you!" Little Red Riding Hood ran and then de wolf chase her down. And the father come with a big saw and cut the wolf up and then the wolf ran away.

This narrative contains many of the elements that the previous one had. The *setting* is very well established, with the main character living in the woods with her parents and the wolf living nearby. The *initiating event* is the wolf catching sight of Little Red Riding Hood and deciding that he wanted to eat her. There is a mini-episode within the story of the visit to the grandmother's house, but the child does not explore the reasons for the visit or the Wolf's intentions or behaviour before that visit. The listener is left to infer that the wolf is saying and doing the things it does to eat Little Red Riding Hood as initially stated. The convoluted *attempt* made by the wolf is therefore not very clear, although the final act of the attempt is directly stated: "Little Red Riding Hood ran and then the wolf chased her down." This final act is followed by a *consequence*, as the father attacks the wolf who, in this telling of the story, runs away. There is no reaction on the part of the protagonist and no mention of what she is thinking and feeling, even towards the end, when she is saved.

This story as retold by the child had elements of direct speech from both the girl and the wolf. This was, however, a recounting of the familiar script of the original tale, rather than the child's attempt to insert character cognitions into the narrative. The child, nonetheless, enjoyed this part of the narrative, using the opportunity to role play the different characters.

Discussion

The development of narrative skills in Trinidadian children in the first two years of primary school is quite evident. The children show markedly improved ability to structure their stories appropriately so that they provide a framework for providing key information about the experience, to deepen characterization and to begin to interrogate issues of right and wrong and essential morality. This ability reflects a cognitive shift from Bruner's landscape of action to the landscape of consciousness.

The structure of earlier narrations is consistent with that found in other studies in which it was found that the narratives produced were concerned primarily with the identification and labelling of actors, objects and actions.[33] This comparison helps to concretize what is a fairly decontextualized activity and represents an aspect of narrative development. The children do not simply label the objects and characters in the narrative, but incorporate an action-focused analysis in which they examine the interrelation between the agent and the object, which Bruner calls *arguments of action*.

The children, as can be expected with current cultural practices and the demands of formal education, follow linear Western story-grammar formats. This story-grammar frame, however, in most instances encases Creole language structures. Some of the children produced their stories almost entirely in Creole. Others showed good facility in code switching between the two, especially to foreground and background information. However, telling a story seems a heavy task for even the most talkative children, perhaps because the concept of a story to them reflects a formal structure, aligned with reading and books and requiring the formal language that is encapsulated in Standard English.

One interesting pattern that the stories reveal is the lack of evaluative language to describe mental states. The children only used evaluative devices to describe states of being like the "big, bad wolf", but in these cases it is most often a simple repetition of a frame that they have heard before. The children give little or no insight into how they or the characters are feeling as they experience the various events and actions. Research has shown that children that age are well on their way to developing *theory of mind*, the ability to attribute beliefs and mental states to other people.[34] Yet, the children do not attribute feelings of fear or anger or happiness to the characters in their stories.[35]

Such a pervasive pattern suggests that the labelling and expression of emotion may have cultural bases within the wider community or, at the very least, the communicative styles of the children's communicative partners. Research has found, for example, that conversations during shared reading are important in the development into planes of consciousness. In *Conversations*, D. McArthur found discussion of story characters' feelings and explanations for characters' actions to be the main topics for discussion in parent-child dyads centred around storytelling. She opines that this may be because "emotions may be the most salient of all the intangible topics from the plane of consciousness".[36] The findings of that study show a correlation between the type of story-based discussion in which the child engages regularly with conversation partners and children's early ability to engage with evaluative devices in their own independent narrative productions. This issue, like others related to how children learn to make and master narratives, remains an important area of research, providing insight into enculturation and development.

Although the frequency of evaluative expressions in the narratives was quite low, it did not in itself hinder the coherence of the discourse. The children told their stories and, with prior knowledge and contextual assistance, the listener was able to comprehend the details of the story. This comprehension is consistent with what Shiro suggests: While the skilful inclusion of narrative devices enhances a narrative and the child's role as a storyteller, it is not necessary for the coherence of the discourse.[37]

The findings of the study lead to the conclusion that Trinidadian children do show significant development in their narrative development in their early school years. This development is in the form of more finely detailed narrative structure and more complex language and may include the use of evaluative devices that signal the cognitive and emotional workings of characters as they interact with events. Further studies on narrative development should use multidimensional measures to accurately evaluate children's ability to build a macrostructure through language, as they emerge as independent and capable story makers.

Notes

1. A *parlour* is a small neighbourhood snack shop.
2. Jerome Bruner, *Acts of Meaning* (London: Harvard University Press, 1990), 11–43.

3. Roland Barthes, "An Introduction to the Structural Analysis of Language", *New Literary Theory* 6, no. 2 (1975): 237.
4. Michael Bamberg, *The Acquisition of Narrative: Learning to Use Language* (Berlin: Mouton de Gruyter, 1987).
5. Peggy Miller, Randolph Potts, Heidi Fung, Lisa Hoogstra and Judy Mintz, "Narrative Practices and the Social Construction of Self in Childhood", *American Ethnologist* 17, no. 2 (1990): 292.
6. Shirley Brice Heath, "Taking a Cross-Cultural Look at Narratives", *Topics in Language Disorders* 7, no. 1 (1986): 84.
7. Roberto Franzosi, "Narrative Analysis – Why (and How) Sociologists Should Be Interested in Narrative", in *The Annual Review of Sociology*, ed. John Hagan (Palo Alto, CA: Annual Reviews, 1998), 521.
8. W. Labov, "The Transformation of Experience in Narrative Syntax", in *Language in the Inner City: Studies in the Black English Vernacular*, ed. W. Labov (Philadelphia: University of Pennsylvania Press, 1972), 359.
9. Carole Peterson, Beulah Jesso and Allyssa Mccabe, "Encouraging Narratives in Preschoolers: An Intervention Study", *Journal of Child Language* 26 (1999): 50.
10. R. Berman and D. Slobin, *Relating Events in Narrative: A Crosslinguistic Developmental Study* (Hillsdale, NJ: Erlbaum, 1994), 25.
11. Other approaches include High Point Analysis, Conversational Analysis and Critical Discourse Analysis.
12. N. Stein and C. Glenn, "An Analysis of Story Comprehension in Elementary School Children", in *New Directions in Discourse Processing*, volume 2, ed. R. Freedle (Norwood, NJ: Ablex, 1979), 54.
13. M. Lahey and L. Bloom, "Variability and Language Learning Disabilities", in *Language Learning Disabilities in School-Aged Children and Adolescents*, ed. G.P. Wallach and K.G. Butler (New York: Macmillan College Publishing, 1994), 356.
14. D. Boudreau and R. Chapman, "The Relationship between Event Representation and Linguistic Skill in Narratives of Children and Adolescents with Down Syndrome", *Journal of Speech, Language and Hearing Research* 43 (2000): 1150.
15. Chien-Ju Chang, "Telling Stories of Experiences: Narrative Development of Young Chinese Children", *Applied Psycholinguistics* 25, no. 1 (2004): 83.
16. C. Westby and G. Rouse, "Culture in Education and the Instruction of Language Learning-Disabled Students", *Topics in Language Disorders* 5, no. 4 (1985): 16; E. Hall, *The Dance of Life* (New York: Anchor Press/Doubleday, 1983) suggested that there was a continuum of contextualization of communication and that cultures may vary along this continuum. These authors suggest that this is a relative rather than an absolute difference.

17. Peggy Miller, Angela R. Wiley, Heidi Fung and Chung-Hui Liang, "Personal Storytelling as a Medium of Socialization in Chinese and American Families", *Child Development* 68, no. 3 (1997); Q. Wang and M. Leichtman, "Same Beginnings, Different Stories: A Comparison of American and Chinese Children's Narratives", *Child Development* 71, no. 5 (2000): 1329–46.
18. Miller et al., "Personal Storytelling", 564.
19. M. Minami and A. McCabe, "Rice Balls and Bear Hunts: Japanese and North American Family Narrative Patterns", *Journal of Child Language* 22, no. 2 (1995): 423.
20. Shirley Brice Heath, *Ways with Words: Language, Life and Work in Communities and Classrooms* (Cambridge: Cambridge University Press, 1983).
21. Tempii Champion, *Understanding Storytelling among African-American Children: A Journey from Africa to America* (Mahwah, NJ: Lawrence Earlbaum, 2003), 3.
22. Ruth Page, "Variation in Storytelling Style amongst New Zealand Schoolchildren", *Narrative Inquiry* 18, no. 1 (2008): 177.
23. Miller et al., "Narrative Practices", 294.
24. Studies have shown that social class is an important variable in the socialization of different narrative styles. An investigation is again beyond the scope of this study, which uses a fairly homogeneous geographical and SES sample.
25. Cynthia James, "From Orature to Literature in Jamaican and Trinidadian Children's Folk Traditions", *Children's Literature Association Quarterly* 30, no. 2 (2005): 170.
26. Ibid., 165, 167.
27. David Bloome, Laurie Katz and Tempii Champion. "Young Children's Narratives and Ideologies of Language in Classroom", *Reading and Writing Quarterly* 19 (2003): 206.
28. N. Stein, and C. Glenn, "An Analysis of Story Comprehension in Elementary School Children", in *New Directions in Discourse Processing*, volume 2, ed. R. Freedle (Norwood, NJ: Ablex, 1979), 53–120.
29. Martha Shiro, "Genre and Evaluation in Narrative Development", *Journal of Child Language* 30 (2003): 171.
30. It can be asked why the dog wanted to chase the cat, but what is considered a characteristic of dogs can be viewed as reason enough.
31. Valerie Youssef and Winford James, "Grounding Via Tense-Aspect in Tobagonian Creole: Discourse Strategies across a Creole Continuum", *Linguistics* 37 (1999): 597–624, suggest that creole speakers use these tense and aspect markers to

establish the foreground and background aspects of narratives. In this case, an inconsistent use of this pattern could suggest that the children in this study have not yet mastered that morpho-pragmatic skill.

32. Developmental psychologists like E. Turiel, *The Development of Social Knowledge: Morality and Convention* (Cambridge: Cambridge University Press, 1983), claim that children require cognitive and emotional-evaluative skills to make moral judgments. In the early stages, their perception of good and bad is fixed and absolute, based on breaking clearly established rules or being told so by an authority figure.

33. Compare A. McCabe and C. Peterson, eds., *Developing Narrative Structure* (Hillsdale, NJ: Erlbaum, 1991).

34. Compare Nicole Guajardo and Anne Watson, "Narrative Discourse and Theory of Mind Development", *Journal of Genetic Psychology* 163, no. 3 (2002): 305–25.

35. This is a consistent pattern because the children do not label their own feelings in the recounting of their own personal experiences.

36. D. McArthur, L. Adamson and D. Deckner, "As Stories Become Familiar: Mother-Child Conversations during Shared Reading", *Merrill-Palmer Quarterly* 51, no. 4 (2005): 405.

37. Shiro, "Genre and Evaluation", 192.

Part 4.

PEDAGOGY

9.

Black Heart/White Heart
The Chronicles of Narnia as Literary Text in a Creole Space

» NICHA SELVON-RAMKISSOON

THE NATIONAL SECONDARY SCHOOL language arts curriculum of Trinidad and Tobago recommends *The Chronicles of Narnia* on its reading list for level 1 students. The curriculum professes to be "student-centered, seek[ing] to provide personally satisfying experiences for each student, and is growth oriented".[1] *The Chronicles of Narnia* is C.S. Lewis's most popular work and is generally accepted as belonging to the canon of children's literature. The protagonists of the books are English children who are magically transported to Narnia for various adventures, including the saving of Narnia from a number of impending crises. Talking animals and other characters drawn from Greek, Roman, Celtic, Norse and Irish mythologies acknowledge the lion Aslan as their (oftentimes absent) sovereign and saviour.[2]

Critics of this series of seven fantasy novels investigate the treatment of race, religion, gender, power relations, sexuality and childhood innocence in the texts. The Caribbean's creole culture is marked (among other things) by an integration of races and religious beliefs, a complex linguistic system, and its own rich tradition of myths, legends and folklore. In this chapter, I will explore discursive practices in the text under the umbrella of *literary linguistics*, which is the application of linguistic theory to literature. I will specifically examine how linguistic forms accommodate varying points of view and perspectival shifts. The linguistic systems of deixis, pragmatics and syntax will also be considered to comment on structural framing and narratorial positioning in the text.

An examination of the discursive practices of *The Chronicles of Narnia*, as well as the ideological implications inherent in these practices, can reveal complications that may be encountered in the use of these texts in the classroom, which occupies a part of the "creole space". Approaches can then be defined for dealing with these complications in the modern Caribbean language arts classroom.

Discursive Practices and Ideological Implications

Point of View

Conceptual perspective gives insight into the mental positioning of the speaker/author of a discourse in terms of viewing location and focalization. It involves drawing on "the physical perception through which a situation or event is apprehended", as well as examining "the ways in which narrative events are mediated through the consciousness of the 'teller' of the story".[3] Ideological perspective gives insight into the values, conceptions, assumptions and beliefs of the speaker or author and frequently even those of the audience. This perspective "is encoded in a variety of ways, such as through modal systems, transitivity, lexical choice and code choice".[4] The manipulation of these two perspectives in *The Chronicles of Narnia* allows the speaker/author to implicitly and powerfully control how readers interpret the text.

Conceptual perspective is achieved through multiple viewing positions, and in this particular discourse, the viewing perspective can be described as *zero focalization*, that is, the viewing position of the omniscient narrator, in which the narrator says more than any of the characters know.[5] At times, there is direct authorial intrusion, where the narrator infuses his personal ideals and values. This intrusion is possible because the discourse is constructed in the oral tradition of a narrative being told by a raconteur to an intimate audience. In the chronologically first book *The Magician's Nephew*, the first paragraph reads: "This is a story about something that happened long ago when your grandfather was a child. It is a very important story because it shows how all the comings and goings between our world and the land of Narnia first began."[6]

Across the chronicles, this omniscient narrator continues to use the second-person object and third-person inclusive pronouns. In *The Horse and His Boy*, he states that the Calormene style of curtseying is "not at all like ours" (*Horse*, 300), and in *The Silver Chair* he includes in parentheses: "When I was at school one would have said, 'I swear by the Bible.' But Bibles were not encouraged at Experiment House" (*Chair*, 551).

This type of constant omniscient intrusion signals an internal narratorial viewpoint, one that "is mediated through the subjective viewpoint of a particular character's consciousness".[7] In an interesting combination of narrative techniques, the chronicles fit into both of Fowler's classifications for internal narrative perspective.[8] The author at times adopts the first-person mode of narration (internal type A), marked by foregrounded modality – "I expect most witches are like that. They are not interested in things or people unless they can use them; they are terribly practical" (*Magician's Nephew*, 47) – *verba sentiendi* – "I think, myself, I would rather have been in Polly's position" (*Magician's Nephew*, 63) – and categorical assertions – for instance, "It is a very important story" (*Magician's Nephew*, 11).[9] This highly subjective approach to narration is further manifested in the author's use of generic statements – "of course he remembered as every sensible person does, that you should never, never shut yourself in a wardrobe" (*Lion*, 133) – and his judgment on other characters – "You see the foolish old man [Uncle Andrew] was actually beginning to imagine the Witch would fall in love with him. The two drinks probably had something to do with it, and so had his best clothes. But he was in any case as vain as a peacock; that was why he had become a Magician" (*Magician's Nephew*, 49).[10]

This internal type A model, however, is usually used for homodiegetic viewing positions, but this narrator is not a character in the text; therefore, he recounts events from a heterodiegetic point of view. To account for this seeming contradiction, the narrator also employs the second internal mode (internal type B) of the omniscient narrator who has access to characters' thoughts and feelings: "Up until now I think Fledge and Polly had had the idea that they would go in with Digory. But they thought so no longer. . . . Only a fool would dream of going in unless he had been sent there on special business. Digory himself understood at once that the others wouldn't and couldn't come in with him" (*Magician's Nephew*, 91). The combination of both types of internal narration is even more perceptible in contiguous phrases such as, "I think (and Digory thinks too) that her [Jadis's] mind was a sort which cannot remember that quiet place at all" (*Magician's Nephew*, 47). In fact many of the narrator's statements begin with this transitive mental cognition process ("I think"), so his viewing position and character judgments are conspicuous.

In each of the texts, the focalizing character is one or two English children or a young Narnian Prince/King. For example, in *The Horse and His Boy*, Shasta is the child focalizer, and even though the four Pevensees children are introduced in the first line of *The Lion, the Witch and the Wardrobe*, it is clear that Lucy is the narrator's choice as child focalizer. Inevitably, both young and old readers will tend to align themselves with these focalizing characters. The audience will, to varying extents, share the focalizer's fears, frustrations, prejudices, pains and triumphs.

Paradigmatic/Syntagmatic/Pragmatic Links

The Chronicles of Narnia is a complex tale that involves multiple characters, an array of subplots, parallel cataclysmic events and resolutions, interchangeable physical and mental landscapes, anachronous temporal settings and meta-themes. The use of paradigmatic, syntagmatic and pragmatic links is necessary for the cohesion of this complex discourse.

Paradigmatic temporal linkage is accomplished through flashbacks (for example, in *Prince Caspian*, chapters 7–9), and flashforwards (for example, in *The Magician's Nephew*, chapter 15). Duration also assists the reader in gauging the immediacy or remoteness of events along the temporal span of the story. This is absolutely necessary for subplots that do not conform to standard notions of time and end on the "same day and same hour of the day" (*Lion*, 196). These links are reinforced by various characters' retelling of stories, most times on account of eavesdropping or accidental overhearing (for example in *The Horse and His Boy*, chapter 8). We are often invited into that character's consciousness by the narrator himself when he at times makes analeptic or proleptic connections: "So the Dwarf settled down and told his tale. I shall not give it to you in his words, putting in all the children's questions and interruptions, because it would take too long and be confusing and, even so, it would leave out some points that the children only heard later. But the gist of the story, as they knew it in the end, was as follows" (*Prince Caspian*, 333).

In keeping with syntactic constructions of children's literature, sentences are frequently right branching, and the clauses are mainly linked by coordination, temporality and causality.[11] In the previous quotation, two of the three sentences are right branching, coordinated by the conjunction "and", with the subordinating conjunction "because". The reader is easily guided through a past event ("the Dwarf settled down and told his tale"), an aspectual action completed by the narrator ("I shall not give it to you in his words"), and a progression into the distant past ("But the gist of the story, as they knew it in the end, was as follows"). The narrator's mediation of the recounting of the events is accommodated by a cause-and-effect relationship: The Dwarf's imperfect account would be too long to record verbatim; hence the need for the narrator's editing. Anaphoric and cataphoric references are further used to link people, things, ideas and concepts between and among sentences. This extensive employment of endophoric references ranges from anaphoric pronominal references (his, it, they), to cataphoric phrases (as follows).

Lexical choices also operate in the text as paradigmatic links. The coining of the blend Calormene (coloured men) affords the narrator numerous opportunities to inextricably tie all the qualities and activities of these enemies of the Narnians to the colour of their skin. In *The Last Battle*, a new character, Puzzle, is introduced, and he is referred to interchangeably as "donkey" and "ass" by both the narrator and by another character, the ape, Shift. One can interpret the relationship of these lexical paradigms as reflecting the speaker's favourable or unfavourable judgment on Puzzle's actions at any given point in time. For example, the narrator introduces him as a donkey, but later on refers to him as an ass when he is outsmarted by Shift. When Puzzle tries to contradict one of Shift's schemes, Shift retorts, "What does an ass like you know about things of that sort? You know you're no good at thinking, Puzzle, so why don't you let me do the thinking for you?" (*Last Battle*, 672). As Puzzle begins to surrender to the scheme, Shift tries to pacify him: "And please don't let us have any more arguing. You know you don't understand these things. What could a donkey know about signs?" (*Last Battle*, 674).

Allegorical representations of characters, including the Pevensee children, gradually unfold paradigmatically across the chronicles to define characteristics that are contiguous with general thematic concerns. Peter becomes "King Peter the Magnificent . . . a great warrior"; Queen Susan the Gentle is "tall and gracious"; King Edmund the Just is "great in council and judgement"; Lucy the Valiant is "always gay and golden-haired" (*Lion*, 194, 195). The lion, Aslan, is a Christlike figure closely resembling the exophoric Christ of the New Testament. The children even meet "Father Christmas". One can interpret the qualities of the children as desirable Christian values in keeping with the mores of Narnia constructed by the Christ/Aslan ruler.

Pragmatic analysis of the discourse can reveal patterns of positively and negatively expressed values, as well as asserted and assumed evaluations of the narrator. This analysis raises two concerns of the text: the Calormene and modern education. In *The Last Battle,* there is a culminating description of the Calormene: "The next thing is that these were not the fair-haired men of Narnia; they were dark, bearded men from Calormen, that great and cruel country that lies beyond Archenland across the desert to the south" (*Last Battle*, 679). Throughout the series, Calormen(e) collates with dark and cruel. The name of the country and the people is the same but for the final *-e*, damning both the physical landscape and human inhabitants in one blow. These negatively expressed values are presented as assumed evaluations, and no one in the text, not even the Calormene themselves, debunk these propositions.

In *The Horse and His Boy*, the Calormene are the focus of a conflict with the Pevensee children-cum-royalty, and the depiction of this group is often juxtaposed against the "normal" Narnian cultural existence. The descriptions are usually filtered through the consciousness of the protagonist Sashta: "In the village he only met other men who were just like his father – men with long dirty robes, and wooden shoes turned up at the toe, and turbans on their heads, and beards, talking to one another very slowly about things that sounded dull" (*Horse*, 205). While there are only two lexical items in this sentence that have negative connotations (that is, "dirty" and "dull"), by semantic association, "wooden shoes turned up at the toe", "turbans" and "beards" all take on negative values. Even the Calormene way of talking is unflattering; the intensifier "very" preceding another adverb "slowly" concretizes this assumed evaluation. The Calormene use proverbs and quote poets in their everyday conversations, and add "may-he-live-forever" after the name of their ruler, Tisroc. The reader is also invited to share the narrator's evaluation of their speech: "Aravis and Cor prepared themselves to be bored, for the only poetry they knew was the Caloremene kind and you know now what that was like" (*Horse*, 309). The dichotomy of Calormene and Narnian lifestyles is presented throughout the narrative as positive versus negative, good versus evil:

> For one thing they were all as fair-skinned as himself, and most of them had fair hair. And they were not dressed like men of Calormen. Most had legs bare to the knee. Their tunics were of fine, bright, hardy colours. . . . Instead of turbans, they wore steel or silver caps . . . a few were bareheaded . . . and instead of being grave and mysterious like most Calormen, they walked with a swing and let their arms and shoulders go free, and chatted and laughed. One was whistling. You could see they were ready to be friends with anyone who was friendly and didn't

give a fig for anyone who wasn't. Sashta thought he had never seen anything so lovely in his life.

And immediately, mixed with a sizzling sound, there came to Sashta a simply delightful smell. It was one he had never smelt in his life before, but I hope you have. It was in fact, the smell of bacon and eggs and mushrooms all frying in a pan. . . . It was all new and wonderful for Shasta for Calormene food is quite different. He didn't even know what the slices of brown stuff were for he had never seen toast before. He didn't know what the yellow soft thing they smeared on the toast was, because in Calormen you nearly always get oil instead of butter. And the house itself was quite different from the dark, frowsty, fish smelling hut of Arsheesh and from the pillared and carpeted halls in the palaces of Tashbaan. (*Horse*, 231, 286)

Positively evaluated adjectives are used in describing the Narnians' dress, walk, demeanour and food. The narrator also strategically comments on the Narnians' fair skin and hair before proceeding with these descriptions. He links the images of the Narnians' skin colour to their qualities in much the same way that he does that of the Calormene. Again, by association, these apparently innocuous lexemes, such as "oil", "pillared", "carpeted" and "palaces", take on negative connotations similar to the lexemes "dark" and "frowsty". And yet again, these observations are contained in a character's consciousness ("Shasta thought he had never seen anything so lovely in his life; there came to Shasta a simply delightful smell"), within which the reader is invited to share by the omniscient narrator ("It was one he had never smelt in his life before, but I hope you have").

On the topic of an attempt to modernize secondary school education, the narrator does not covertly voice his opinion through a character. He declares openly of "Experiment House":

I shall say as little as possible about Jill's school which is not a pleasant subject. It was co-educational, a school for both boys and girls, what used to be called a mixed school; some said it was not nearly so mixed as the minds of the people who ran it. These people had the idea that boys and girls should be allowed to do what they liked. And unfortunately what ten or fifteen of the biggest boys and girls liked best was bullying the others. All sorts of things, horrid things, went on which at an ordinary school would have been found out and stopped in half a term; but at this school they weren't. Or even if they were, the people who did them were not expelled or punished. The Head said they were interesting psychological cases and sent for them and talked to them for hours. And if you knew the right sort of things to say to the Head, the main result was you became rather a favourite than otherwise. (*Chair*, 549)

This author's technique for representing the modernization process is embedded in a familiar pattern. On this occasion, he adopts the first-person mode of narration (internal type A), marked by foregrounded modality ("I shall say as little as possible about Jill's school which is not a pleasant subject"), inclusive of evaluative adverbs ("unfortunately") and adjectives ("horrid"). He uses a number of categorical assertions ("These people had the idea that boys and girls should be allowed to do what they liked"), primarily for the purpose of demeaning co-educational schools and, by extension, a modern approach to education. Co-educational schools are not, for the narrator, "ordinary" schools, and because of this, "horrid" things can be allowed to go on unpunished. The narrator's thoughts and feelings on these schools are further verified by the unnamed "some", who also further suggest that the school's administrators were psychologically unfit for their posts. The pun on the word "mixed" is used to support the notion of their ineptitude. For Calormene appearance and conduct as well as modernized education, the narrator employs a type of contrastive analysis to juxtapose the "normal" and "abnormal". In so doing, there is the presupposition that the reader, too, shares the same notions as regards values of normalcy and deviance.

Ideological Implications

Hollandale identifies three levels of ideology that often occur in written discourse and, by extension, children's literature. The first he refers to as an overt, often proselytizing or didactic level.[12] By adopting the first-person mode of narration as well as that of the omniscient narrator, the chronicler is able to overtly work along moralistic themes. It is clear that vices such as pride, greed, lying, betrayal, flattery and back chatting are the reasons for characters' downfall in the text, while the ones who give unconditional obedience are rewarded. Even when the didacticism is not explicit, the reader can infer the narrator's values. In the quotation "When I was at school one would have said, 'I swear by the Bible.' But Bibles were not encouraged at Experiment House", it can be inferred that the narrator supports the former practice involving the use of the Bible and condemns its neglect.

The second level of ideology that Hollandale identifies is a covert one, in which characters are used to articulate world views.[13] In *The Last Battle*, Tirian, the last of the Narnian kings, who is described as having "a fearless, honest face", says to the ape: "Ape . . . you lie. You lie damnably. You lie like a Calormene. You lie like an Ape" (*Last Battle*, 687). The implications here are that all Calormene lie, and, by comparing Calormene with Ape, that they both have other similar qualities. The dwarfs, who are sketched as a rude, jeering bunch in *The Last Battle*, yell at the Calormene: " Had enough, Darkies? Don't you like it? Why doesn't your great Tarkaan go and fight himself instead of sending you to be killed? Poor Darkies." They are mildly reprimanded for this slur by King Tirian, "Come here and use your swords, not your tongues" (*Last Battle*, 732). As a further example, after Shasta learns that he is really from fair-skinned Archenland parents who named him Cor and that Shasta was the name given to him by the Calormen, Aravis says: "Cor is a nicer name than Shasta" (*Last Battle*, 300). This world view is even more significant given the fact that Aravis is also from Calormen.

The third level of ideology identified is an underlying type of ideology that is couched in the climate of belief of the writer's time that undeniably informs the fiction.[14] In *The Chronicles of Narnia*, this fictional foundation is built on Christian doctrine and values. There are literally hundreds of intertextual links to the Bible and other Christian literature conjoined with metaphorical and symbolic references contained in the discourse. Indeed, Aslan is symbolic of the Christ figure. The hegemonic values of any given time will influence writers of the day, and it is always a thorny task to assign modern ideologies as yardsticks to judge books written in another place and time. It is vital though for educators to develop some sensitivity to the hegemonic values that have shaped discourses that are used as literary texts in formal educational settings.

One way to determine dominant values of these chronicles is to examine the lifestyle of the favoured hegemonic group. The Narnians eat the "right" kinds of foods, wear "suitable" clothing, have a "correct" way of walking, hold "appropriate" names, speak in a "proper" manner and possess the monopoly on religious legitimacy. In *The Voyage of the Dawn Treader*, the narrator describes the child Eustace before his adventures and re-education in Narnia: "He didn't call his Father and Mother 'Father' and 'Mother', but Harold and Alberta. They were very up to date and advanced people. They were vegetarians, non-smokers and tee-totallers, and wore special kind of underclothes" (*Dawn Treader*, 425).

The "right" diet is not a vegetarian one, an opinion that is incongruent with the eating habits of some vegetarian groups in the Caribbean. Factions in this region that refrain from tobacco or alcohol for religious and other reasons may be classified into this satirized group of "up to date and advanced people". In terms of clothing, comparable to the Calormene, turbans and long beards are also customary for some local ethnic and religious groups. The act of naming has many implications for power relations and, historically, Caribbean peoples have had to change their African and Asian names to more anglicized ones to access education, jobs, housing and other social opportunities. It is not uncommon to hear individuals within an ethnic group scoff at names that reflect their own heritage, much in the same way that the Calormene, Aravis, tells her fellowman of his new Narnian name: "Cor is a nicer name than Shasta." Perhaps, though, one of the most important values to address (especially in relation to the language arts curriculum) is that of notions of "correct" and "proper" languages as opposed to "incorrect" or "broken" languages that differ grammatically and stylistically. The language attitudes within the text are reminiscent of those prevalent in creole spaces. Caribbean creoles have generally been viewed as substandard to the lexifier languages or official languages or both. Interestingly, proverbs and sayings provide pragmatic context for regional creole discourse, yet these are the same stylistic features derailed in the text. Finally, while Christianity is a major creed in the region, it shares religious liberty with other faiths, and interfaith activities are encouraged.

One of the themes in this text that has received much attention from critics is that of race relations. The dark-skinned Calormene are characterized as evil, greedy, cruel, deceitful, pretentious, egotistical, extravagant, stupid, spoilt, useless woodsmen; lazy sentries; misguided religious zealots; cowards, wantonly violent ... the list of negative qualities gets longer with each episodic adventure. To compensate for their dysfunctional existence, they own slaves. As aforementioned, their bad ways are inextricably tied to the colour of their skin, as are the good qualities of the Narnians. In *The Last Battle,* when the children are preparing to ambush the Calormene by smearing themselves with a special dark juice, the Narnian King Tirian warns that "After this has hardened on us, we may wash in water and it will not change. Nothing but oil and ashes will make us white Narnians again" (*Last Battle,* 697). The black/brown versus white colour diatribe runs counter to the multi-ethnic and multiracial continuum that epitomises the Caribbean Creole space. One way of maintaining this physiological composition is through interracial marriages. In *The Horse and His Boy,* however, this practice is frowned upon. King Peter asks his sister, Queen Susan, "Have you settled in your mind whether you will marry this dark-faced lover of yours . . . ?" When she responds in the negative, he is relieved: "I should have loved you less if you had taken him" (*Horse*, 234).

Gender relations in *The Chronicles of Narnia* is another theme that has been expounded upon by critics. Phillip Pullman accuses the narrator of being "monumentally disparaging of women".[15] In *The Last Battle*, Susan, who had formerly been a queen in Narnia, is described by her brother King Peter as "no longer a friend of Narnia" since, according to the new queen, Jill, "She's interested in nothing nowadays except nylons and lipstick and invitations" (*Last Battle*, 741). For three of the books, the villains are not collective entities, but a single archenemy: a strong, domineering, manipulative witch. There is no male equivalent throughout the entire discourse. Critic Karin Fry posits that the narrator, through characters' voices in the discourse, "[has] positive and negative things to say about both male and female characters, suggesting an equality between sexes. However the problem is that many of the positive qualities of the female characters seem to be those by which they can rise above their femininity . . . The superficial nature of stereotypical female interests is condemned."[16]

Caribbean women have traditionally been highlighted as the cohesive force of their families, as well as the embodiment of survival. Their potency and fortitude are celebrated in Caribbean oral and written discourse. Creole proverbs in the oral tradition attest to their unwavering strength (for example, one's breasts are never too heavy for one's chest), and in the literature they are often celebrated for their long-suffering and resilience, at times in contrast to their European counterparts. Perkins and Mohammed, in an interview with contemporary Caribbean women, report that these women consider "agency" and "self-perception" as obstacles for obtaining what they want in life. This affects their self-confidence and assertiveness.[17] While the assertive woman in the texts has been associated with having evil and contentious ways, the loss of this assertiveness contributes to feelings of agentlessness and decreasing intuitive awareness among modern-day Caribbean women.

Closely linked to gender are thematic concerns of childhood and innocence. In the text, only "bad" children talk back to their elders. In *The Lion, the Witch and the Wardrobe*, Edmund is portrayed as a spiteful bully, so it is he and not Lucy who talks back to his elder sister: "And who are you to say when I'm to go to bed? Go to bed yourself" (*Lion*, 111). This low tolerance of "back talk" is also shared by the Calormene. Shasta is boxed in the ear for it by a soldier: "Take that you young filth, to teach you how to talk to free men" (*Lion*, 229). The philosophy of children being seen and not heard has been damaging to the psyche of the Caribbean child.[18] The same is true of the philosophy of unconditional obedience of the child, yet in these chronicles, unquestioning obedience is seen as model behaviour. Only those who conform are blessed, any deviance is ruthlessly crushed. The obedient child is also expected to be humble. Young Prince Caspian is asked by Aslan, "Do you feel yourself sufficient to take up the Kingship of Narnia?" to which he replies, "I – I don't think I do, Sir, I'm only a kid." This is an acceptable response from a child for Aslan says, "Good, [if] you had felt yourself sufficient, it would have been a proof that you were not" (*Lion*, 411).

Growing up and subsequent loss of innocence are two unfortunate intermediate states between childhood and full adulthood, as can be garnered from the depiction of Susan's journey through these conditions. Eustace reports her loss of faith in Narnia, which can be read as a loss of innocence: "whenever you've tried to get her to come and talk about Narnia or do anything about Narnia, she says 'What wonderful memories you have! Fancy your still thinking about all those funny games we used to play when we were children.' " Her two female acquaintances join in denunciation of her attempts to "grow up": " 'Grown-up indeed,' said the Lady Polly. 'I wish she would grow up. She wasted all her school time wanting to be the age she is now, and she'll waste all the rest of her life trying to stay that age. Her whole idea is to race on to the silliest time of one's life as quick as she can and then stop there as long as she can.' " Jill confirms this position: "She always was a jolly sight too keen on being grown-up" (*Lion*, 741).

This aversion to Susan's growing up and loss of innocence exemplifies the popular literary construction of "the child as a pure point of origin in relation to language, sexuality and the state . . . children's fiction emerges, therefore, out of a conception which places the innocence of the child and the primary state of language and/or culture in a close and mutually dependent relationship".[19] These ideologies of childhood innocence and primacy must be interrogated within the Caribbean context, especially in light of the didactic deliberations in the text.

The chronicle's narrator gives his opinion of modernization attempts in secondary school education; as seen earlier, his most scathing criticism is documented in *The Silver Chair*. One cannot escape the irony of using this text in an education system that is attempting to move from a traditional philosophical background to a more progressivist one. The Trinidad and Tobago language arts curriculum was first conceived under the Secondary Education Modernization Programme (SEMP). One can submit, therefore, that many of the values of *The Chronicles of Narnia* are incompatible with creole culture (which is heavily influenced by Caribbean history and philosophy), as well as contemporary attempts at progressivist education.

The Caribbean Classroom

The inspiration for the title of this chapter comes from an exchange between a teacher and her student in a local form 1 classroom during a language arts period. The class was asked to categorize individual characters in *The Lion, the Witch and the Wardrobe* into groupings of "black heart" or "white heart", according to each one's actions throughout the text. The student in question raised two issues. He noted that the main threat to the children in the story was a white witch (so why the designated assigning of black/white heart?) and that some characters, for instance Timnus the Faun, could not decisively be placed in either category. He recommended a third grouping – "grey heart" – in which to place characters that could be described as neither totally bad nor totally good. His teacher applauded his critical thinking.

Umberto Eco comments on polysemous texts and readers' ideological responses to such texts. He proposes that some readers will question a text to reveal underlying ideologies; it can be argued that the aforementioned student questioned the text based on his process of reasoning. However, Eco also hypothesises two other reader responses: assumption of ideologies and aberrant readings of the discourse.[20] In an online discussion on the themes of race, religion and sexuality in *The Chronicles of Narnia*, twenty-two out of twenty-five respondents expressed similar sentiments of having enjoyed the books a great deal when they were younger, and feeling that any prejudiced treatment of these themes went "right over [their] heads".[21] It is quite possible for Caribbean students to also engage in aberrant evaluations of the text, or to unconsciously absorb precarious ideologies within the discourse.

Policymakers and educators may view children as vulnerable and susceptible to errant ways of thinking and may determine that part of their professional responsibility is to protect their charges from exposure to manipulation.[22] However, I do not recommend censorship of *The Chronicles of Narnia* (or any book on the language arts reading lists). Not dealing with issues that seemingly contradict a value system is not equivalent to protecting children. In fact, educators must accept that no text is value free and that in any given discourse, there will be tension between narrated ideology and readers' value systems. Educators must therefore devise ways to navigate between these two boundaries.

Language arts teachers should be sufficiently trained in literary-linguistic analysis to be able to examine discursive practices in any literary text. This kind of analysis also explores point of view from various angles and uncovers how these perspectives affect ideology. Van Lier advises that "one of the first tasks of language awareness is to examine the so called 'normal' and to see if it really is the way it's supposed to be and the way we want it to be".[23] Teachers (as guides and learners themselves) can benefit from an investigative practice that allows them to cross-examine issues of "normalcy".

Secondary school students are expected to develop skills in literary analysis of texts, especially literary devices and discussion of chronology and plot. *The Chronicles of Narnia* provides a wide range of opportunity for analysis as literary text through its fantasy element, connection to the epic tradition (life as journey, battle and so on) and rich use of literary devices (allegory, metaphor, symbolism and so on). The chronological arrangement of the plot and the order in which the sequels are presented can be surveyed to illustrate the concepts of chronology, plot and story.

As guides in the pedagogical process, teachers can manipulate how much time is spent discussing certain topics. They may choose to obfuscate some themes until a more suitable time, while foregrounding others: children in the text as brave, shapers of their own destiny, making choices for survival and displaying filial love. Issues can be interrogated as they are raised by the students themselves, which may be an indicator of their ability and readiness for evaluating more controversial ideas. According to education psychologist Jerome Bruner, schools waste time by postponing the discussion or teaching of important areas that are assumed to be too difficult or contentious. He subscribes to "the hypothesis that any subject can be taught effectively in some intellectually honest form to any child at any stage of development", and from this hypothesis comes his notion of the *spiral curriculum*.[24] He sees the spiral curriculum as one that facilitates students' gradual conceptualizing of subject-content and problem-solving abilities by "revisit[ing] basic ideas repeatedly, building upon them until the student has grasped the full formal apparatus that goes with them".[25]

Classroom practitioners can generate much discussion and interest in *The*

Chronicles of Narnia by allowing students to reinterpret the text and context. Narnian geography can be explored, and its flat world can be reordered to resemble the Caribbean archipelago. Students may be able to find similarities among Caribbean mythological figures and the Greek, Celtic and other mythological figures of the text. They may also wish to provide alternative endings to some scenes in the books or to give a specific character a voice to justify or apologize for an action.

Given the profound influence that a writer's time, life experiences and world view has on his work, it may prove to be an insightful exercise for students to research an author's biography with the intention of understanding the influences that shaped his ideology. Students may uncover that, while an author might try to experiment with novel – perhaps even revolutionary – ideas, threads of thoughts that are reflective of the era in which the author lived could persist. Learners can then be directed to their own ideological condition to begin a process of interrogation of taken-for-granted assumptions of their own time.

Conclusion

The conceptualizers of the English language arts curriculum explain that "the curriculum also immerses students in the literatures of different cultures in order to encourage them to develop respect for diversity and aesthetic values, and at the same time to support their language learning process".[26] This exposure to literatures of other cultures should not inhibit the development of "the values and competencies that will prepare [students] to see themselves as citizens of Trinidad and Tobago, the Caribbean region, and of the world; to value the diverse cultures and language experiences that characterize our society".[27] One of the intended learning outcomes of the curriculum is to "use language to reflect and support creative and critical thinking".[28] This curriculum is founded on a constructivist approach to learning, in which "learners actively create and construct their own meanings or understandings".[29] Thus, open dialogue and uninhibited expression of discourse between clients and practitioners of the curriculum will not only allow for cross-examining of pertinent issues related to *The Chronicles of Narnia* and other literary texts, but will also facilitate enjoyable exploration of this literary classic.

Notes

1. Curriculum Development Division, Trinidad and Tobago, Ministry of Education, *The Secondary School Curriculum: Form One, Two, Three Language Arts* (Port of Spain: Ministry of Education, 2008), 1–11.
2. *Aslan* is the Turkish word for lion.
3. The former is also referred to as "perceptual point of view". See Gerald Prince, *Dictionary of Narratology* (London: University of Nebraska Press, 2003), 71; and the latter as "psychological point of view". See Paul Simpson, *Language, Ideology and Point of View* (New York: Routledge, 1993), 11.
4. Barbara Lalla, "Creole Representation in Literary Discourse: Issues of Linguistic and Discourse Analysis", in *Exploring the Boundaries of Caribbean Creole Languages*, ed. Hazel Simmons-McDonald and Ian Robertson (Kingston: University of the West Indies Press, 2006), 173.
5. Gerard Genette, *Narrative Discourse* (New York: Cornell University Press, 1980), 188.
6. C.S. Lewis, *The Magician's Nephew*, 11. This book is included in the compilation by C.S. Lewis, *The Chronicles of Narnia* (New York: Harper Collins Publishers, 2001). All subsequent quotations from this novel, as well as from the other novels in the series, are taken from this edition, and references to the novels appear parenthetically in the text.
7. Simpson, *Language, Ideology and Point of View*, 39.
8. Roger Fowler, *Literary Criticism* (Oxford: Oxford University Press, 1986), 127–47.
9. *Verba sentiendi* are words denoting thoughts, feelings and perceptions.
10. A more detailed example is in *The Lion, the Witch and the Wardrobe*, in which the narrator focuses an entire chapter (nine) on Edmund, most of which he uses to outline his faults.
11. John Stephens, "Analyzing Texts for Children: Linguistics and Stylistics", in *Understanding Children's Literature*, ed. Peter Hunt (Ithaca: Cornell University Press, 1980), 65.
12. P. Hollandale, *Ideology and the Children's Book* (New York: Signal 55, 1988), 3.
13. Ibid.
14. Ibid., 4.
15. Phillip Pullman, "The Dark Side of Narnia", *Guardian*, 1 October 1998, 2.
16. Karin Fry, "No Longer a Friend of Narnia: Gender in Narnia", in *The Chronicles of Narnia and Philosophy: The Lion, the Witch and the Worldview*, ed. Gregory Bassham and Jerry L. Walls (Chicago: Open Court, 2005), 155.

17. Patricia Mohammed and Althea Perkins, *Caribbean Women at the Crossroads: The Dilemma of Decision-Making among Women of Barbados, St Lucia and Dominica* (New York: University of the West Indies Press and International Planned Parenthood Federation, 1998), 97.
18. H. Evans and R. Davies, "Overview of Issues in Childhood Socialization in the Caribbean", in *Advances in Applied Developmental Psychology*, volume 14. *Caribbean Families: Diversity among Ethnic Groups*, ed. I.E. Sigel, J. Roopnarine and J. Brown (Stamford, CT: Ablex Publishing, 1997), 5.
19. Jacqueline Rose, *The Case of Peter Pan or the Impossibility of Children's Fiction* (London: Macmillan, 1984), 8, 9.
20. Umberto Eco, *The Role of the Reader* (London: Hutchinson, 1981), 22.
21. http://www.boxxet.com/The_Chronicles_of_Narnia/news:add-a-personal-message (accessed 13 March 2009).
22. Peter Hunt, *Understanding Children's Literature* (New York: Cornell University Press, 1980), 2.
23. Leo Van Lier, *Interaction in the Language Curriculum: Awareness, Autonomy and Authenticity* (London: Longman Group, 1996), 19.
24. Jerome Bruner, *The Process of Education* (New York: Vintage Books, 1960), 33.
25. Ibid., 13.
26. *Secondary School Curriculum*, 22.
27. Ibid., 23.
28. Ibid., 24.
29. A.C. Ornstein and F.P. Hunkins, *Curriculum: Foundations, Principles and Issues* (Boston: Pearson, Allyn and Bacon, 1998), 254.

10.

Using *For the Life of Laetitia* to Teach Character Development to Form 3 Special Students

» KAREN SANDERSON COLE

ADOLESCENT PREOCCUPATIONS WITH CONCEPTS of identity, decision making, and coping with change are some of the themes addressed in *For the Life of Laetitia*, by Merle Hodge. These themes were selected to teach "character development" to a group of form 3 "special students", using the approach of *critical literacy*. Critical literacy is an approach that seeks to maximize the connections that can be made between the home or cultural environment of the learner and the formal education system. Quantitative and qualitative methods of assessment were used to monitor the effectiveness of the intervention. The findings bear out the founding principle of critical literacy: that a context-specific approach to teaching, in which the text and activities are related to the cultural and social environment of the learner, will positively assist lower-achieving students to grasp and respond relevantly to the issues posed in literary works. However, these students need more time to achieve the mastery level required.

Introduction

In a postmodern era of Internet chat, cell phones, portable play stations and the like, the teacher of literature is continually challenged to find new and interesting ways to engage the attention of the adolescent at the secondary level. The ante is upped when the target population is the twelve to sixteen age group and is literacy challenged. Traditional approaches to teaching have focused on the "listen-to-me-and-learn" model, according to Thelma Cey.[1] Using this approach with students who are literacy challenged often proves too big a leap, given the difficulties of these students with reading and writing. This method does not promote knowledge that is meaningful, context appropriate and engaging.

Whatever their level of skills, however, students need tools to enable them to communicate their thoughts and feelings across the barrier of limited grammar, spelling and reading skills. Special students also need to develop critical literacy skills to successfully participate in the wider discourses of their society. Critical literacy provides a foundation for addressing some of the problems that literacy-challenged children have in the classroom because it uses the knowledge students already have. It aims to find ways to make links between this knowledge and the target literacy goals. It provides a means, according to Barbara Comber, of getting the most out of students' schooling experience.[2] A reorientation of teacher expectations is needed, which may mean, as Comber argues, that teachers need to redefine what they accept as "school literacies" because "we cannot even fully predict all the genres and sites in which textual and information practices will be crucial in the coming decades".[3]

Critical literacy seems more compatible with an increasing trend in education towards a constructivist approach. *Constructivism*, according to Thelma Cey, is based upon key principles, such as the personal construction of reality of the learner, simulated authentic learning environments, active learning and collaboration.[4] Creating these learner-centred environments presents even more challenges to the teacher already faced with the pressure of having to cover more information in rapidly decreasing time, but effective learning requires that strategies be sought to capitalize on students' experiences.

This chapter comes out of research undertaken to prepare a group of sixteen "specials" for the national secondary assessment examination in literature, in which character development is a significant theme. The aim of the study was therefore to use critical literacy as an approach to teach a unit on character development. The objectives were to enable students to apply critical analysis to evaluate character responses to given situations, to justify their assessment and opinions of characters by providing textual support and to develop genre competence in answering literature-based questions.

Background

Morale is usually low among students who are placed in government secondary schools known as junior secondary schools in Trinidad and Tobago. Few students who take the Secondary Entrance Assessment examination indicate these schools as their first choice. *Special* for these children means that they have not met the basic level of literacy acceptable for entry into secondary school, and remedial efforts are necessary to help them approach the required standards. Not meeting the entry requirements for secondary school does not mean that all are at the same level in their literacy. Competencies vary, which creates an additional challenge in preparing material appropriate to their needs.

Traditional approaches to teaching literature do not assist these students in formulating opinions on issues raised in a given text or in making the necessary links to their lives that make the study of literature meaningful. At the junior level, literature-based questions have a predetermined structure. The first two questions ask for factual knowledge: name of book, name of character. The next two questions ask for application skills: explain, predict, discuss. What this has meant for students who have basic deficiencies in decoding texts is that performance on writing-based examinations is poor. Student difficulties are evident in a number of ways. First, their responses show a lack of information about the characters in the text or the predicament the character faces or both. Second, students seem unable to explain the events related to character or make connections or links outside the text.

Target Group

The special class used in the study was considered one of the better ones, in that there were more students with basic competency in reading and writing than other special classes in the school. The class consisted of sixteen students: seven boys and nine girls. Most of the students could read at the level of the standard 2 primary school student. Two children (one boy and one girl) could not read at all. Another boy was at the second-year kindergarten level in reading, and one other boy was at the standard 1 level. The girls were generally better readers. Despite their low competence in reading, most students seemed embarrassed to admit they did not enjoy reading. Given a questionnaire, eleven responded positively to the question "Do you love to read?" but their responses on the other questions did not bear this out: Only four owned books outside of mandatory school texts and, of the texts read, only one was not a novel studied in class. Maximum participation is generally received via oral work, that is, the teacher reads while students listen or attempt to follow in their texts.

Theoretical Base

The field of critical literacy is wide and has spawned a number of different approaches. At their root, though, is a belief that knowledge is ideological: Reality cannot be known definitively, and textual meaning is culturally and historically defined. Critical literacy builds on the work of Paulo Freire, who believed that the teaching of literacy should be combined with the social context of the learner. Words, he argued, could not be separated from the context in which they were used, and situating them in their real-life context engages the reader in a critical analysis of the word.[5] This concept has been adapted in the study of literature in different ways. According to a document produced by the Tasmanian government for its English-language teachers, critical literacy is based on "an active, challenging approach to reading and textual practices".[6] It encourages the development and use of questioning what lies beneath the surface of the text. It focuses on the purpose of the text, the culture in which it is created and the agency of the individual to participate in the changing of the world or social order.

In "A Tale of Differences: Comparing the Traditions, Perspectives and Educational Goals of Critical Reading and Critical Literacy", Cervetti, Pardales and Damico argue that there are fundamental differences between critical literacy and critical reading that, when not properly understood, lead to a misappropriation of practices. They argue that critical reading rests on four assumptions: knowledge, reality, authorship and goals of literacy instruction. In this model, reality exists as an objective reality: a reference point against which experience can be tested for reliability. Knowledge, on the other hand, is gained through experiencing the world. Cervetti et al. see critical literacy as a process of construction, not exegesis; therefore "one imbues a text with meaning rather than extract(s) meaning from it".[7]

With specific application to literature, critical literacy stresses the evaluation of characters in terms of how children, teenagers and young adults are constructed in the text; why the composer of the text has represented the characters in a particular way; and the manner in which the text portrays different age, gender or cultural groups. There are a variety of strategies available to a teacher who wants to use a critical literacy approach. In "The Questioning Circle", knowledge of text, reader and world forms the basis of questions that are asked about a given text.[8] Students are encouraged to question the content presented, their personal response and the wider world in which the text can be seen.

Olson suggests that teachers use a combination of literary and non-literary strategies to develop critical literacy: clustering ideas to brainstorm and organize information, anticipation guides that can help students tap into prior knowledge and reading charts to assess attitudes before and after reading.[9] Other strategies such as REFUSE – *r*eally ask questions, *e*xamine all the consequences, *f*ind alternatives, *u*se persuasion, *s*tate all consequences, *e*xit from the situation – can help students develop a tool to analyse character dilemma in literature, as well as evaluate situations in their own lives. Pincus also provides a list of activities that assist learners in charting the sequence of steps involved in assessing a decision.[10]

Thus, a critical literacy approach can be particularly useful in motivating and improving the literacy level of challenged students by homing in on the literacies that they already possess. Adapting various teaching strategies that tease out the connections that can be drawn between the informal and formal environment underpins this objective.

Design of Study

Ten sessions were organized to assess the intervention. Applying critical analysis to evaluate character responses to given situations was an objective in all of the lessons. Text, reader and world formed the basis of the organization of each unit. Text consisted of newspaper articles, cartoons, greeting cards, written transcripts of students' speech and edited versions of the main text, *For the Life of Laetitia*. The reader was the student, and the world existed in the applications to the wider society, which students were encouraged to make during each lesson. Specific strategies, such as Directed Reading Thinking Activity (DRTA),[11] were also used to help develop comprehension skills, along with REFUSE[12] to encourage students to assess the logic of decisions made. Teacher-made assignment sheets combined yes/no charts and paragraph assessments to provide quantitative and qualitative data for determining the extent to which students understood assignments

Each lesson focused on an aspect of adolescent development. Lessons 1 to 3 addressed character response to social challenges; lesson 4, the impact of family support on academic success; lesson 5, suicide; lesson 6, coping with adjustments;

and lessons 7 and 8, "the art of refusal". Lessons 9 and 10 were used for evaluation and feedback.

Each lesson was structured with an opening activity to highlight students' pre-knowledge of the theme to be studied. Oral discussion was encouraged. An extract from the text would be read, problem vocabulary would be addressed and then students would be put to work on specific activities. In each lesson, students were required to justify their responses to issues raised. Students were put in groups of four to allow for discussion and collaboration but were expected to respond individually.

The Text

For the Life of Laetitia, by Merle Hodge, was chosen because it presents a number of character dilemmas to which the target group of students could relate. The main character is a twelve-year-old girl making the transition from life in a small village as part of a large, extended family to life in the city with a father she barely knows, in his nuclear family. She must also cope with the changes that come as a result of successfully sitting the national secondary placement test, which propel her from the primary to the secondary school level. Over the course of her first year of secondary school, Laetitia must cope with unfair treatment from a teacher, her relationship with a father she barely knows and increasingly feels alienated from, the suicide of a close friend and accepting responsibility for the consequences of her actions.

Results

The research objectives were to use a critical-literacy approach to get students to apply critical analysis in evaluating character responses to given situations, justify their assessment and opinions of characters by providing textual support and produce a written paragraph to express evaluation of character and situation.

Applying Critical Analysis to Evaluate Character Responses to Given Situations

Lesson 2 provides an example of the assessments used to evaluate the extent to which students were grasping the idea of applying critical analysis to evaluate character responses. The theme was one to which they could quickly relate: unfair judgement of students by a teacher. Mrs Lopez, one of Laetitia's teachers, makes it clear that the homes from which the students come make it a waste of the government's money to educate them. The primary instrument used was a pre-reading and post-reading chart. Students were told to read five statements and answer "yes" or "no" to each one. An extract from the novel, which the students had to orally summarize, was read. They were then told to refer to their sheets again and answer the same questions. They were then asked to select a specific statement from the sheet and, using evidence from the story, justify their response. Responses collected showed a number of inconsistencies, which suggested that students did not fully understand what was required of them.

Table 10.1: Student Responses Before and After Reading Text

Statements	Before Reading		After Reading		No response
	No (disagree)	Yes (agree)	No (disagree)	Yes (agree)	
1. Grandparents are not fit to bring up children	9 (69%)	4 (31%)	6 (46%)	5 (38%)	2
2. Children from single-parent homes cannot do well in school	8 (62%)	5 (38%)	6 (46%)	6 (46%)	1
3. Fathers are seldom responsible for children	1 (18%)	12 (92%)	3 (32%)	9 (69%)	1
4. It is a national waste of money to educate poor children	13 (100%)	0 (0%)	11 (85%)	4 (31%)	1
5. Children of parents without education will never be better than their parents	11 (85%)	2 (15%)	8 (62%)	4 (31%)	1

Table 10.2: Student Responses in Paragraphs

Statements	No (disagree)
1. Grandparents are not fit to bring up children	3
2. Children from single-parent homes cannot do well in school	1
3. Fathers are seldom responsible for children	3
4. It is a national waste of money to educate poor children	5
5. Children of parents without education will never be better off than their parents	1

Analysis of Tables

The number of students who disagree with the statements is almost always greater than those who agree, both before and after reading the text. The only exception to this trend occurs with the view of fathers being seldom responsible for their children. In this case, twelve students, or 92 per cent, agreed with statement 3 on fathers. Even after reading the text, in which evidence to the contrary is provided, the number disagreeing with the statements remained greater than or equal to the number of those who agreed. Thirty-one per cent (four students) responded using supporting evidence from the text. With regard to statement 3 on fathers, for example, one student wrote: "fathers do be responsible in their own way", and one other responded that "Laetitia's father responsible because he take Laetitia to go home by him". Fifty-four per cent (seven students) responded based on their personal experience. Students did not see any ambiguity in the statement on whether or not grandparents are fit to bring up children, interpreting this based on their own experience of growing up with their grandparents. One response, for example, was "my two brothers grow up under they grandparents and they are very good children". The statement on the government wasting money to educate poor children drew much ire from students, evident in responses like "poor would tern out to be bandits" and "some children . . . was not able in class so they would not pick up fast so they are wrong".

Comparing the results of the pre-reading and post-reading chart, the results suggest that, at the end of lesson 2, while there were changes in the views held by students concerning the statement, more than 50 per cent were not able to use supporting evidence based on the text to justify their answers.

Justify Assessment and Opinions of Characters by Providing Textual Support

By lesson 4 on family support, all students demonstrated ability to extract evidence from the table to compare and contrast the circumstances of the two characters, Laetitia and Anjanee. In this lesson, they were asked to assess the elements of family support that impact academic success, compare and contrast the family support the two characters receive and evaluate the effect of this support on a child's success at school. Both oral and written responses were accepted. Some of the written comments were critically insightful. On the importance of financial support, one student said, "I read somewhere in the book where Anjanee's mother does give her money to come to school but not all the time." Another student noted that "Laetitia's father gives her money to come to school but he doesn't use encouraging words". On Anjanee's lack of support, one student wrote: "Anjanee can also be successful as well if she rely want to do well at school, by studying every day without studying what is going on in her life and try to be better than her parent."

Develop Genre Competence in Answering Literature-Based Questions

Results of examination-type questions in lesson 8 and in class 9 show that there was some improvement in developing genre competence. However, students needed a lot of assistance to keep on track. After eight lessons, the accuracy of providing an appropriate answer improved, but students still did not produce a paragraph. The average length of the response rose to about three lines, which was an improvement. This improvement suggests that students, when given "props", such as blanks to fill, were able to successfully complete them; but in free responses, students' skills failed.

In lesson 9, students were given a question from a past paper to answer. Here, again, the response was not expansive, but when the responses were corrected and given to the students to answer again, answers were fuller. The stronger students' answers ranged from three to six lines. Students showed an improved

Table 10.3: Scores of Eight Students Who Participated in Final Evaluation

Student	Marks Scored	Percentage
1	7	54
2	5	38
3	11	85
4	9	69
5	7	54
6	1	8
7	1	8
8	8	62

Notes: Maximum possible mark = 13; standard deviation = 1.83.

understanding of the need to support answers with reference to the text and also of the need to provide reasons for their answers. Significantly, no additional characters were made up, and no one included any nursery or fairy tales, which were problems before the intervention.

A level of mastery of 54 per cent is considered acceptable. Five students (63 per cent) attained this level of mastery.

Discussion

Making the link between everyday experiences and what happens in the literary world was the most important approach to teaching character development to literacy-challenged students. When they can see themselves in a text, they are motivated to involve themselves in it, despite the difficulties. Even though creating excitement in the classroom does not equate with a significant increase in student learning, student participation and interest in classes were very encouraging. They chided each other for not following the story. Edited versions of the text sections helped students to focus on the issues. These were necessary as well because the novel interrupts the linear order of events at times. By lesson 5, students had a grasp of the method being used, that is, an affective introduction and then the text dilemma, so much so that one student remarked: "Miss trying a set of psychology with us in these English classes these days!"

The intervention did not help all students in the class. Students need a baseline of literacy skills to fully participate in each lesson. For two students in particular, the stretch seemed too much. However, because students remained involved in the classroom activities, there were fewer instances of misbehaviour, and once present, they did not run away from classes (although other teachers complained about them on both accounts). The onus is on the teacher to commit to finding the best ways to hone in on students' individual and collective skills and build on them. A number of approaches must be used, and there will not be a textbook formula for addressing all of their needs.

For the teacher, the experience underscored the importance of being able to understand how people learn. The process helped the teacher to see the issues presented in the novel from new perspectives, and the challenge of finding ways of creating activities for students was a source of motivation.

Recommendations

Individual strategies and social realities must be merged to help low-achieving students succeed in the secondary school system. Special students need longer blocks of time in which to work: forty to forty-five minutes are not sufficient to improve mastery of a task, even though time has to be balanced against shorter attention spans and high frustration levels. Students often need to be redirected to a task, but with enough time they will complete it. Students also need time to do and redo assignments to assist in building the literacy skills they need. Being able to chart their progress while redoing assignments helps to build confidence that they, too, can achieve. Students also had problems in thinking through an issue in a sequential manner. Breaking up an activity into small chunks with explicit questions after each section was helpful, as was providing strategies such as REFUSE in giving them a checklist they could use to evaluate their own progress. More time has to be devoted to individual help; the teacher sat with each child, which also motivated them to try.

Links have to be made for students so that they can make connections between the opportunities education offers and the quality of life in their own communities. They are not doomed to the lives of their parents or grandparents and those around them. At the same time, parental support is important. Parental support is needed to curb the problem of student absenteeism – although *For the Life of Laetitia* offers us, in the experience of Anjanee, a grim picture of the conditions that make it almost impossible for parents to provide the support that is necessary. But this is not always the case. One parent admitted that her child was kept at home any time the child indicated she did not wish to attend school. Attendance over the course of the intervention varied. At the last session, only eight students were present.

Administrative issues also have an impact on the progress or lack of progress in the classroom. During the course of the study, classes were disrupted for a number of reasons ranging from the spraying of the school to eye testing (three days) to a spoilt classroom lock (also three days to repair). School administrators must increase their level of sensitivity to the impact of external stimuli on the classroom environment.

The findings of the study bore out the founding principle of critical literacy: a context-specific approach to teaching, in which the text and activities are related to the cultural and social environment of the learner, will positively assist lower-achieving students to grasp and respond relevantly to issues and dilemmas posed in literary works. More time, however, is needed to achieve the mastery level required.

Notes

1. Thelma Cey, "Moving towards Constructivist Classrooms" (paper submitted for EDCOMM 802.6, University of Saskatchewan, Saskatoon, Saskatchewan, 10 February 2001), 3.
2. Barbara Comber, "Critical Literacy: Maximizing Children's Investments in School Learning" (draft discussion paper presented at the Resource Teachers Literacy Training Programme, Christchurch College of Education, New Zealand, 12–13 July 2002).
3. Ibid., 13.
4. Cey, "Moving".
5. For a fuller discussion of significance of Friere's contribution to development of critical literacy see Ira Shor, "What Is Critical Literacy?", *Journal for Pedagogy, Pluralism and Practice* 4, no. 1 (Fall 1999): 1–27. http://www.lesley.edu/journals/jppp/4/shor.html.

6. Department of Education, "Critical Literacy", Tasmania, School of Education Division, http://www.education.tas.gov.au/curriculum/standards/english/english/teachers/critlit.
7. Gina Cervetti, Michael J. Pardales and James Damico, "A Tale of Differences: Comparing the Traditions, Perspectives and Educational Goals of Critical Reading and Critical Literacy", *Reading Online* 4, no. 9 (April 2001), http://www.readingonline.org/articles/cervetti/index.html.
8. L. Christenbury, "The Questioning Circle", in *Making the Journey: Being and Becoming a Teacher of English Language Arts* (Portsmouth: Boynton-Cook/Heneman, 1994), 245–46.
9. C.B. Olson, *The Reading/Writing Connection: Strategies for Teaching and Learning in the Secondary Classroom* (Boston: Pearson Education, 2003).
10. Debbie Pincus, *Feeling Good about Yourself: Strategies to Guide Young People toward More Positive, Personal Feelings* (Carthage, IL : Good Apple, 1990).
11. In DRTA, students are encouraged to assess book titles, pictures, or other pieces of information for clues about the content of an article. These predictions are recorded in a chart on the board and are confirmed or rejected as the article is read.
12. Mary Karsten, *Developing Healthy Self-Esteem in Adolescents* (Parsippany, NJ: Good Neighbor Press, 1995).

11.

"We Supposed to Have Fun"
Voice and Resistance in the Primary School Classroom

» ROWENA KALLOO

> Big belly Arthur eat chataigne parata,
> To be the most musical farter.
> He could play anything,
> From "God save the King",
> To old school like Sinatra.
>
> Piggy on the railway picking up stone,
> Up come ah engine truck . . .
> Those were happy days,
> Really happy days,
> School days was really happy days.
> –The Mighty Sparrow, "Happy Days", 1963

THE MIGHTY SPARROW'S POPULAR calypso, "Happy Days", reminds us of the intimate link between childhood in Trinidad and Tobago and primary education.[1] Its lyrics are mischievous children's rhymes that have been sung on local playgrounds across the generations. Through the eyes of the nostalgic adult, the calypso might signify a time that was happier, perhaps simpler and innocent.

However, if we foreground the voice of the child rather than the adult, a child's world that is the counterculture to the official world of the school becomes evident. The mischievous twist of the lyrics conveys a sense of children who are not simply passive recipients of knowledge or experiences but are actively interpreting and reconstructing their experiences of schooling. In this counterculture, children have a voice, which is not often heard within the classroom.

The calypso provides a cultural context to raise the questions that are the focus of this chapter: Why should children's voices be part of the dialogue in education? What do children's experiences contribute to understanding pedagogy and primary education in Trinidad and Tobago? These questions are discussed through the voices of standard 4 students[2] in a denominational primary school in Trinidad, as they speak to a defining experience of schooling in this country: the rigorous preparation for the Secondary Entrance Assessment (SEA).[3]

I begin this chapter by addressing questions on the relevance of children's voices. A brief methodology of the study is outlined before the presentation of children's conversations, framed by the culture of the school, classroom and the voice of the teacher. The data are contextualized by a discussion on the historical and cultural implications of the SEA for primary education in Trinidad and Tobago. This chapter closes with a reflection on the implications of children's expressed concerns for moving beyond postcolonial traditions of schooling to more democratic, enriching and imaginative forms of primary education.

Defining Voice

The concept of voice emerges from the interpretivist paradigm of the social sciences. For the interpretivist, social reality is constructed by the individuals who participate in it, and reality is therefore shaped by historical, political and social context in which individuals exist.[4] Voice is therefore a central component of unearthing social reality. Bogdan and Bilken describe the quest of the phenomenologist as an attempt to "gain entry into the conceptual world of subjects, by seeking to give their voice legitimacy".[5]

Voice as agency speaks to persons' rights to participation, to be heard and to have their issues regarded and acted upon. Michelle Fine argues that the process of education is to allow "children, adolescents, and adults their voice – to read, write, create, critique and transform".[6] Voice, then, is not simply a tool for entry into the world of children, but also a representation of the legitimacy of children's words and an acknowledgement of their status as "creative participants in the world".[7]

Why Voice?

There are cognitive, psychological and ideological perspectives on the voice of children. These perspectives span concerns from optimizing learning to issues of social justice. I will discuss four such perspectives.

Voice is Central to Constructing Meaning

Lincoln refers to this aspect of students' voices as the *scientific context*.[8] The work of the cognitivists, Piaget, Vygotsky and Bruner, has established that learning is an active process in which learners construct new knowledge through interaction with their physical and social environment.[9] Constructivism argues that the school's role is to provide students with the experiences necessary to construct new and more powerful conceptual knowledge. Lincoln writes, "since schooling is one of the most powerful shapers of both learning and acquiring world-view, it makes sense to attend to ways in which children actively shape their contexts".[10] Within this scenario, students' voices are necessary for teachers to understand the experiences that children bring to the classroom. This knowledge of children's experiences allows teachers to develop meaningful frameworks for conceptual understandings.

Research into how students actively construct understanding and make sense of their world spans a wide range of subject areas: mathematics, reading and science.[11] Of interest to Trinidad and Tobago, in particular, is the research into street science by June George.[12]

George analyses the intersection between local, traditional knowledge of the natural world and that of conventional science. The latter is based on an epistemology valuing logic, questioning and tentativeness, and the former is grounded in the weight of social authority. George and Glasgow have suggested that the epistemological schism requires the creation of "border crossings" into an alternative paradigm, and to cross, students must have the opportunity "to air and discuss their beliefs with regard to scientific topics . . . being studied at any particular time".[13] Voicing then becomes a prerequisite to children constructing more powerful and indigenized models of knowledge.

Students' Voices Are Necessary to Build a Democratic and Participatory Culture in Classrooms

The Trinidad and Tobago Educational Policy Paper (1993–2003) suggests a need to create and sustain a humanized and democratized system of education for the survival of our democracy.[14] Despite the goals of the White Paper, research cited by Phillips, Jules, the United Nations Development Programme, and Deosaran strongly suggests that systemic and classroom variables work against the humanization and democratization of schools and classrooms.[15] These researchers highlight the way in which the stratified system of education and the uneven starting points of children within the local system reproduces or at least creates the milieu for sustaining social inequities. Phillips, investigating juvenile delinquency in the junior secondary schools of Trinidad, uncovers a complex intersection of school malaise, community deprivation and multiple levels of abuse, which children in her interview claimed to have experienced. It was by providing a platform for students' voices that the research was able to draw attention to the hidden curriculum of the school, in which the main agenda, as Phillips states, is not the subject of the official curriculum, but an attempt by students to satisfy their pressing needs for comfort, love and security.[16]

Deosaran's work cites the gap in academic performance and school cultures between the traditional, denominational secondary schools and the comprehensive schools that house the majority of students. Despite this cultural gap, he notes the lack of civic mindedness evident in the pervasiveness of bullying across all schools, regardless of academic performance. Although largely ignored by school personnel, bullying is identified by students as having a major impact on their physical and psychological safety in secondary school.[17] Indeed, the UNDP report concludes that a critical consideration at the secondary level is the "need to treat the individual with dignity and worth".[18] These conclusions derive their legitimacy because students' voices informed the data, and it is difficult to conceptualize either democratization or humanizing of the school system if children and youth are silenced within their schools.

Voice Acknowledges and Reaffirms the Personhood of the Child

Lincoln argues that there has been a progressive shift in societal understanding of children: from notions of the child as chattel property to "children as both the inheritors and the inheritance of the future".[19] The White Paper on Education in Trinidad and Tobago echoes these sentiments in its vision for education, describing education as an enterprise of futuristic visioning that can create "individuals with the intellect and capacity to develop and lead societies, communities, villages and families of the future".[20]

Trinidad and Tobago, as a signatory to the Convention on the Rights of the Child, acknowledges its commitment to the three Ps of the convention: provision, protection and participation. In so doing, it accepts in principle that rights have shifted from a concept of welfareism to entitlement based on issues of social justice.[21]

Voice Is a Fundamental Tool in Children's Psychosocial Development

Psychosocial theory describes the formation of adaptive personality traits – "prime adaptive ego qualities" – as individuals' progress through life. Traits emerge because of the ability to resolve a number of psychosocial crises that occur at each stage of development, and the resolution at one stage promotes growth at later stages. Ability to resolve such conflicts results in adaptive ego qualities, such as hope, industry and identity, to name just a few.

The ages of six to twelve, the primary school years, are critical to the development of the ego quality of industry, through which children are motivated by the desire for mastery, competence and the external rewards associated with industry. Industry may be the precursor to the development of positive attitudes towards work in the adult years.

Education, largely through school, provides students with opportunities for mastery, but also with teachers who are models for commitment to learning. Teachers can give students a sense of how much more there is to learn and the motivation to acquire goals and standards for developing more advanced skills.[22]

Equally important is the development of social skills, which at the elementary school level can often be overshadowed by the emphasis on building basic skills like literacy and numeracy. Newman and Newman have argued that, without social skills, children remain unable to master their environment.[23] Primary education therefore plays a pivotal role in children's development, cognitively, psychologically and socially.

Further, Helen Bee observes that the reciprocal nature of relationships at this stage is important, because there are lessons that can only be learned in social interactions.[24] Bee's observation of reciprocity points to the integral role of children's voices in their own psychosocial development and in dialogue with an important other: the teacher.

Caribbean Culture and Children's Voices

> And don't come home here and tell me he [teacher] had to beat you, because I will give you my share of licks too.[25]

In Caribbean culture, the difference in status between children and adults is clearly demarcated. The quote above, from the novel *Salt*, reflects a well-recognized relationship between the home, the school and the child. Within this tradition it is disrespectful for a young person to "answer back", that is, provide an opposing point of view to an adult. In local parlance, to do so is considered being too "womanish" or "mannish", signifying unacceptable disrespect to adult authority. Indeed, Janet Brown, in documenting parental attitudes to children's rights in Jamaica, observed that parents viewed rights with "suspicion", as "foreign constructs", imported and alien to Caribbean parenting practices.[26] Brown states, "[p]arents seemed fearful that children would hear in the new rights language, permission to speak their own mind, to argue back when in disagreement, with parent or authority, or to insist on privileges and independence not yet earned".[27]

Such attitudes may be rooted in a more global perspective of the qualitative differences between childhood and adulthood. Douglas Sturm has proposed that the experimentation and playfulness of childhood and children's dependency on adults not only demarcates childhood from adulthood but also "constitutes a normative boundary, specifying what possibilities are appropriate to the class of persons assigned to either side of that boundary".[28] This boundary, Sturm argues, constitutes a boundary of "domination", in which the adult gains the right to have authority over the child, and which can serve to negate the agency of children.

Sturm provides an alternative conceptualization of childhood. He suggests that "children, even while undergoing diverse stages of development, are, like adults, creative participants in the world community . . . and should be respected as such".[29]

Despite the cultural reservations described, several initiatives by the private and state sector have begun to provide opportunities to hear the opinions of youth and children. Some of these include student councils, which are being encouraged by the Ministry of Education, the Royal Bank of Trinidad and Tobago Young Leaders' Projects and the United Nations Children's Fund-sponsored Caribbean Child Research Conferences.[30]

Despite these initiatives, less emphasis has been placed on the voice of the elementary-school child. More commonly, as previously elaborated, issues of youth apathy and violence act as an impetus to provide teenagers with a forum for voice. It is only within recent times that work such as that by Jerome Delisle et al., presented at the 2009 "First They Must Be Children" conference, and this author's work, have deliberately sought to investigate the voices of children at the primary school level.[31] Regardless, I have attempted to argue that there are cogent ideological and educational reasons that support the need for the academic and wider community to hear, not just our teenagers, but our younger children, as well. By providing a platform for children's voice, the academic goes beyond speaking to issues of school policy and practice. A platform for voice recognizes the status of children as important contributors to their school community.

Focus of the Chapter

This chapter presents the voices of standard 4 students as they speak to their experiences in preparing for the SEA. The data are excerpted from my doctoral thesis, an ethnographic study on the dynamics of teacher-pupil relationships in a standard 4 classroom.[32] The research provided a platform for children's voices, and their embrace of this platform is itself a testimony to their resistance to silencing.

This chapter uses children's voices to interrogate the nature of their experiences at a pivotal point in their primary education. In so doing, it addresses the following questions: How do children interpret the demands of being a standard 4 pupil? How do they situate themselves as creative agents within the autocratic boundaries of schooling? How do they negotiate the curriculum with their significant other: their teacher? What are the larger lessons of schooling and childhood that children wish for us to learn?

Methodology

This study used Lawrence Lightfoot's Portraiture as its method of inquiry.[33] *Portraiture* is an ethnographic method that represents the culture of a group in narrative form through the constructs of context, voice, relationships and emergent themes. These constructs speak to the epistemological assumptions that underpin the qualitative paradigm and, more specifically, the ethnographic tradition. Portraiture attempts to describe rather than control the complexity of the social milieu and recognizes that voice is a central interrogating tool. Portraiture, like ethnography generally, represents human culture in its complexity, searching deeply rather than broadly for its truths. These imperatives determined the small sample size: one class and its participants in one school.

The data presented here were collected over a two-year period between 2000 and 2002. During this period, I observed five classes, one class each from standard 1 to standard 3, and two standard 4 classes, one of which was the pilot class. Each class was observed for two weeks each in the first term and for one day in the third term. In each class, I interviewed the teacher and students and collected and reviewed archival data, such as students' report cards, demographic data, textbooks, exercise books and photographs of the school compound and classes. The principal and vice-principal were also interviewed. The archival data served to triangulate interviews and to create the context of the study. All interviews were tape-recorded and transcribed. Most of the observational classroom data for the standard 4 class described here was collected in the first two weeks of the September-to-December term. During this term, I attended the school for the full day, sitting in the classrooms as a non-participant observer, following children out to the playground where the interviews took place, sharing snacks and conversations and building relationships in which children could feel safe to give voice to "their" stories.

From CEE to SEA[34]

Several educators have argued that the SEA has assumed disproportionate significance in the organization of the primary school curriculum in Trinidad and Tobago.[35] Delisle describes the SEA as a standardized test that evolved from the now-defunct British Eleven-Plus, which was a "corrupting legacy". While justifying the importance of examinations as tools that can provide data to improve classroom practice, he argues that the SEA exam distorts both the mission and organization of primary school, with its narrow focus on preparation for testing. In so doing, it has led to a de-emphasis on classroom testing, the early segregation of students and largely homogeneous approaches to instruction.[36]

The grip that SEA exerts on primary education in Trinidad and Tobago is located in the intersection of historical and political events as primary and secondary schooling developed in the islands. These events include the early inception of mass post-emancipation primary education, aspirations of the black masses for social mobilization, secondary education as one of the few social mechanisms for such mobilization, and a select and elite secondary school system available only to the most competent of black academics or the fee-paying bourgeoisie.[37] When one considers that, as late as 1916, there were fifty thousand elementary students, but the total enrolment at the four recognized secondary schools was just seven hundred, the fierceness of the competition for secondary school places can be easily understood.[38]

By independence, in 1962, the college exhibitions for denominational schools had been replaced by the Common Entrance Examination (CEE). The CEE acted as a meritocratic mechanism that allowed children across boundaries of race and class to enter the limited secondary schools that existed at that time. However, in the 1970s, when secondary education expanded through the establishment of the junior secondary and senior comprehensives,[39] allowing access to a wider range of middle- and lower-income students, the examination had already shifted from its purely meritocratic objectives to a hotly contested race for the denominational schools. In 2000, Trinidad and Tobago had attained universal secondary education, the examination had changed name and format three times, its sorting function was well established and school choice had become embedded in the popular psyche as a right of the people.[40]

The SEA has an enormous impact on children's lives. SEA preparation is characterized by a routine of drill and practice, past papers and extra lessons and the inevitable reduction of playtime. For most children, these sacrifices may not allow them to access the small number of coveted denominational schools.

Despite this reality and the sacrifices asked of children during this period, children's voices are conspicuously absent from decisions concerning the examination and its preparation. However, given the research on children's cognitive and psychosocial development and the goals of democratic and participatory schooling in Trinidad and Tobago, it is reasonable to suggest that children's voices would be integral to academic, developmental and institutional outcomes.

Background: School Traditions

The standard 4 class under present study is in a Catholic primary school, with a low- to middle-income clientele, in a low- to middle-income suburb. All names have been altered to ensure anonymity. The principal described his staff and students as "good people", reflecting a desire to do well by the children, to be "family". The school revolved around a daily routine of prayer, didactic teaching and autocratic discipline including the use of corporal punishment. Steelpan lessons, a parang (folk music) group, singing classes, a cricket team, library periods, the Christmas play, end-of-term class parties and the celebration of Catholic traditions filled the school year. At the time of this study, society was debating the abolition of corporal punishment in schools, and the principal and staff were experiencing the anxiety of possible change. The long-standing rituals and traditions of this school, juxtaposed with changing social understandings of the child as a subject of rights, created a dynamic that foreshadowed the themes of classroom life.

Standard 4A

This particular standard 4, comprising ten boys and seven girls between nine and eleven years, was labelled the A class. "A" was a label of academic competence rather than giftedness, and there was a range of abilities in the class. Their teacher was an experienced professional, who had been teaching for at least fifteen years. She was new to the school, and this was her first term.

The classroom was without walls, a space surrounded by blackboards, like so many primary classrooms in Trinidad. The blackboard that separated it from the neighbouring standard 5 class had a fist-sized hole through which the children could peek at one another. Standard 4A was part of the upstairs school, the downstairs school being infants and the lower school.

Standard 4 was also the beginning of the preparation for the SEA, which is administered in the second term of standard 5. SEA examined only English language and math. In the last revision of the examination, which brought with it the change of name, the science and social studies components were removed to decrease the pressure of the workload on students. The result was that, in some of the more competitive schools, these subjects were not taught at the upper levels. However, the new standard 4 teacher, Mrs Fortune, taught both social studies and science, although she mainly focused on math and language.

Serious Work

Although the teacher had just met her class, she quickly established its routine and culture. Learning in standard 4 was serious work, and this seriousness revolved around perceptions of the examination. As the teacher explained:

> I would like to take these straight up and work with them . . . to Common Entrance. Don't know how much they are ready to really . . . get as much work done, because . . . It's not a tea party. It's work! . . . . You have to work as well as enjoy the work, . . . It's (the) seriousness that goes along with, you know . . . (May 2002)

Serious work meant a continuous diet of drill and practice after the introduction of a concept, certain attitudes and skill mastery. Students were expected to focus, to work at a brisk pace and have priorities that were academic and are not merely for personal enjoyment:

> **Teacher:** If you work quickly and quietly you would finish on time and wouldn't have to stay in lunchtime. You all focusing on the wrong thing, colouring! This is not an art class. (Day 3, math lesson illustrating fractions in tenths on squared paper)

Accuracy meant the correct answer was expected, and wrong answers would not be tolerated:

> **Teacher:** Any foolish sentences and I'm reading for the whole class to hear! I want well thought-out sentences that make sense! (Day 2, English lesson, feedback on students' sentences)

The expectation of high standards of performance by all children with consistent, homogeneous outcomes was equally important. After giving a short class test in English, the teacher had students call out their marks for their peers. During this exercise she said:

> **Teacher:** See who fails? All the talkers! If Sandra can get 70 per cent and others 70 to 80 per cent everybody should be able too! (Day 9, test feedback)

Expectations of accuracy, seriousness, focus, speed and significant written output were all tools for achieving high marks on standardized testing.

When two boys did not complete their homework, with the excuse that they were ill, the teacher began to scold the class, using the exam as the measure by which they should judge the consequences of their actions:

> **Teacher:** Whatever you do, and however you do, you reap the benefits later on. So when we see people like Sandra going to a good school later on we can look at the work she did. And when we see somebody else going to a school he doesn't like, you can look to see.

While feedback was ostensibly given with the aim of improving children's academic performance, it also relayed messages about students' competence ("see who fails"); character ("the talkers") and the relative status of members of the class (Sandra versus the rest). It is easy to observe how insidiously notions of failure in the exam slip seamlessly into failure of the child.

Superman Hand: Children's Voices

The children understood that their teacher's passion was directed to their achieving success, but "serious" work was not easily tolerated. The following dialogue brings out the tensions that SEA preparation created and the multiple perspectives through which children interpreted the curriculum:

> **Alice:** Miss, I find she giving us enough work, because I does work fast and most of the people in class does work slow. That is why they would say that.
>
> **Claudette:** You must be superman . . . Miss, today we get plenty work. Twenty sentences. We look like superman [*laughter from the rest of the group*] . . . What we look like? We have superman hand, so we could just put your eyes on the pencil and the pencil writing your work! (Week 2, excerpts from a lunch-break interview)

The following conversation began in response to the question, "How do you feel about your new class?":

> **Sandra:** Miss, I had like her first till the beginning of the term. She kind of good. She does give us work. . . . But sometimes, I doesn't like how she does want us to write fast, because she think we should be writing fast since we in standard 4, and I know we going in standard 5; but most of us does write slow, and we does have to study plenty.[41]
>
> **Charlie:** She quarrelling with us because we is be laughing. But Eccles and them is be making jokes and I cyah hold back my laugh!
>
> **Lawrence:** She want everybody to stay long and droopy. (Group interview)

The children's grumblings reveal the disjuncture between their age-related needs and the demands of the work. The work places stress on their

- Physiological needs: for water, to use the toilet, to have a snack, in the face of the teacher's demand that they "finish first in everything".
- Developmental capacity: as inherent in the amount of concentration and writing of which they are capable, as well as the amount they must accomplish: "I know we going in Standard Five, but most of us does write slow."
- Emotional and psychological needs: for fun, to laugh and be a child ("she quarrelling with us because we is be laughing"; "I cyah [can't] hold back my laugh") and adult demands to uphold a serious demeanour ("If we smile, she say that is disrespect").
- To feel safe from threats and fear of threats: "She want people to laugh so she could give them licks!"

There is a subtle difference in the perception of "serious", of which neither teacher nor students seem fully aware. For the teacher "serious work" is fruitful labour, but for the children, it is "droopy face" work, a seriousness whose quality is the antithesis of childhood. The teacher's concept of "serious work" seems impervious to the children's psychological needs, as she is focused on the goal of examination success and the perceived opportunities that will benefit those who enter the high-performing, denominational secondary schools. Ironically, despite the status and social significance of the SEA,[42] neither the examination nor its preparation through drill and practice provides students with opportunities for authentic learning, although schools try to compensate for this loss by having an enriched curriculum in the term following the examination.

Hard Work Is Good

Despite students' grumblings, they described their teacher as "a good teacher" because she gave them "work". On one occasion, students willingly stayed in to complete an assignment and did without their break, justifying their actions by noting: "Miss says we work too slow" (Yasmin), "so we want to finish before the others" (Harry).

The children voluntarily tried to appease the teacher, accepting her opinion that they needed to improve their performance; their actions reflect the legitimacy of the teacher as the authority figure. The children also reflected the culture of respect given to education. As such, the children tended to give schoolwork and hard work a positive value.

Here was Lawrence's view of hard work:

RK: What makes teachers favourites for you?

Lawrence: When they give you games (physical education) and thing, and some hard work.

RK: Hard work is good?

Lawrence: Yes, Miss.

RK: Why is hard work good?

Lawrence: Don't know; it does help you learn better, Miss.

Even students like Claudette, who complained she lacked a "superman hand" and struggled with her studies, expressed a positive value for work. Here she describes the benefits that she could derive from education:

> I like to do work . . . it good to do more work to learn more things about animals, science and to do it well for when you get your own business and thing. . . . Well I want to try to do my best in class, so like I could beat Sandra and I could pass for a good school and when I leave school I could get a good job. . . . I could have money to build my own business, big business, a restaurant or something. (Student interview 4, 8)

Children's protests were not directed at opposing teacher authority or supporting "laziness", but rather at the frustration of being forced to operate beyond their capacities. However, despite the students' belief in hard work, their capacity to adhere to the work regime was mitigated by their physical, emotional and psychological developmental needs.

The teacher's actions were supported by a belief in which children, rather than the system, were at fault for their failure: The talkers failed, not the system. The belief system was a function of the teacher's biography: the experiences of her life world and cultural pressures, inadvertently promoted by the cultural status assigned to success on the SEA. This personal belief system acted as a masking theory, as it hid those aspects of learning and teaching that would impute the system, and allowed the reproduction of the didactic and traditional forms of knowledge, which promoted success on standardized testing. In that sense, the culture of examination preparation was forcing the teacher to ignore students' developmental needs. The result, however, was the creation of a debilitating tension in the teacher-pupil relationship, in which the teacher's intentions were never fully appreciated or understood by many of the students in the classroom.

The Talkers: Voice as Resistance

> **Claudette:** Harry, I, Netty, Linda, Eccles and Charlie, we real like to talk in that class. Sometimes if Miss doing work we only talking right through, and Harry, Harry does real make up the rudest thing. It does sound kind of good you know, it not all that rude it just kind of – yeah. (Student interview 2, 8)

There was no doubt that students in standard 4A did not simply react to Mrs Fortune's demands. As the student quotation above suggests, instances of disobedience were often deliberate acts of resistance. Resistance was subtle, understated and carefully timed. Children could not risk overt aggression because of the absolute power of the teachers, yet through their understated acts of resistance, they found a space in a classroom that actively, albeit unconsciously, suppressed their voice.

There were several reasons why children deliberately resisted the demands for silence in the classroom. One reason simply had to do with the human need to bond, communicate and share with someone of their age. Here, some of the "talkers", as the teacher labelled them, describe their reasons for talking.

> **Claudette:** I don't find that talking does distract me because when Miss [class teacher] give us the work, I was talking to Collin while I was writing and I finish nearly everything before the bell ring.
>
> **Harry:** So I think talking is good, so you could write more faster.

Another reason triggering disobedience was the pull of their different learning styles:

> **Claudette:** And you could have a music in your head and a rhythm. I does kind of ride the rhythm and write and I listen to the rhythm and . . . that doesn't distract me.

A predominant reason for resistance was to offset boredom, to have some fun. Some of the children described the classroom as a boring place, lacking in stimulating and engaging activities.

> **Harry:** I think it is very boring . . . because we do not get games very often and Miss [class teacher] send us inside [referring to an incident during which they were punished by the teacher's banning of physical education] . . . and when she teaching she does talk so tired, everybody does get so tired.

Children's responses to the teacher's style reflect the diversity of learners and personalities in any one classroom, yet each child was offered the same diet of knowledge and teaching/learning strategies. The teacher's pedagogy was not idiosyncratic but actually reflects a didactic teaching style that is typical and pervasive in schools in Trinidad and Tobago. Despite the didactic style, the teacher did provide individual attention to students, and students positively acknowledged these efforts.

Partial compliance as a means of offsetting boredom and creating the interactivity and fun necessary for engagement provided psychological rewards that could override the cultural goals of examination preparation. The goal of partial compliance was not – as in other studies of students' resistance in European and American cultures – to prevent the teacher from doing her work or even to evade work.[43] The students evaded work when they could no longer comply with its onerous demands. Their resistance can be better perceived as an attempt to communicate to their teacher their physiological and psychological needs and to create a sense of themselves as agents. In this context, resistance is a response to silencing, an attempt to create an avenue through which children could make a stance for their right to engaging, authentic and creative learning.

No Sweat

Children's differentiated resistance to rules was not only related to learning style but was also dependent on maturity and could be gendered, again reflecting the diversity of needs among this age group. An example is the resistance to the "no sweating" rule, which was not just the teacher's rule, but an expectation of many teachers in the school. Teachers frowned on students who played so vigorously they entered class with their shirts damp from sweat. Children could be punished by being hit or scolded. This was a rule that was particularly difficult for the boys, who found it almost impossible to obey, even when they could faithfully repeat the teacher's reason. The diverse nature of their responses is illustrated in the following conversation:

RK:	Yesterday your teacher say, you all cannot run about and get sweaty. What do you think about that rule?
Justin:	That is a good rule because if you come in the class sweaty, you would smell stink and you can't do any work in the class. That is why Miss put the rule from the start when we come in the class.
RK:	Okay, do you intend to stop playing football on a lunchtime?
Justin:	Yes, Miss.
RK:	You're not going to play any more. Did you play yesterday?
Justin:	Yes, Miss.
RK:	So how come you played yesterday?
Justin:	I didn't have anybody to play with me, so I went and play football yesterday.
RK:	What about Vaughn? What you think about the no-sweat rule, Vaughn?
Vaughn:	Miss, I don't like to sweat.
RK:	So you weren't playing football yesterday?
Vaughn:	Yes Miss, but I didn't run about so much, Miss.
Student:	Miss, and we was not sweating so much.
Charlie:	If I become a big footballer now, and playing for Trinidad and win the World Cup, what she go say now?

The conversation illustrates the dilemma in which children are placed when their physiological needs are in conflict with their cultural socialization for obedience and the contradictory logic they must use to support their positions.

For the Love of Children

Despite the discourse of tension and conflict that characterized standard 4A, Mrs Fortune cared deeply for her children. At least three of the students were allocated places in denominational academic schools, a rarity in this largely working-class school, as the scores to enter these schools represented the top 10 to 20 per cent of students. In the second term, one of the girls described her as "very, very, very kind" because she helped her with her work.

After the teacher noticed a negative comment about her in one of the students' questionnaires, she was upset and attempted to make a connection between the removal of corporal punishment from schools and children's increasing rebelliousness, which included the challenging of her authority.[44] However, in the midst of this criticism, when I asked her how she coped with this new dispensation, she said sincerely that she loved her class: "You know me, I love my class and you know they will get me mad or angry at some point but I just warm up in another way, another spirit . . . You know they're warm and a nice bunch. And I suppose many of them have their shortcomings because of their home setting too . . . Children react because of some things, you know." Standard 4A always contained the odd, contradictory behaviours that did not seem to blend with either the students' or the teacher's opinions of each other. I observed children sharing poems and life stories with their teacher and the teacher listening with empathy.

Mrs Fortune's expression of affection and the children's attempts to communicate with their teacher on personal matters reflect a desire by teacher and child for transactions of affection, for the development of community. Community transformed the teacher and her students from being merely victims of the system, grappling with tangible cultural pressure to develop a product: examination success. Through the desire for community, teacher and students discarded their prescribed roles and related to each other in personal and humane ways. In these rare scenarios, although the adult-child difference in status did not disappear, it was not overshadowed by either party's need to dominate the other. The teacher listened and empathized, as in the case of Justin, or admired and affirmed, as in the case of Andres's poems. Justin and Andre were often critical of the teacher's management and pedagogical style, reflecting the tensions between teacher and students previously described. However I observed Justin candidly sharing stories of his drug-infested neighbourhood one-on-one with his teacher, and Andre bringing the poems he composed for the teacher to read. When I found the teacher and Justin deep in conversation, she was not denying his story, not doubting whether it was true, exaggerated or otherwise; she was an empathetic listener. The relationship here was not simply task oriented, but one in which the adult used her power to support the student, rather than control the individual.

Such interactions are significant because they intimate that teachers and students are not solely defined by the prescribed roles of postcolonial schooling. They are first human beings and have the emotional and affective needs of all human beings to be part of a community. These incidents also highlight the ways in which teacher and students use their agency to redefine themselves and step outside the boxes predefined and orchestrated by larger sociopolitical and cultural forces. Such agency has implications for places in which interventions in the system should be located, whether at the symbols of tradition, such as in the changes to the examination culture, or at the microcosm of schools among students and teachers in their classroom.

"We Supposed to Have Fun": Lessons from Children's Voices

> We are children and we suppose to play, have fun as a child so when you grow up you wouldn't have time for that, so let us enjoy being a child . . .

Children recognize the potential of school to provide an avenue for a better life. Their belief in the power of education is uniquely Caribbean and echoes the historical antecedents of schooling as an instrument of mobility. Through their voices we recognize that

1. Postcolonial structures of curriculum and examination, which define schooling by promoting autocratic relationships and linear models of knowledge transmission, are inimical to children's psychological and cognitive well-being.
2. Children's agency is directed to the expression of their rights – to be heard and seen – and the need for affirmation and mutual respect.
3. Children have a deep desire to develop transactions of affection that affirm the human spirit with the most important person in their school life: their teacher.

The children's voices in standard 4A also spoke to their capacity for rationality, to understand context and purpose in its more nuanced form and therefore to contribute to their community in meaningful ways.

When Charlie stated categorically that the no-sweat rule was bad because one day he could be a "big-time footballer", he signified the meaning of childhood and its promise for the future. Childhood events hold the key to the next decade, whether through the production of "big-time footballers" or female restaurant entrepreneurs.

These data suggest that the absence of children's voices in the dialogue about education is no signifier of the importance of that voice. Further, whether or not children are provided with a platform for voice, they have the capacity to make themselves heard: whether through resistance to authority or by seizing opportunities that become available.

Children's voices also provide a deeper context for teachers' voices. When Mrs

Fortune passionately states her love for her students, one can hear the conflict that the teacher faces between the need to at once be a caring human being and to be an authority figure constricted by cultural norms that negate the kinds of relationships that affirm a partnership of learning. In that sense, voicelessness is not just a symptom of childhood but is also imposed unwittingly on the teacher.

The teacher-child bond does not exist in a vacuum; it is shaped by the historical, political and cultural facets of the community. It must be a collective duty, rather than the job of individual teachers, to construct an environment that can allow schools and teachers to redefine themselves in ways that honour children's voice and agency and in so doing create the humanized and democratic environment that the society envisions as its future.

Notes

1. Carl Campbell, *Colony and Nation: A Short History of Education in Trinidad and Tobago 1834–1986* (Kingston: Ian Randle, 1992). Primary school was the only free education for the masses of the population from immediately after post-emancipation until the 1950s, when the thrust to independence led to increasing emphasis on the expansion of secondary education (71–75). Note, however, that while the whole book illustrates this point, the pages cited are about only the expansion of secondary education. Not only was primary schooling intimately tied to childhood but also to the development of whole communities that revolved around the school and its church for their intellectual and spiritual life.
2. The classes at primary level are referred to as standards. Standard 4 is the equivalent of grade 4, and children in this grade are usually nine to ten years of age. However, due to retention policies in the school, this class of seventeen students had one child who was twelve years of age.
3. Rowena Kalloo, " 'No Easy Thing': A Portraiture of the Dynamics of Teacher-Pupil Interactions in a Standard Four Primary Classroom in Trinidad" (PhD diss., University of the West Indies, St Augustine, 2008).
4. W. Jerry Willis, *Foundations of Qualitative Research: Interpretive and Critical Approaches* (Thousand Oaks, CA: Sage, 2007); Walter R. Borg and Meredith D. Gall, *Educational Research: An Introduction* (New York: Longman, 1989).
5. Robert Bogdan and Sari Knopp Bilken, *Qualitative Research for Education: An Introduction to Theory and Practice* (Boston: Allyn and Bacon, 1998), 23–24.
6. Michelle Fine, "Silencing in Public Schools", *Language Arts* 64, no. 2 (1987): 172.

7. Douglas Sturm, "On the Suffering and Rights of Children: Toward a Theology of Childhood Liberation", *Cross Currents* 42, no. 2 (1992): 155.
8. Yvonna S. Lincoln, "In Search of Students' Voices", *Theory into Practice* (Spring 1995): 88.
9. Peter Smith and Helen Cowie, *Understanding Children's Development* (Oxford: Blackwell, 1991), 315–73; David Woods, *How Children Think and Learn: The Social Contexts of Cognitive Development* (Oxford: Blackwell, 1992), 1–54.
10. Lincoln, "In Search of Students' Voices", 89.
11. On mathematics, see Megan L. Franke, Noreen M. Web, Angela G. Chan, Marsha Ing, Deanna Freund and Dan Battey, "Teacher Questioning to Elicit Students' Mathematical Thinking in Elementary School Classrooms", *Journal of Teacher Education* 60, no. 4 (2009): 380–92. On reading, see Elizabeth Bondy, "Seeing It Their Way: What Children's Definitions of Reading Tell Us about Improving Teacher Education", *Journal of Teacher Education* 41, no. 5 (1990): 33. On science, see Bonnie L. Shapiro, "What Children Bring to Light: Towards Understanding What the Primary School Learner Is Trying to Do", in *Contemporary Analysis Education Series: Development and Dilemmas in Science Education*, ed. Peter Fensham (London: Falmer Press, 1988), 73–95; and Richard F. Gunstone, "Learners in Science Education", in *Development and Dilemmas in Science Education: Contemporary Analysis Education Series*, ed. Peter Fensham (London: Falmer Press, 1988).
12. June George, "Culture and Science Education: A Look from the Developing World", American Institute of Biological Sciences, http://www.aibs.org/action-bioscience/atom.xml; Joyce Glasgow and June George, "The Boundaries between Caribbean Beliefs and Practices and Conventional Science: Implications for Science Education in the Caribbean", in *Education For All in the Caribbean: Assessment 2000 Monograph Series*, ed. Lynda Quamina-Aiyejina (Kingston: UNESCO, 1999), 28.
13. Glasgow and George, "The Boundaries between Caribbean Beliefs and Practices and Conventional Science", 22–23.
14. C. Keller, Preface, "Education Policy Paper 1993–2003 White Paper" (Port of Spain: Ministry of Education, 1993). The Education Policy Paper 1993–2003, is also referred to as the White Paper on Education, as opposed to the Green Paper, which is the version put out for public consultation. The Green Paper was laid in Parliament on 12 March 1993, xviii.
15. Research cited by Daphne Phillips, "Juvenile Delinquency in Junior Secondary Schools in Trinidad: The Hidden School Curriculum" (prepared for the

American Sociological Association Annual Conference 2008, Boston, 2008), http://www.allacademic.com/one/www/www/index; Vena Jules, *A Study of the Secondary School Population in Trinidad and Tobago: Placement Patterns and Practices* (Trinidad: Centre for Ethnic Studies, University of the West Indies, St Augustine, 1994); UNDP, *Trinidad and Tobago National Human Development Report 2000: Youth at Risk in Trinidad and Tobago* (Port of Spain: UNDP, 2000); Ramesh Deosaran, *Benchmarking Violence and Delinquency in the Secondary School: Towards a Culture of Peace and Civility*, volume 2, The General Report (Trinidad: Ministry of Education, 2004).
16. Phillips, "Juvenile Delinquency".
17. Deosaran, *Benchmarking Violence*.
18. UNDP, *Trinidad and Tobago National Human Development Report 2000*, 49.
19. Lincoln, "In Search of Children's Voices", 88. Interestingly Mary John, *Children's Rights and Power: Charging up for a New Century* (London and New York: Jessica Kingsley Publishers, 2003), argues that the concept of childhood promoted by Philippe Ariès, *Centuries of Childhood*, trans. Robert Baldick (Harmondsworth: Penguin, 1979), which posits that childhood did not count in sixteenth-century Europe, is counteracted in later research on medieval society in England by Nicholas Orme, *Medieval Children* (New Haven, CT: Yale University Press, 2001). John takes Orme's position that the Middle Ages could have been more enlightened in its treatment of children than we have been led to believe. Tara Inniss, on the African family during slavery in Barbados, also challenges the colonial accounts that suggest that, during slavery, African families showed little affection or care for their children. See Tara Inniss, " 'Even Little Black Children Cannot Be Reared Like the Lambs and Calves of the Field': Children, Family and Community in Plantation Society, 1790–1838" (paper presented at "First They Must Be Children: The Child and the Caribbean Imagi/Nation: A Cultural Studies Conference", University of the West Indies, St Augustine, Trinidad, 21–22 May 2009).
20. Keller, "Education Policy Paper", xviii.
21. Christine Barrow, "Introduction: Children's Rights and the Caribbean Experience", in *Children's Rights, Caribbean Realities*, ed. Christine Barrow (Kingston: Ian Randle, 2001), xv–xvii.
22. B.M. Newman and P.R. Newman, "Middle Childhood (6–12 Years)", *Development through Life: A Psychosocial Approach* (Washington: Wadsworth, 1999), 263–99.
23. Newman and Newman, *Development through Life*.
24. Helen Bee, *The Developing Child* (New York: Harper Collins College Publishers, 1995).

25. Earl Lovelace, *Salt* (London: Faber, 1996), 56. All references from Lovelace are taken from this edition.
26. Janet Brown, "Parental Resistance to Child Rights in Jamaica", in *Children's Rights, Caribbean Realities*, ed. Christine Barrow (Kingston: Ian Randle, 2001), 113–31.
27. Brown, "Parental Resistance", 114.
28. Sturm, "On the Suffering and Rights", 153.
29. Ibid., 160.
30. "Success/Laventille Secondary Tops RBTT's Young Leaders", *Trinidad and Tobago Newsday*, 27 May 2010, Business Section, http://www.newsday.co.tt/business/0,121480.html; Allison Hickling, "Third Annual San Marino-UNICEF Awards Honour Children's Advocacy Groups", 17 March 2009, *LAC VOX Forum*, UNICEF, http://www.lacvox.net/?p=584#more-584.
31. Delisle et al., "Sisterhood".
32. Kalloo, "'No Easy Thing': A Portraiture of the Dynamics of Teacher-Pupil Interactions in a Standard Four Primary Classroom in Trinidad".
33. Sarah Lawrence-Lightfoot and Jessica Davis Hoffman, *The Art and Science of Portraiture* (San Francisco: Jossey-Bass Publishers, 1997).
34. CEE stands for Common Entrance Examination. This examination was instituted in 1960 and replaced the separate entrance examinations that the traditional secondary schools implemented for selection of students to their institutions. Before the CEE, a small number of select students sat the college exhibition examination, which gave free access to fee-paying secondary schools. Children sat CEE at age eleven, and it was open to all children, regardless of social class. The CEE provided a more meritocratic and transparent method of assigning students to secondary schools. As explained in the main body of the text, for many years the inadequate number of secondary schools on the island created fierce competition for the few secondary schools available. Preparation for this examination took the form of copious drilling of students, along with extra lessons in the later grades of the primary school. The CEE was replaced by the SEA in 2000. This exam differed little from its predecessor, except that the science and social studies components of the test were removed.
35. Task Force for the Removal of the Common Entrance Exam 1998, "Report of the Task Force for the Removal of the Common Entrance Examination" (presented to the Honourable Minister of Education 1998, Trinidad and Tobago, 1998), 12; Jules, *A Study of the Secondary School Population*; UNDP, *Trinidad and Tobago National Human Development Report 2000*.

36. Jerome Delisle, "Can Standards-Referenced, Large-Scale Assessment Data Lead to Improvement in the Education System?: Judging the Utility of Student Performance Standards in the Primary School National Assessments of Educational Achievement", *Caribbean Curriculum* 15 (2008): 72. The distorting effect of this examination was observed soon after independence, when R.T. Green, "The Common Entrance Examination as a Selection Procedure", Memorandum No. 3 (Ministry of Education and Culture, Trinidad and Tobago, 1966), refers to primary schools dropping subjects such as history and geography and teaching being restricted to subjects being tested, to get their most "promising student over the C.E.E. hurdle" (10). Twenty years later, the Task Force for the Removal of the CEE has similar sentiments: "the examination itself began to exert an inordinate influence on the primary schools and the curriculum and teaching practices within the system" (12).
37. Entrance to secondary schools for the working-class black Trinidadian was largely available through the college exhibition, which was instituted in 1872. Initially, it was awarded only to boys and provided disproportionately small numbers of children access to the few church-based secondary schools established. In *Inward Hunger: The Education of a Prime Minister*, Eric Williams noted that in 1922, at the time he was entered for the exam, exhibitions had increased marginally from four to eight (London: André Deutsch, 1981), 30. In 1950, the number of exhibition winners rose to one hundred. See Carl Campbell, *Endless Education: Main Currents in the Education System of Modern Trinidad and Tobago 1939–1986* (Kingston: University of the West Indies Press, 1997).
38. Campbell, *Endless Education*, 28.
39. The junior secondary and senior comprehensives represented a two-cycle secondary education system. In this sense they contrasted with the continuous five or seven years of full-day secondary education in one school, which was offered at the established denominational and government secondary schools.

 The junior secondaries operated a shift system, where students attended school in either the morning or afternoon period. This immediately opened access to large numbers of students to secondary education, with minimal school infrastructure. However, it created problems of large numbers of unsupervised students for at least half a day. It offered a broad, compulsory, curriculum for the eleven to fourteen age group. Students were exposed to an academic core of English language, Spanish, mathematics, integrated science, the creative arts and technical vocational subjects. Students then entered the senior comprehensives (fourteen to eighteen years), where they did a compulsory academic core and were given the option to specialize in a range of elective courses in the academic, technical-vocational, commercial, agricultural and creative arts disciplines.

40. The Report of the Task Force for the Removal of the Common Entrance Examination supports this observation, noting that "the provision of additional schools by the Government over the succeeding years did not remove the demand for the traditional schools as these were viewed as the institutions of greatest prestige by parents" (12).

41. Errol Fabien is a popular local comedian.

42. *Authentic* is used here from a progressivist viewpoint, in which learning is described as authentic when it relates to students' real-life experiences. It is through such relationships that children can actively construct meaningful knowledge.

43. Paul Willis, "Elements of a Culture", in *Life In Schools: The Sociology of Pupil Culture*, ed. Martin Hammersely and Peter Woods (London: Open University, 1993), 61–76; Angela Spaulding, "Micropolitical Behaviour of Second Graders: A Qualitative Study of Student Resistance in the Classroom", *The Qualitative Report* 4, nos. 1–2 (2000), http://www.nova.edu/ssss/QR/QR4-1/spaulding.html; John Beynon, " 'Sussing Out' Teachers: Pupils as Data Gatherers", in *Life in Schools: The Sociology of Pupil Culture*, ed. Martin Hammersely and Peter Woods (London: Open University, 1993), 121–44.

44. These were questionnaires I distributed to the class during the 2002 return visit, in which I tried to find out if children's opinion of their teacher's strict discipline had changed between terms 1 and 2.

12.

Do Teachers Make Science Learning Fun and Relevant?

» RAWATEE MAHARAJ-SHARMA

Introduction

DECADES OF RESEARCH HAVE revealed that the best and most memorable learning experiences take place in an unintimidating and comfortable environment and are fun. Relevance, too, makes learning interesting and "alive" or "real" for students. Educators and researchers advocate that the learning process ought to involve a smooth interaction between fun and relevance for it to be meaningful. Despite the obvious logic in this argument, many teachers in Trinidad and Tobago seem unable to strike that delicate balance. It is against this background that the current chapter was conceptualized. This chapter reveals that science teachers generally do not employ a variety of teaching/learning strategies to introduce fun and relevance into the science teaching/learning experience. Furthermore, when contemporary strategies are used, the frequency with which they are used to deliver science lessons is very low. Except for games and practical hands-on activities, teachers deliver science instruction mainly by the traditional "chalk and talk" method. In addition, this chapter shows that there is often a mismatch between teachers' choice of activity and the intended learning outcome for which the activity has been selected.

Literature

In many classrooms, motivating students and keeping them engaged in classroom learning are major challenges for teachers. Often, students are bored and inattentive, as they have difficulty seeing the connection between schoolwork and their lives outside the classroom. Educators at all levels of the education system agree that students of all ages are greatly affected by and sometimes preoccupied with what is going on around them. Rather than viewing this as a detractor of learning, teachers can capitalize on this preoccupation to make classroom learning engaging, stimulating and meaningful.

In work done by Rothman, a survey of twenty-five thousand eighth graders revealed that almost half indicated they were bored in school most of the time because they did not see the "value" of the learning to their lives.[1] Other studies revealed poor student engagement in classroom activities because students claim that the learning experience is boring and irrelevant.[2]

This chapter's research is set in Trinidad and Tobago and attempts to explore the teaching/learning activities primary school teachers use to effect learning in their classrooms. Fifty-two standard 3 (level 5 of primary school) teachers participated in the research conducted via classroom observations, interviews and questionnaires. At the primary school level, the Ministry of Education mandates that all curriculum subjects be taught to all students from infants up to standard 5. Since the researcher is a tertiary-level science educator, the focus was on teaching/learning activities teachers adopted for science lessons.

In Trinidad and Tobago, the summative assessment for academic mobility and employment is a series of high-stakes external examinations at all levels of primary and secondary schooling. Teachers, school administrators, parents and even students are "driven" by the competitive desire to attain 100 per cent passes and the highest possible grades. In addition, the curriculum is extensive, so teachers often feel they cannot cover the respective syllabuses in the allotted time, arguing that it is possible to do so only if they adopt rote learning and drill and practice strategies. Hartman and Glasgow, as well as Roblyer, report that, under these conditions, students do not enjoy learning and do not see the relevance of the learning.[3] They suggest further that the vastness of the curriculum coupled with the competitive culture can box teachers into the traditional delivery paradigm.

The following research questions tailored this chapter:

- What categories of activities are students exposed in the science teaching/learning process?
- Which activities make learning fun (*fun learning activities*)?
- Which activities make learning relevant (*relevance learning activities*)?

Regarding best practice in science education, Johnson, Lee and Fradd report that if classroom learning becomes relevant to students, so that they understand how the learning applies to their everyday lives, they are more likely to be participative and alert in class.[4] Lee indicates that the introduction of structured play in the learning process stimulates and encourages students to meaningfully contribute to concept building and discussions in science.[5] Furthermore, Loucks-Horsley, Hewson, Love and Stiles identify specific activities and strategies that teachers can easily use in the classroom to promote fun for students as well as to establish the relevance of the learning.[6] These activities can be easily adapted for use in Trinidad and Tobago and, as suggested by Rogoff, Matusov and White, depending on teacher creativity, some of these activities can be easily integrated into science lessons to achieve the desired learning outcomes.[7]

Methodology

Fifty-two standard 3 primary school teachers, randomly selected from rural and urban areas across Trinidad and Tobago, formed the sample for this study. All teachers were graduates of the Bachelor of Education programme at the University of the West Indies, St Augustine, and had more than five years' teaching experience at the primary level. At the standard 3 levels, the average age of students is about nine years. This age group was chosen because at this stage of development students begin to form opinions about the subjects they like and those they do not.[8] In Trinidad and Tobago, the Revised Primary School Science Syllabus document, issued by the Ministry of Education, guides science instruction delivery.

The data collection procedure was divided into three phases. In phase 1, a questionnaire, consisting of three open-ended explorative questions, was administered to the participants and elicited from teachers what teaching/learning strategy or strategies they normally employed to create a typical science lesson for their standard 3 students. They were asked to indicate the rationale for each strategy. They were also asked to indicate how often, on average, over a three-month period, they would use each strategy.

Phase 2 involved classroom observations of the participants by the researcher. In this phase, the participants were observed while involved in actual classroom teaching of science. All teachers were observed at least twice, but some were observed more often because of challenging infrastructural issues (such as inadequate room facilities and unavailability of functioning teaching aids) that arose in the classroom when scheduled visits did not proceed as planned. The lessons were also videotaped to fully capture the use of specific strategies the teacher employed in the delivery of lessons. Randomly selected science lessons that formed part of the normal course of work were observed and videotaped on each occasion. The aim was to identify specifically the particular teaching/learning strategies the teachers used to deliver science lessons. The researcher used an adaptation of a science lesson observational checklist designed by Shepardson[9] to record the strategies used and the role of the teacher and the learners during the teaching/learning process.

In phase 3, a sub-sample of twelve teachers was selected, with the aim of seeking maximum diversity regarding teachers' range of teaching/learning strategies, as suggested by J.H. McMillan and S. Schumacher.[10] These twelve teachers were invited to participate in a semi-structured interview that explored the extent of congruency or discrepancy or both between what teachers said they normally did when teaching science (phase 1) and what they actually did when they were observed teaching science (phase 2). They were asked to explain the choice of strategies used in the observed teaching and why they chose the particular strategy or strategies. They were also asked to indicate whether they would classify the strategies they used as *fun learning strategies* or *relevance learning strategies*. In the interviews, teachers' written responses and their classroom enactments were discussed and compared to explore the congruency or discrepancy or both. Teachers were encouraged to provide explanations for any discrepancies identified.

Data Analysis

Phase 1

Teachers' written responses from the questionnaires were reviewed and categorized to produce a list of all the teaching/learning strategies they normally used. Responses were analysed to reveal why teachers used a particular strategy and how often they used each particular strategy in their science teaching.

Phase 2

The science-lesson observational checklists and the videotapings of the lessons were compared and reviewed several times to accurately identify and classify the particular teaching/learning strategies used in the delivery of the science lessons.

Once this was performed for all the recorded lessons, the findings were cross-checked against the list of strategies generated for each teacher in phase 1. The goal was to determine if the strategies respective teachers said they used to teach science were in fact the ones they actually used.

Phase 3

The interview responses obtained from the subset of teachers were transcribed, and the transcriptions were reviewed to ensure that there were no misrepresentations of the interviewees' responses. The transcriptions were subsequently coded to reveal the specific reasons offered by teachers regarding why they used the particular strategies observed. Furthermore, the transcriptions were analysed to capture teachers' views on how they would classify the various strategies. Codes related to fun and learning as a fun process were placed in one category, and codes related to making learning relevant for the students were captured in a second category. The final aspect of the analysis in this phase involved looking closely at the two categories (fun and relevance) and comparing the strategies in these categories to the reasons teachers articulated for using the strategies; the goal was to see if there was congruence between the reason or reasons they suggested for using a strategy and their classification of that particular strategy.

Results and Findings

Phase 1

The analysis revealed that this sample of primary school science teachers used a range of teaching/learning strategies to deliver science lessons to their standard 3 students. Most teachers articulated why they would use a particular strategy. Some of their reasons related to the topic being taught, but a number of teachers indicated that they would choose a particular teaching strategy either to make science learning fun for their students or relevant to the lives of their students or both. Interesting, though, was the variation in frequency with which each of the strategies was actually used by the teachers; some strategies were used quite often and others very seldom or not at all. The data revealed the following among the strategies used by the fifty-two primary school teachers who participated in this study:

- Games
- Hands-on activities
- Role play
- Storytelling
- Song/poetry
- Information communication technologies (ICT)/multimedia
- Building models
- Fieldwork

Clearly teachers understood and appreciated the value of adopting creative and contemporary teaching/learning strategies to encourage and promote learning in science, as they indicated the following in their responses to why they would use these strategies:

"If children learn by doing, they see the relevance of the learning to them. . ."
"If students have fun learning, they will participate fully in the process . . ."
"Learning ought to be fun . . ."
"The strategy would make science learning fun and relevant to the student . . ."
"Storytelling makes learning fun. . . ."
"Young children love to play, so a game will make learning fun for them . . ."
"ICTs and multimedia help students to visualize, so they see the relevance of science."
"A game can make learning fun, but it can also show relevance of the learning . . ."
"Science learning should occur by doing . . . hands-on involvement . . ."
"Getting physically involved by doing aids in understanding the relevance . . ."

Teachers therefore understood the need to adopt creative and contemporary activities to encourage and promote science learning. Furthermore, the strategies in the list suggest that teachers appreciated the benefits of curriculum integration and cross-disciplinary practices in science education.

Phase 2

Careful examination of the videotapes and the observational checklists, however, revealed that, while teachers indicated on the questionnaire that they used a variety of strategies, the frequency with which these were used was in fact very low. The frequencies refer to the total number of times the teachers, collectively, were observed; for example, the total number of lessons observed was 127, so a percentage of 23 per cent of the time means 23 per cent out of the total 127.

From among the lessons observed, with the exception of games and hands-on activities, all other strategies/activities identified by teachers (phase 1) were only very sparingly used in the classroom. Even more surprising was that none of the teachers indicated on the questionnaire that teaching via the traditional chalk-and-talk method was a frequently employed activity. The observational checklist, however, revealed that this method was used on average 20 per cent of the time. This is almost the same frequency with which hands-on activities were observed to have been used – 23 per cent – while the use of games as a teaching/learning strategy/activity was the most frequently used strategy, as it was observed to have been used 45 per cent of the time in the science classes. The frequency with which each of the strategies identified in phase 1 was actually used in science teaching/learning is shown in table 12.1.

Table 12.1: Frequency Distribution of Specific Teaching/Learning Activities

Teaching/Learning Activity	Frequency
Games	45%
Hands-on activities	23%
Role play	6%
Storytelling	2%
Building models	2%
Song/poetry	< 1%
ICT/multimedia	< 1%
Fieldwork	< 1%
Chalk and talk	20%

Phase 3

Analysis of the interview data in conjunction with the data from phases 1 and 2 allowed for the further categorization of each of the strategies/activities actually used by the teachers to deliver science lessons into either fun learning strategies or relevance learning strategies. This categorization is presented in table 12.2.

During the interviews, teachers offered several reasons to explain the choice of /rationale for the particular strategy or strategies they used in the classroom to deliver their science lessons. Teachers often reported that they chose "a strategy that was easy to manage with a large class". Teachers unanimously agreed that games were the easiest of the strategies/activities to use in their science teaching. The following were some comments made by teachers during the interviews:

Teacher 1: "Time is always a challenge . . . and when you have to finish a certain amount of work. . . . songs and poetry and drama is just a waste of valuable teaching time. . . . chalk and talk gets the most done. . . ."

Teacher 2: "I understand the need to use different activities . . . but how can you manage experiments and role play . . . in a small classroom that is cramped with thirty-six students. . . ."

Teacher 3: "I tell them stories sometimes, but after that I have to still write the notes on the board. . . . they don't internalize it. . . . they respond better to games."

Teacher 4: "I would love to use the computer to show videos. . . . This will help them to visualize. . . . but the principal has major problems with that. . . ."

Table 12.2: Categorization of Teaching/Learning Activities

Fun Learning Activities	Relevance Learning Activities
Games	Fieldwork
Song/poetry	Hands-on
Models	Role play
Storytelling	ICT/multimedia
ICT/multimedia	

Teacher 5: "Hands-on science has many benefits . . . I know this from when I was a student. . . . so I try to do some of this with my students. . . . there are no facilities at the school, so I bring the stuff from my home. . . ."

Teacher 6: "Games are easy to make up. . . . they like it . . . and I can make these up easily so it doesn't take up much of my time. . . ."

Teacher 7: "I tried model building once. . . . it failed . . . the students just clowned around with the plasticine. . . . I had to teach it over again the next day. . . ."

Teacher 8: "Games yes. . . . this makes learning fun. . . . Hands-on activities yes . . . this makes it real to them. . . . but I don't do anything else. . . . most times it is chalk and talk. . . ."

Teacher 9: "If I have to do something different, I choose the simple activities like games. . . . the others are too difficult to manage in my class. . . ."

Teacher 10: "I only use a different activity if the students seem bored . . . maybe a game . . . or a story. . . ."

Additional Findings and Insights

Further analysis of data/findings from the three phases of the project, but particularly from phase 3, revealed that for many teachers, selection of a classroom teaching/learning strategy occurred "on spur": very little deliberate planning went into the choice of strategy teachers employed in the classroom. Chalk and talk seemed to be the natural inclination among the teachers. Some would use loosely structured games such as "heads and tails" or "context clue crosswords" in the main body of their lesson, most often for reinforcement. Others used similar games at the end of the lesson, sometimes as formative assessment and at other times just to "make up time". According to the teachers' responses, their main reason for using games as a teaching/learning strategy was to make science learning a fun activity for students: an activity they would enjoy.

A number of the teachers subscribed to the scientific approach and in this regard used some amount of experimentation/hands-on learning when teaching science. However, in most of the instances observed, this approach was used as a verification-type activity of principles or concepts that were earlier introduced to students in the traditional paradigm. Very little inductive reasoning, inquiry or explorative learning was built into the hands-on activities. Despite this shortcoming in the hands-on approach adopted by teachers, their responses indicated almost unanimously that the main reason for their choice of the hands-on strategy was to make science learning relevant for their students.

Generally, teachers were not guided by any overarching "big picture or plan" in the delivery of science instruction; the sequential coverage of the syllabus document was their only guide. As was evident from the analysis emerging from phase 3, teachers employed the strategies/activities deemed easiest on the occasions when they diverged from the traditional form of delivery: games and hands-on activities.

Limited ICT/multimedia competence was a challenge for some teachers who had access to the facilities but were unable to effectively integrate these into their science teaching. Most teachers who took part in this study, however, did not have access to ICT/multimedia facilities at their schools. Almost all the teachers surveyed in this work identified limited space as a challenge, indicating that contemporary activities, specifically experimentation/hands-on activities, required at least some physical movement, which they viewed as "too difficult to manage" given their space constraints. Storytelling, song and poetry were used on two occasions by the same teacher, but it was clear that the teacher was operating outside his comfort zone on these occasions. Models, too, were used on two occasions by two different teachers, but the strategy was limited to the use of commercial models to demonstrate parts and processes to students. No opportunity was provided for students to construct models of their own in the lessons observed. On one occasion, a teacher took the class outside into the schoolyard to look at the varieties of leaves and to classify leaves based on their shape, texture and the nature of their edges. This was interpreted as fieldwork.

Conclusions

Except for the traditional chalk and talk, games and hands-on activities were the most popular strategies teachers reported they used to promote teaching/learning in their science classrooms. Teachers indicated that, when games were used, the aim was to infuse fun in the teaching/learning experience, while hands-on activities were employed in instances in which teachers wanted to make the learning relevant for the students. The researcher believes that there are some interpretions/implications that can be drawn from this work that might be worthy of consideration when discussing science classroom practice in the context of appropriate teaching/learning strategies for effective delivery of science instruction:

1. An unsatisfactory variety/range of teaching/learning strategies was used to promote fun in learning and to establish relevance of learning for the students, and the frequency with which contemporary activities were used was low (table 12.1).
2. Activities such as debates, reports, projects, artwork and cartoons were not at all mentioned by teachers in the entire study; and even though games were used 45 per cent of the time, primarily to promote/encourage fun, there was no apparent structured approach to inserting these games into the classroom learning.
3. Hands-on activities were used 23 per cent of the time to make science learning relevant to the students, but it seems that infrastructural improvements are needed in schools to encourage teachers to increase the frequency with which this strategy is used in their science classrooms.
4. Storytelling and building models were used only 2 per cent of the time in science teaching. Song and poetry, ICT/multimedia and fieldwork as teaching/learning strategies were used less than 1 per cent of the time in the science classrooms. The reasons for these observations are worth exploring in subsequent work.
5. Teachers' creativity levels were low, and they were hesitant to adopt new approaches in the absence of support and encouragement.

Recommendations

- The findings of this study and the researcher's reflection on the process suggest that there is a missing link: Many of our teachers currently teach the way they were taught, simply because they have not been extensively trained to do any differently. This gap must be bridged with targeted programmes and courses designed to develop teachers' competency in the effective use of appropriate science teaching/learning strategies.
- We must institute an efficient support network for science teachers into which they can log to discuss issues, share ideas and source possible remedies for challenges they may encounter in delivering science instruction. In addition, structured monitoring and evaluation are needed to guide teachers when they opt to use less traditional approaches in their science classrooms.

- Perhaps less formal forums, such as collaborative public meetings in the form of panel or round-table discussions, could be planned at convenient times and places to allow teachers to share their ideas and experiences with their peers. These forums would open up the possibilities to which teachers are exposed and could encourage them to try activities their peers use.
- Eventually, though, it comes down to personal will and attitude. Teachers must have these and must see themselves as change agents in education. Only then will genuine effort translate into meaningful practice.

Notes

1. K.J. Rothman, "A Sobering Start for the Cluster Busters Conference", *American Journal of Epidemiology* 132, no. 1 (1990): S6–S13.
2. J.I. Goodlad, *A Place Called School* (New York: McGraw-Hill, 1984). Compare Herreid, *Start with a Story: The Case Method of Teaching College Science* (Alexandria, VA: ASTA Press, 2007); T.W. Malone and M.R. Lepper, "Making Learning Fun: A Taxonomy of Intrinsic Motivations for Learning", in *Aptitude, Learning and Instruction*, volume 3, *Conative and Affective Process Analyses*, ed. R.E. Snow and M.J. Farr (Mahwah, NJ: Lawrence Erlbaum, 1987), 223–53.
3. H.J. Hartman and Neal A. Glasgow, *Tips for the Science Teacher: Research-Based Strategies to Help Students Learn* (Thousand Oaks, CA: Corwin Press, 2002); M.D. Roblyer, *Integrating Educational Technology into Teaching* (Columbus, OH: Merrill Prentice Hall, 2006).
4. C.J. Johnson, "Bioterrorism Is Real-World Science: Inquiry-Based Simulation Mirrors Real Life", *Science Scope* 27, no. 3 (2003): 19–23; O. Lee and S.H. Fradd, "Promoting Science Literacy with English Language Learners through Instructional Materials Development: A Case Study", *Bilingual Research Journal* 23, no. 2 (2001): 76–88.
5. O. Lee, "Teacher Change in Beliefs and Practices in Science and Literacy Instruction with English Language Learners", *Journal of Research in Science Teaching* 41, no. 1 (2004): 65–93.
6. S. Loucks-Horsley, Katherine E. Stiles, Susan E. Mundry, Nancy B. Love and Peter W. Hewson, *Designing Professional Development for Teachers of Mathematics and Science* (Thousand Oaks, CA: Corwin Press, 1998).
7. B. Rogoff, B. Matusov and S. White, "Models of Teaching and Learning: Participation in a Community of Learners", in *The Handbook of Cognition and Human*

Development, ed. D. Olson and N. Torrance (Oxford: Blackwell, 1998), 388–414.
8. Trinidad and Tobago, Central Statistical Office, *Statistics at a Glance* (Port of Spain: Central Statistical Office, 1998).
9. D.P. Shepardson, *Assessment in Science: A Guide to Professional Development and Classroom Practice* (London: Springer, 2001).
10. J.H. McMillan and S. Schumacher, *Research in Education: A Conceptual Introduction*, 5th ed. (New York: Longman, 2001).

Contributors

GISELLE RAMPAUL is Lecturer in Literatures in English, Department of Literary, Cultural and Communication Studies, University of the West Indies, St Augustine, Trinidad and Tobago.

GERALDINE ELIZABETH SKEETE is Lecturer in Literatures in English, Department of Literary, Cultural and Communication Studies, University of the West Indies, St Augustine, Trinidad and Tobago.

BEN BRAITHWAITE is Lecturer in Lingusitics, Department of Modern Languages and Linguistics, University of the West Indies, St Augustine, Trinidad and Tobago.

KATHY-ANN DRAYTON is Lecturer in Speech-Language Pathology, Department of Modern Languages and Linguistics, University of the West Indies, St Augustine, Trinidad and Tobago.

RYAN DURGASINGH is an MPhil student in Literatures in English, Department of Literary, Cultural and Communication Studies, University of the West Indies, St Augustine, Trinidad and Tobago.

ROWENA KALLOO is Assistant Professor, Centre for Educational Programmes, University of Trinidad and Tobago, Valsayn campus.

BARBARA LALLA is Professor Emerita of Language and Literature, University of the West Indies, St Augustine, Trinidad and Tobago.

RAWATEE MAHARAJ-SHARMA is Lecturer in Science Education and the coordinator of the Bachelor of Education programme at the School of Education, University of the West Indies, St Augustine, Trinidad and Tobago.

SANDRA POUCHET PAQUET is Professor Emerita of English and Director of Caribbean Literary Studies, University of Miami, Florida.

JENNIFER RAHIM is Senior Lecturer in Literatures in English, Department of Literary, Cultural and Communication Studies, University of the West Indies, St Augustine, Trinidad and Tobago.

KAREN SANDERSON COLE is Assistant Lecturer in the Foundation English programme, Department of Modern Languages and Linguistics, University of the West Indies, St Augustine, Trinidad and Tobago.

NICHA SELVON-RAMKISSOON is a PhD candidate in Linguistics, University of the West Indies, St Augustine, and Lecturer in Language, Literature and Education, University of Trinidad and Tobago.

CPSIA information can be obtained at www.ICGtesting.com
Printed in the USA
BVOW031104090812

297457BV00002B/2/P